NO JUSTICE IN JAMAICA

How the Jamaican Judicial System
Destroyed My Life and
My Business—and
How It Can Happen to You

DWIGHT CLACKEN

"Powerfully and frighteningly real: This novel recounts in gripping details of the venomous machinations of politicians, public officials and professionals who have corrupted Jamaica for their own aggrandizement. The Justice system, especially in the courts, is the arsenal that empowers the rich and powerful while the will of the less fortunate is broken by oppression. Corruption is rampant; a vibrant culture of honesty and uprightness is destroyed. Money and connections rule. This book leaves me with the novel question -- Is there hope for Jamaica to rid herself of this serpentine leadership?"

KM

ISBN-13:978-1519539489
ISBN-10:1519539487

Edited by Dan Crissman, NY Book Editors
Book cover design: Howard Moo Young
Interior image Credits: Cartoonists - Las May and Clovis
Special reference Credits to Jamaica Gleaner, Jamaica Observer, Jamaica Star, RJR News, Grace Kennedy Foundation Lecture, 2013.

Contact the Author:

Facebook: /dwightclacken

Linkedin: Dwight Clacken
dclacken4@gmail.com

Disclaimer
The Author bears no responsibility for broken links referred to or mentioned in this book. Should you have a difficulty accessing any of the links herein, try to copy and paste into your preferred browser or Google search the title.

CONTENTS

Preface xiii

Part I - My Jamaica 1

Chapter 1 - The mood in a battered Nation 3

Chapter 2 - My Early life 13

Montego Bay 19

Lucea, Hanover. 20

Chapter 3 – Working in a newly Independent Jamaica 23

The Changing Jamaica 25

Chapter 4 - The Terrible Seventies 29

The Making of Delinquents 38

My Working Journey Continues. 40

A Culture in Rapid Change. 40

Chapter 5 – New Beginnings and the Birth of EML 47

A Vote against Communism (The Seaga Era) 50

The Second Manley Administration. 58

A Return to Rackets 59

Chapter 6 - The FINSAC era—and My Troubles Begin 61

FINSAC, from a Small Businessman's View 62

Lessons from FINSAC 65

Where is the Leadership? 66

The First Signs of Trouble 67

The New Zealanders 71

Chapter 7 – Broken Trust 79

New Millenium . . . More of the Same? 84

Time to Part Ways 85

Chapter 8 - The Journey for Justice Begins 89

The Consent Order 89

Paul Cole's Jamaican Lessons Commence 92

That Poor Old Lady 99

Like a Stuck Record 102

KPMG's Paul Cole Throws in the Towel 105

The Public Accountancy Board Outshines the Supreme Court 107

EML's Auditor Investigated by the PAB 109

A change in the country's Leadership 111

Chapter 9 – A Hint of Change to Come 115

Even More Delays 117

A running start for Golding 122

Golding's promises and his challenges 126

More Hurdles? 130

Reliance on Professionals 131

A shocking result 133

The Armadale Tragedy 135

The Fight Continues 138

Chapter 10 – The Tivoli Incursion 141

Why Dons Still 'run tings' 144

Stalemate 146

The stage seemed set 149

Appeal Court and Privy Council earns no respect 151
A final message to investment 152
Going through futile reminders ... for the records. . .155
The realities I must face.. 156
Continued strident pursuit of elusive justice 157
The 'top' continues to command no respect 160
The 2011 General Election 160
My efforts continue. 161
The stand continues 163
A sudden and overly late response. 164

Part II – Jamaica Today 167

Chapter 11 – Jamaica 2010s 169
JEEP 170
Endemic CRIME 171
Ponzi Schemes 172
Lotto Scams 174
Ticket Extortion by Government. 181
Police corruption, brutality, sanctioned killings 183
Police brutality 185
Foreign help with investigations. 189

Chapter 12 – Extortion, Kickbacks, Bribery, and More 195
Begging again for an IMF Bail out. 199
Raid on the National Housing Trust (NHT). 206

Chapter 13 – The Broken Justice System. 211
Judges 211
Court Resources 219

Resident Magistrates Court .221
Lawyers 222
OCG (Office of the Contractor General) 223
The Ministry of Justice 225
Director of Public Prosecutions (DPP). 237
The Azan Affair 240
The Role of Social Clubs and Charitable Groups in Jamaica 242

Chapter 14 - Who is to Blame . . .and Why? 245
Lending agencies 248
Tolerance of the Powers that Be. 248
When is the right time?. 249
International Professionals and Contractors 249
Government Boards 251
Private Sector Corruption 254
The Church. 257
The Media. 258

Chapter 15 – Corruption Harms Investment 261
Questions from investors 264
Total Collapse. 267

Chapter 16- Solutions. 275
The major solutions: Narrow our focus; we can't solve them all at once. 278
Impeachment – Seaga's Call?. 280
Avoiding the Caribbean Court of Appeal 283
Making Professionals Accountable. 284
The need for an IMF. 285

The Security Forces 286
Broken Promises 288

Chapter 17 – Closure 297
An appeal to Jamaicans living overseas 298

ACKNOWLEDGMENT

To my friends who, empathized, advised and encouraged me during my tumultuous pursuit of justice, I thank you. There were days when I was depressed and your support challenged me to continue going about my daily work and also to write my story. Thank you for your patience in listening to my hurt and outrage a million times.

I am grateful to those who read and critiqued my tentative manuscripts until they became cohesive. I thank those who knew that I enjoyed fishing and who invited me on fishing tournaments in a token to clear my thoughts because, indeed, I was incensed with rage when I realized the intensions of my venal opponents.

My family, you were my rock. Lynne, how would I have survived this without you? You consoled me when I became temperamental. You reassured me even though you were hurting and losing the same as I was. EML was pioneered by both of us; it was your work and your dream too. My darling you are an amazing woman.

This novel is to all of you who believed in me. Bless your kind hearts.

PREFACE

It is amazing how we have done it. This is the epitome of self-destruction - the type that blows away the ash so no fabled phoenix can rise from it.

Jamaica, Jamaica. What a beautiful country! What a fun-loving nation! And yet, hundreds of its citizens bear down on the embassies daily, seeking a one-way ticket to another country. Is it just that we have a weak economy, a problem easily addressed with better-qualified officials? No. It is that justice, law, and order—the lifeblood of every progressive nation—no longer exist here.

Any country that mishandles justice is doomed to failure. Any nation that does not vigorously protect the sanctity of the rule of law is bound to turn on itself. Any nation where "justice" can be bartered, tweaked, or ignored is en route to a failed state. Any nation where "justice" is no longer a right but a privilege, the power-mongers and their rapacious cohorts stand to gain heftily at the expense of the masses—the very masses that the political "comrades" swore to protect forty years ago.

When "justice" is treated as commerce—that is, who can afford to make the purchase gets what they want, such as the careful selection of judges and jurors, conveniently timed disappearance of critical court documents, and professionals who are prepared to skew opinions or evidence—the people must take matters into their own hands.

Is it any wonder that we have one of the highest crime rates in the world? Never have we seen such brilliant people as our professionals who use their "brilliance" to trick, confuse, and thwart the unfortunate for their own aggrandizement. Never have we seen individuals who are well aware of the nation's problems but are too seduced by the material gain from a dysfunctional system to have any desire to change it.

Jamaica, a nation that is gifted with innovative thinkers, appears bereft of individuals who possess the ideas and the will to effect change.

I have learned the hard way. As a businessman who slaved to build a company and who also could have been named one of Jamaica's most successful entrepreneurs with time, I have suffered—not only from my unjust partners but from more than 12 years of struggling in the system of justice that I sought as recourse. Today I reluctantly agree with my friends who insist that I was ridiculous not to have taken justice in my own hands. I am all too aware now just how broken the system is.

Little did I know that when I confidently believed that a matter which should have been settled in no more than 90 days would have taken more than 12 years. Despite more than 70 visits to the Supreme Court and numerous ignored and wasted attempts seeking accountability from various government departments, my case has still barely moved a day forward. This is not because of the complexity of the case but rather from the maneuverings in the system that seemed to be intended to waste time. Some may scoff at this book as just another bitter tirade against the system. Some may even say that it "doesn't concern them" or that "it isn't their business" and "the author is just unfortunate." I advise you to rethink your stance. Too many of us have an "I don't care, it is not my business" mentality, which hinders our ability to effectively tackle the problems in our society. A rape becomes only a two-day outrage because "it is not my daughter, thank God." A young man of promise is gunned down and the response is "thank God it is not my son." A slaughter of an entire family is no longer met with outrage but relief that "it is not in my community, that is why me nuh live a dem place deh." Once we are not the victims we hardly care; our response is to barricade ourselves with high-tech security systems and gated communities while the root of the problem remains.

Is it really that we are selfish, or is it that we cannot rely on the system to protect us? Therefore we have to "see and blind, hear and deaf".

In the movie *Dancehall Queen*, a compelling reflection of life in Jamaica's inner city, the character Priest tells the protagonists after brutally killing one of their own, "Walk and live, talk and b@**#t dead." I once found this warning to be hilarious, but in subsequent years I've been forced to acknowledge the macabre truth of his edict. The truth about how Jamaican society perceives justice is simple: Mind your own business and you will be OK.

I, however, am defying this warning to tell my story in these pages. The cost will be what it will. Never did I imagine that I would have suffered more than 12 years, battling against a corrupt system. My ordeal is not unique; it is all too typical of how cases are handled in Jamaica.

Could it be that our court is the source of corruption? I assumed that there was a system of justice that preserved the rights of the innocent and ensured that the guilty would face their comeuppance. I could not have been more wrong.

This book is a warning to those who may believe that they are insulated from an unjust system. It is for those who may believe they will never face 'Your Honour' with their livelihood on the line. It is a call for all to take a stand before Jamaica is reduced to rubble.

Jamaicans do not take well to biting criticism, however constructive. They interpret it as 'tearing down the country'. Comments like 'not all Jamaicans are like that' or 'we are a beautiful country' or 'what about the positive things' have intercepted the need for accountability.

We produce people who are famous around the world. Jamaica is a beautiful country with many decent, law-abiding citizens, which is why we should lash out in the first place. To everything there is a season and a time for every purpose. The time has come (in fact, it has passed) to stamp out corruption in our system of justice. It is not the time for us to be in denial about the real challenges to Jamaica's future. It is not the time for us to lose ourselves in the euphoria of Reggae music, prolific athletes, and our magnificent landscape.

We are in a bad way and if our country is to recover we must be prepared to confront our problems rather than shoot the messenger.

Too many Jamaicans focus on how something was said or a little word or phrase that might seem offensive, and in so doing they lose sight of the grave matter at hand. We love to major in the minor; the tail wags the dog. Until we stop this petty nonsense we will continue to lose ourselves in the maze we have created.

Jamaica does not need another toothless commission, committee, arm, agency, movement, or watchdog to combat our problems. They have all been established only to appease. Jamaicans are understandably cynical at the call for any new investigative body. What good are they when they are tainted by one interest or another? What good are they when the teeth of these bodies belong to politicians and their friends to bite only when it suits? What good are they when many of those who should come under investigation are themselves on investigative bodies?

We are in a deficit in every area of growth, morality, values and attitudes. How we moved from being one of the fastest growing countries in the 1960s to a nation in crisis seems impossible. We have taken laziness and called it "inefficiency", have taken carelessness and called it "mismanagement", have taken slackness and called it "inconsistency", have taken stealing and called it "hustling" [1], and have called swindling hard earned tax dollars "overruns". We have diminished the magnitude of vagrant behaviors in our most essential offices by euphemistic taglines. When an action is too outrageous to escape scrutiny, we remove a thieving official and place him or her in another important position to 'thief some more' is the message. Is there any hope for this country? Or should we believe the prophesies on the streets that 'dawg a go nyam dawg' [2] in Jamaica.'

I believe that the real question is, "Who is willing to do what it takes to turn this country around?"

In other countries, the shame of exposure would silence and tarnish the offending individuals and even their families. In Jamaica, it 'blow off.' It is ironic that we admire these countries and sometimes adapt policies that are askew to our culture, yet the best practices that are the vanguard of protecting the rights and freedoms of all are selectively overlooked.

It is not for me to even speculate on guilt or innocence of any particular person. What I do know is that public officials, when implicated in a crime or a scandal, should step aside in the interest of preserving the image of the office that they serve. It is the decent thing to do. We should not cause the honour of public office to become sullied or besmirched with aspersions. That there is greatness within us is without question. Yet we are often our own worst nightmare. Today our leaders beg investors to come to Jamaica but who will come in this hostile environment?

In observing the transition of Jamaica over recent years I have been through phases of disappointment, shock, and most painful, the feeling of hopelessness. I have used my case as one measure and it is shocking. Despite all the odds against us that might have been brought about by 'connections' on the other side, the acts of corruption suffered or used against us we continued to ignore the people who said "pay off someone to apply pressure". We refused to be part of that, and I beg of others not to do it. This can't be allowed to go on forever. There must be justice at some point.

Corruption and injustice are alive and vibrant in the Jamaican system. The pulling of strings exists more than ever. The delays and corruption in the Court's Registry is still alive and well, more than it was 12 years before; probably better camouflaged but nevertheless there.

I continue to disagree with the voices of peace who say God will deal with those who are evil. I also disagree with those who say "take the law in your own hands," not because I believe that it will not work but because of the way I was brought up. I will never agree with those in the system who say "Yes the system is corrupted, but just accept whatever is offered for settlement, whether it be 30% or 50% or a pittance." This I find absolutely irresponsible. To do that would make me a contributor to the very corruption I am so vehemently against, in effect, helping to perpetuate it.

Why not fight it? How will we ever put an end to this scourge if we continue to give in and to reward it? If fighting it does not end it then at least let it be seen that we contributed to changing it, even a little.

History has been repeatedly changed because good people fought against it. Obviously I am no Martin Luther King, a hero of mine, but just imagine the loss had he thrown in the towel? Can you imagine if after his first march he just gave up? Can you imagine the state of the world if Nelson Mandela did that? As Martin Luther King once said, "Injustice here is a threat to justice everywhere." To give in to it is to encourage and breed more injustice.

So many critics or even enforcers of the laws are under the misconception that we need new laws and changes to the old laws. Yes, some new laws are needed from time to time. Yes, changes to old laws are required. This is perfectly understandable since innovations in culture and technology will create the need for some changes. A traffic light–related law would obviously not have been necessary in the 18th century. Likewise, in today's world libel laws often obstruct justice and ought to be overhauled. Laws giving more teeth to the justice system are often necessary and welcome, but to excuse the breakdown of law and order by blaming a shortage of laws is to justify wrong at the expense of a few lawmakers. No law can ever make sense if there is no enforcement!

This book is a desperate cry for help—a late cry indeed, but no less necessary—to the Jamaican Diaspora, to other developed countries, and to anyone interested in saving this nation. In these pages, I will use my own story to expose the evils of the current system and to open the eyes of the world to how they can bring about change. I am tired of our leaders hiding their own failures behind proclamations that 'Jamaica is the greatest country in the world, a country with the greatest people'. We are a nation in crisis. I seek your support to help make our country, Jamaica, the pearl of the Caribbean once again.

Although I cannot adequately expose the ills in Jamaica over the past 40 years in a single book I have tried to touch on various samples that might give some indication of what has and is happening. I am indeed ashamed that the failure of the country has been so devastating to its people by my generation, in particular to the poor for whom I have the greatest empathy.

This is simply the telling of my story, my life, my experience, my disillusion, and my pain. See me, Dwight Hugh Clacken, as a man who has the courage to tell his story and to challenge the country of his birth to make an about turn. I have taken the step to write. What step will you take?

PART I:

My Jamaica

CHAPTER 1

THE MOOD IN A BATTERED NATION

Jamaica in 2009 ranked among the most violent and corrupt in the democratic world—certainly the most violent and corrupt in the English-speaking Caribbean. Six years later nothing has changed, nor is there any reason to think that it will anytime soon.

Murder, a crime that not so long ago was viewed with abhorrence in every corner of the island, is now a normal activity that gets little or no attention from the population. We have become immunized against these ghastly atrocities and nothing short of a decapitated corpse at our doorstep can rouse us to respond.

Why? Why are the people so brutish against each other? Why do they take the law into their own hands? Isn't there a process that preserves their rights? Hmm. And yet, how accessible is justice to the masses who happen to be the poor? Can the poor afford to pay high profile lawyers? Can the poor afford to pay for the whole lengthy arduous process to get justice? Can the poor afford the costly price to pull strings?

The poor have learned that justice via our courts is not for them. They have learned that Justice is not a right; it is a privilege mainly reserved for a few. The not-so-poor are aware but can call on "connections" to achieve whatever they desire – good or bad. Getting anything done is typically preceded by a question like "whom do we know there?" The rest comes naturally.

While we scoff at what we hear about the workings of the inner city style of justice, one thing is sure: if what is rumored is true, the underground is the closest model to fairness and expediency that we have in this country. The dons are said to maintain an elaborate system with lawyers, witnesses and jurors. Cases are tried and sentencing is meted out swiftly. There is no trial in the garrison that runs for months or years. It would appear that if many cases were brought to them, we would have a less corrupt system - and yet, we are the ones who boast numerous degrees and who claim to be upstanding citizens who are watchdogs of the preservation of law and order.

The rich maintain their influence through money-power and political clout. Jamaica belongs to them. You may not want to accept this view of the land we all love but, wait until you Mr. Poor gets in a tangle with Mr. Who's Who and you shall understand the depths of rot in the courts. It is not simply that 'Your Honour' might make an unjust ruling; you may not even get to reach to 'Your Honour'. The delays alone will expend any resources that you imagined would sustain your pursuit of justice. The wealthy know this. Politicians know this. Professionals know this. The 'connected' know this.

They all know that when you are put off for years, you will be frustrated and resigned to accept anything. Even if your loved one is brutally killed, after years have passed, the economic realities force you to settle; after all, *"dem done dead already"*.

There is no doubt that corruption is rife and in many instances fuelled by politicians, although they will no doubt take great offence to this classification. The rape, pillaging and abuse of the peoples' money and rights has been documented repeatedly and I am hard pressed to recall even two politicians who have served time in prison during the past 30 years. Billions budgeted to do the nation's business have been stolen (or, as they call it, "misappropriated"), lining the pockets of fellow members of the 'establishment' who in turn distribute it amongst the poor who grab for it like starving dogs. These handouts are scarce benefits that the poor and uneducated need for survival in a country where work is rapidly diminishing. They are used as a weapon of enslavement, yet the uneducated view it as a helping hand. The will of such a person to stand up for self-determination, liberty, and justice is therefore threatened by deprivation or even starvation.

Meanwhile, kept uneducated, the beneficiaries of benefits unwittingly strengthen the hands of their leaders by securing votes to keep them in power. This power remains in the hands of leaders for as long as the beneficiaries remain dependent.

In order for any businessman to succeed it requires careful calculation of how to maneuver within the system; who to contact, who to bribe and how much, who to owe a favor like a promotion; who to have arrange removal of the competition. The consequences for the businessman who does not participate in the 'runnins' [1] are dire—a minimum of subtle persecution that could put someone out of business, often in the form of harassment from government agencies. Depending on how lucrative the business or how stubborn the operators, more fearful eventualities than that can be arranged.

The Ministries with responsibility for the collection of revenue and for setting the terms and standards for the running of the country are infected to a level that renders honest growth absolutely impossible. A simple but blatant example would be the fact that an application for a subdivision of any land for business or for private housing, or even the request for a building permit, is known to be impossible unless the applicant is connected or is willing to navigate through more than twelve departments, pay 'kickbacks', grant favors, or wait years for approval.

Back in the 60s, this was unacceptable and was greeted with shame and rebuke. In the 70s, this was greeted with some discomfort, but less shame and less rebuke. Private individuals started disassociating themselves, by looking the other way while the contracted professionals handling the matter did the dirty work.

One would think that since professionals — the educated among us — ought to be more qualified in ethics, more aware of right from wrong, more trained in the consequences of dishonesty and the impact of corruption. Yes, they should; they are the ones who are in charge of planning, designing, financing, assessing and executing projects that are meant to create employment and provide the basic essentials for a healthy economy.

Let's face it: if all the potential clients of professionals in Jamaica resisted corruption, then the contractors would have no work. It is therefore no surprise, that the professionals are the main contributors to the failure of this nation.

The two major political parties, The Jamaica Labour Party and The People's National Party have dominated the stratosphere of our democratic choice, the latter with 18 years of proven incompetence and rife corruption, and the former too absorbed in its internal affairs to be affected by the plight of the people. They appointed a Contractor General of known resolve and impeccable integrity, but tied his hands and removed his teeth in what must have been an effort to appear that 'something is being done' about corruption.

Meanwhile, those who have resisted the masters are migrating to more business friendly nations—taking their assets with them of course. Those who remain reluctantly give in and join their masters, becoming tainted. They guard the skeletons in their closets with vigor, now effectively silenced. The police, the revenue department, and ministries with responsibility for areas like commerce, utilities, and the courts all fall under the umbrella of "civil servants", the majority is up to their necks in corruption. The minority that resists the temptations becomes blameworthy by omission; while their fingerprints are not documented in wrongdoings they are culpable because their silence gives corruption a smooth transit. There was once a time when we could say that the majority in the civil service was upright, and only a few were tainted. During that very period the few who were tainted were black listed; nobody wanted to risk their reputation by associating with them. Now I fear that it is the majority who carry skeletons while the minority is resolutely silent. But how did the majority become entangled in the web of corruption? This simple scenario explains it. How can you point a finger at someone who is stealing millions when that same person gave you an incentive—maybe a promotion to look the other way or maybe to move a file to the top of a batch. You are implicated with no moral authority to speak out and oftentimes may have to be an accessory to your corruptors who may, upon your unwillingness to cooperate, issue a timely reminder of your past 'indiscretions'. What has caused the minority to be silent? Fear. Fear of not getting a promotion, of losing their jobs…of losing their lives.

We have reached a point with very little chance of reversal. We are truly at or passed the tipping point. Remittances from Jamaicans who migrated away from a "hell under construction" have been a saving grace for many here. After 50 years of independence, the nation's economy is so ravaged that there is little hope of reversal in the near future. A nation where investors are deprived of access to information critical to the state of their investments cannot survive.

All those who sit on air-conditioned committees or pray loudly at the Pentecostal prayer breakfasts are hypocrites, conveniently out of touch with reality. We all know what the problem is yet we fool around trying to blame it on poverty, American influences, unemployment, the absence of father figures, the influence of the mass media, or "slutty" music. We blame it on the symptoms, but we are unwilling to name the root of the problem.

I contend—and uncompromisingly so—that *injustice* forms the nucleus of the cataclysmic problems that threaten our country. Where there is no justice, Pandora's Box and all its miseries are unleashed with fury. For a country that loves to copy others we choose to ignore the strengths of their societies such as an effective justice system, one that reassures every citizen that their rights will be protected regardless of race, social class and financial status. In fact it seems that the motto of our justice system is "You will get by provided that you are of the right race, class, and financial status—and have the right connections."

How did the powers that be turn a blind eye to the decay that threatens and destroys access to our fundamental rights? Those who walk between the raindrops feel that they are not a part of corruption but they have created the puddle that eventually became a murky swamp.

To turn a blind eye is to slip corruption through the doors. Who in Jamaica has the integrity to lash out against injustice? To whose advantage would it be to stomp out this corruption? Who can resist the lure of pocketing millions of dollars of taxpayer's money especially if it is protected from easy detection? Who can resist the bribe? The kickback money assures some the little luxuries of today, the mansions, the big wheels, and the hype. Corruption is worth it since the risk factor is obscure.

Crime and violence in our country are mere links in the chain. Our country that is teetering on the edge of moral and financial ruin is the result of the machinations of politicians, professionals, judges, businessmen, all those who use their superior education, their intelligence and powers of office to manipulate every system, to plunge the poor man into doom, to fatten themselves and to screw up Jamaica land we love. The worst part of it is that these same people stand on every platform crying out for a "change in our nation".

Why can't we stop the hunger for murder in our country? It is because the "little man" knows that he doesn't have the kind of **money** or **"connections"** to get justice in court. Justice in Jamaica is for sale, like a common loaf of bread. Our court rules seem to have become the lawyer's mint. Our justice system, it appears, is not about unraveling the truth, defending the rights of, and protecting the innocent. It is about who has enough sense to pay off a lawyer, bribe a judge, have the registry misplace files or "link" a politician. It is about who has the 'connections' powerful enough to influence which judge should sit on a particular case, how he or she should rule, and when a case can be indefinitely delayed to the advantage of only one side. The victims become poorer, and lawyers and judges get richer.

It is simple. These are the **'untouchables'** who make a mockery of the justice system and who enjoy the break to hide behind excuses created '*out of convenience*' with the protection and support from their 'connections'. Murderers are protected as cases are adjourned over and over, as the victims' family's passion for justice wanes. Witness's memories and courage weaken during the 5 or 10, or 15 years waiting on justice as they look constantly over their shoulders for those likely to kill them. They eventually give in to fear, distance themselves from their statements or avoid showing up at court. Having waited years under the pressures and threat on their lives and of their family, many finally throw in the towel.

Are the courts concerned at the mockery that is made of its power? I don't think so. You would collapse if you hear how some lawyers advise their clients. You would wonder who the real criminals are.

Look at the Police. They are supposedly here to serve, protect and reassure. But instead they do the heavy leg work for the powerbrokers and so many are as corrupt as they come.

As for the poor man, "him get knock". Justice is for the highest bidder. The poor man no longer trusts the police, so he takes the law into his own hands. His justice! To him it is well worth the risk for that is the message that he has been sent. To him the only justice that you will find is the one exacted by your own hands.

Jamaica does not have the framework that assures individuals fair hearings, and the powers that be seem to want it that way. Murderers, scammers, money launderers, fraudsters - all criminals, irrespective of their colour, standing, creed or status, are guaranteed safe passage to freedom and privileges provided that they are tools of the well-to-do and "connected" . . . especially so if they are politically connected. Where therefore is the protection for the innocent?

The punishment for the guilty is often more gain; the justice for the innocent is often one of pain. The zero level of trust in the system is therefore justified. Having no other alternative, jungle justice prevails; to them, the only kind of justice that works. Most believe that we get better justice from the Dons. Why? It is consistently swifter, fairer, and is governed by a clear set of rules with which both parties are familiar. Unlike the flawed system in place, no one dares to lie to the Don because there are clear consequences.

It is no surprise why the Don is given this level of respect. The Don is trusted to be fair, that is why he is chosen over the Jamaican judicial system. Our courts allow and encourage people to play games. One could accurately refer to our courts as 'mafia-run gambling houses' – risky and expensive for the patrons; results are often by arrangement, rarely by chance. With the 'Don' no one plays games.

Because so many of the Police are protected by 'bigwigs' (and, by extension, the courts), most victims are powerless to their actions. We are thankful for those in the force who are upright, for those have not yet succumbed to the lures and pressures of corruption. Injustice here is a tight money powered circle that involves the "Big Man", the Businessman, the Judge, the Lawyer, and the Professional. Common to all these is education. It is so sad, we refer to ourselves as a developing country, yet we have not used education as a means to enhance our citizens. Our leadership has treated justice as if it were an option; as if it were not an absolute necessity and a right that the people should not be denied. The honest man knows that this wickedness originated in high places and is perpetuated and regulated from there as we speak.

How did a country with the most gifted, resourceful, honest, caring and friendly people on earth become a depraved, crime-ridden, corrupt nation so soon after gaining its independence? A country where, after 51 years of Independence, no one flinches with surprise as murder is perpetrated and sanctioned by the powers that be by way of their unfulfilled promises to 'stamp out' crime? In less than 40 years, we were showing a murder rate of more than 1,600 per year compared to 51 murders just preceding Independence in 1961. Who is it that took us down this path? Who are the beneficiaries of this rot? And who are the suckers that endure this slavery? What is it that went so very wrong?

The destruction of the Jamaican economy over less than 40 years is symptomatic of the greed, incompetence, and corruption in leadership over that period. With out-of-control inflation and massive devaluations at intermittent and unpredictable intervals, the strength of Jamaican currency declined from being stronger than US currency to being more than 140 times weaker.

In 1975, fourteen years after Independence, the official rate at the Bank of Jamaica showed little change, but mismanagement, fear, corruption, and uncertainty gave good reason for the start of a debilitating black market. The Bank of Jamaica only started to indicate this in 1978. From there, it was all downhill for the "Paradise of the Caribbean".

Using official rates, this table clearly shows the impact on investors commencing less than 10 years after gaining Independence. By holding Jamaican dollars, time became a tool to fear and has remained increasingly so, even as I write.

In 1968	Ja$1, 000.00 could buy	US$1298.00
In 1972	Ja$1, 000.00 could buy	US$1098.00
In 1978	Ja$1, 000.00 could buy	US$ 952.00
In 1980	Ja$1, 000.00 could buy	US$571.00
In 1983	Ja$1, 000.00 could buy	US$317.00
In 1987	Ja$1, 000.00 could buy	US$181.00
In 1991	Ja$1, 000.00 could buy	US$116.00
In 1995	Ja$1, 000.00 could buy	US$27.00
In 2000	Ja$1, 000.00 could buy	US$22.00
In 2005	Ja$1, 000.00 could buy	US$15.00
In 2010	Ja$1, 000.00 could buy	US$11.00
In 2013	Ja$1, 000.00 could buy	US$ 9.00
In 2015	Ja$1, 000.00 could buy	US$ 8.00

Those of us with personal experience of living through a disaster spanning over 50 years, most of which worsened every day and still continues, are stunned. It is impossible for anyone outside of this experience to understand why people have tolerated it for so long. It says a lot for the ability of our leaders to con a majority of the population back into slavery without a hint of them revolting on a large scale. They have mastered the art of creating a culture to destroy. They have also mastered the art of disguising it to look like a culture of freedom and entitlement. They have certainly fooled the majority, while the politicians, the educated and the well to do, take full advantage of lavish lifestyles and overseas wealth. Only by doing what so many are afraid to do, can one see and understand what has happened to 'paradise'. Only by frankly relating my own personal experiences can I give a true picture—one so alarming that it may be tempting to read it as fiction.

I consider myself more qualified than most to speak on the quality and availability of justice in Jamaica, spanning a period, long enough to give fair comparison. I was lucky to be part of 'paradise' when justice was so sure it was taken for granted that evil could not thrive in

Jamaica. I was present during a change for the worse in the 1970s. I was present during a recovery period in the 1980s, and I was present during the destruction in the 1990s. I fought during the first decade of the 21st century to capture the elusive justice that converted our island paradise to the murder capital of the world, and I failed in that fight.

I saw justice, injustice, and the causes of both throughout that time. I visited almost every ministry of government that impacted justice, from the police to the courts to the Prime Minister himself. I have lived through too much to adequately explain in one volume, but I owe it to Jamaica—especially the underprivileged, the oppressed, the uneducated—to make a contribution towards change since it can no longer be accomplished through the ballot.

Countries that have not yet travelled our path will do well to learn from any gains and pitfalls Jamaica experienced after fifty years of independence.

CHAPTER 2
LIFE BEFORE INDEPENDENCE

I was born in 1947 in Kingston, Jamaica to middle-class parents. My father was a civil servant, and my mother a housewife.

As a boy 4 years old living at Prince of Wales Street in Allman Town, I can recall only few experiences. Naturally, those that stick in my mind are some of the more frightening experiences. During Hurricane Charlie in 1951, our roof came off and I along with my sister and two brothers were moved around under tables and in closets as my parents were busy dealing with the adverse effects of the hurricane. Strangely I recall vividly the sound of glass breaking at a window, but I don't remember much else. My sister claims that I slept through most of it.

My father, a collector of taxes, was transferred to Jackson Town in the Parish of Trelawny shortly after the hurricane. My memories of life in Jamaica thereafter are much clearer. Much of our time at the ages of 4 and 5 was spent at play and a considerable amount at the Christian Brethren Church (Evangelical) where my dad officiated and preached. Sundays was 'breaking of bread' in the morning, Sunday school in the evening, followed by night service. My father started a branch of that church everywhere that government transferred him, pioneering and establishing some eleven branches throughout his lifetime. It is from this base that my high standards were set; it was not unusual to the family to attend the "Gospel Chapel" two or three nights per week in addition to three times on Sunday.

While I revere these as some of the happiest days of my life, we were not without our tragedies. My younger brother Boysie died of accidental poisoning at the tender age of three. Boysie was a kid with extreme tolerance for pain and was almost fearless. He was tough, inquisitive, highly intelligent, and very persuasive. Any 3 year old who can convince 5 and 6 year olds as well as his Nanny to do practically anything has got to be a smart kid. He was definitely a handful for my parents; as I recall, spankings had little effect on Boysie. He was years ahead of his age, and without doubt a leader. His single fear was 'Jonkunnu' (John Canoe) parades, a cultural display by masked dancers emulating various animals and the devil, and backed up by distinctive drumbeats and music. The very sound of drums emanating from a distant 'Pocomania' church gathering would send him scampering under a bed or nearest convenient hiding place. His greatest weakness was an *addiction* to "sweeties," the Jamaican slang for candy.

Boysie, as I recall clearly, had seen Mom place some tablets prescribed for him at a location well out of reach of any normal child under 10 years old. They were placed on top of a closet (called a "press" in those days). Boysie organized and supervised the shoving of a bureau (dresser) up to the press and used the drawers as steps to climb atop the bureau as he reached up to the closet for the tablets. He kindly shared the tablets as if they were "sweeties" among my sister, our Nanny, and I. Our youngest brother was a baby and was not given a share. Of course we all enjoyed the 'sweets'. They were orange in color, sweet on the outside, and the bitter part in the middle we spat out as we sucked away at the 'sweeties'. Boysie 'the organiser', shared himself a much larger portion.

Later that night my sister awakened Mom and snitched. "Mummy Boysie ate the sweeties". Mom rushed to check on Boysie, and his complexion had an unusual hue. We were ten miles from the nearest hospital, which necessitated the traversing of narrow dirt roads. Boysie was rushed to hospital as quickly as possible to have his stomach pumped, but he died in hospital that night during treatment.

It was a tough time for my parents, particularly my mother. She had been visiting with the Post Mistress [1] no more than 80 yards away on the night of Boysie's demise and the Nanny was in charge—or so she thought. Actually, Boysie was in charge. I can't help thinking about the power of Boysie's personality. My sister was never one to be bossed; she ruled the roost. Her strong personality, and her conviction for doing what is proper, was overcome by Boysie's eloquence that night.

Boysie's death was not very clear in my mind. I recall travelling some 90 miles to Kingston with Boysie's body in the coffin spanning the front and back seats of the Vanguard, as my sister and I lay below the coffin, at times pasting our ears to the floor, listening to the road noise through the floor. Throughout the Journey my mother wept uncontrollably as my father consoled her.

After his death we did not discuss Boysie often, but on the few occasions I recall seeing my mother cry when discussing his death she would explain to us that Boysie was in Heaven and that we would see him one day. At that tender age I was confused by her reaction. Why should Mummy be so sad when Boysie was gone to a happy place like Heaven? My father did not cry, or at least I never saw him cry. Not then, nor at any other time in his life. His faith in God seemed to have kept him strong, as I would realize later. He never wavered in his commitment to his God.

As an adult, I have often thought that Boysie's unique personality could have made him a genius or a dangerous mastermind - any of two extremes, but never mediocre. The good Lord might well have decided.

Jackson Town was a quiet and reserved village with some small farms, but larger farmlands in sugar cane made up much of the area. Much of the town was not wired for electricity, and nearly all the roads were dirt.

How could I forget the values instilled during those junior years? Those years stand out in stark contrast to the absence of morals today. Parents—mine included—were strict on discipline and values, and children were respectful of others, particularly of their elders. Very special respect was the norm for teachers, the Post Mistress, pastors, policemen, nurses, doctors, and the elders from other families. We referred to our elders as 'Sir', 'Ma'am', 'Miss' etc. So important were values that it was not unusual for a parent to spank the child of another parent at any time if the rules of good conduct or values were breached. This almost never caused conflict between the parents. In fact, this is an indication of the sense of trust only found where justice was expected and always handed down. I got the impression that a parent who did not correct a disrespectful child was doing that child's parents a disservice.

Respect for our elders was therefore endemic and natural. One evening while walking home from First Hill School in Jackson Town and playing with my "gig" (top) as I travelled, I passed the Post Mistress without saying "good evening" or acknowledging her at all. Indeed I was preoccupied with play. Well, what followed was a good spanking and a sound lecture that had me sneaking home, not daring to tell my parents because I figured that one spanking was enough. These events are fixed in my memory probably because they were early lessons in obedience, respect, values, and all the expectations that are today seen in Jamaica as insignificant.

I remember two men, Lively and Cecil, who were the town troublemakers. Whenever the local shop was broken into, it was either Lively or Cecil. They were most often drunk and although branded as the common petty thieves of the area, my parents would employ them to do odd jobs around the home at various times, even after they were released from prison. They did so without fear of them injuring the children or themselves. I can hear my mother pleading with them on occasions to clean up their lives.

"Cecil, why do you do it?" she would say when he was released from a stint in jail. "There is work around, just work and stop the drinking."

Lively and Cecil never pretended to be innocent when they were guilty and never had a violent bone in their bodies. They just could not stop stealing. They stole for food and liquor, not wealth. They worked hard but drank harder.

My parents made no special effort to protect us from Cecil. I really liked him. I remember being fascinated with 'Cecil's magic' when he 'picked' wasp nests from our orange trees with his bare hands and shirtless body without being stung. Although I have seen this done by two other persons later in my life, I still have not determined the secret to keeping the wasps from attacking. The wasps numbering sometimes 20 or so on each nest would vibrate their wings while the nest was being slowly removed and my experiences of being attacked and stung on many occasions gave me reason to believe that Cecil was special. I never missed the opportunity to nag him, begging him to "pick" more wasp nests.

"How do you do it"? I would ask him.

"Mi wipe up wid mi sweat an grind mi teet wen mi pick dem," he would always say.

However, that didn't work when I tried it. I discovered that apart from the sweat and teeth grinding being ineffective, I would have been better off with my shirt on.

"Serves you right," my mother would say as she wiped down my swollen face and body with some sort of ammonia product.

I guess I was not very persistent at that age because I never had the guts to try it more than once. With that skill Cecil was never out of work as long as wasp nests were around my home. I would never fail to show every nest to my mother, just to see Cecil in action.

At age six, I attended First Hill Elementary School, a late age compared with today. On my first day at school, I got a thorough whipping from an 11 year old student whom I stared at because I noticed that he was sucking his finger. I just could not fathom a habit like that for a boy that age, and I ridiculed him as "Suck Finger Jack." Had I not commented on his habit I might have been spared an extra lick or two. It was also a good lesson in when not to tease. Clarence, an athletic boy about 10 years old, whose family was friendly with my family, came to my rescue and returned the favor in what turned out to be a one-sided fist fight. This served me well as all students at school figured that Clarence would not permit anyone to bully me. It made my journey through First Hill School easier, and I learned to pick on those more like my size.

As young children in Jackson Town, we were always very aware of the "*Black heart man*"— a man who would grab onto little children, remove and eat their little hearts if they strayed into certain areas without their parent's permission and protection or if they returned home in the dark of night. In hindsight I am quite sure that these stories were concocted by parents, probably dating back to the days of slavery to make sure that kids did not stray into unfamiliar areas or speak with people not known to the family. I certainly bolted home on the occasions that the "*Black Heart Man*" alarm was sounded by anyone. Quite often, while playing marbles with our friends along the road, some passing cane worker or small farmer would sound the alarm. This would test our fleet-footedness – fire gashed from every 'foot bottom' as we sped away, and the most athletically gifted would not necessarily lead the way home. Usually the most terrified among us would set the pace.

My parents were very good friends of the Headmaster of First Hill Elementary School, "Teacher Codner," and his wife "Aunt G", herself also a teacher. They parented Cecil (affectionately - "Seecil"), Brenda, Faye, and Anthony (Tony) who was my age. Cecil, Brenda and Faye were older. Brenda and Faye were in High School when we were in elementary school.

On one occasion my parents left Jamaica for 6 months on accumulated leave and we stayed with "Teacher Codner". His farm was about 60 acres, but as a child it appeared like 600 acres. It was a bountiful farm with all the Jamaican fruits you can think of. Electricity was not available in Jackson Town so all was accomplished with manually operated equipment, including horses and mules. Collecting coconuts was done using a horse or mule drawn cart. Removing honey from the honeycomb with a manually operated centrifuge and converting the honeycomb into wax blocks for cleaning wooden floors was typical. Floors were waxed using a brush made by cutting off one end of the husk from a dried coconut. Butter was not bought; it was made. My recollection is that the farm was as close to total self-sufficiency as was possible in those days, and even by today's standards it was very self-sufficient.

The time spent on the headmaster's farm was great fun. His son Tony and I did it all. We rode horses bareback, milked cows, fed the rabbits, attended bee hives (although the bees were not my favorite), we climbed trees including coconut trees to reap the nuts, drove the mule drawn cart collecting dried coconuts, reaped and ate fruits like the cashew fruit, played games with marbles and "gigs," [2] and climbed trees to capture young "white winged" birds from their nests for taming. You name it, we did it. "Extra lessons" were not my favorite times but always formed a part of our duties. It was clearly understood that studies went along with work and play. Aunt G saw to that.

We were never closely supervised in our free time during those days. As long as we did our chores and homework we were free to roam the fields and bushes on foot or on horseback armed with our slingshots. As boys we got up to our tricks, but we knew the consequences and often chose to learn from the "strap" when we fell out of line. On one occasion I recall practicing with my slingshot at Mr. Burnett's turkey, hitting it in the head and sitting out the rest of the day measuring in my mind what would happen if it died. It didn't, and it spared me having to tell Teacher Codner about it.

I can't recall ever being punished unfairly in those days. Floggings at school seemed always administered when deserved. I got my fair share at home or when I spent time at the home of the headmaster and failed to do my chores on the farm or for offences like disobedience. It was never regarded as pleasant but in hindsight it was always deserved.

Somehow it appeared that people were more honest and fair in those days and we accepted it as part of our culture. Every flogging that I got was justified - even the spanking from the Post Mistress was fair. During that time the feeling of injustice was unknown to me.

Montego Bay

My father's transfer to Montego Bay (Mobay), snatched from me the fun days of Jackson Town. Montego Bay was quite a contrast to the rural Jackson Town. A faster moving town, Mobay was more businesslike with less play but nevertheless I had my fair share of fun. There I struggled to keep up with the brighter boys in class at Cornwall College. Fifteenth place out of thirty students was the best I achieved, and that was good enough for me. I was still in play mode.

Secondary school at Cornwall College required walking to and from school, covering over two miles each day. Of course, the trek home was more interesting than walking to school and by then the rumours about "Black Heart Man" had disappeared completely. Life seemed now more rushed but the standard of discipline was no less. Parents intervened less with the behavior by children of other parents. This I suppose was because by then the base was already established and respect had become entrenched to the point where it was automatic. The customary parental interference continued in the lower age groups nevertheless. By no means were we all angels in those days, but we certainly were respectful of others.

Floggings or 'canings' at high school remained standard, yet normally they were never delivered in anger. We all knew right from wrong, we just hoped to never be caught. On a particular occasion at age ten I was unjustifiably 'caned' at school, and I recall the anger that it left with me. Up to the age of nine I had not personally experienced any form of injustice. Just imagine, even at that tender age injustice was immediately recognized as unacceptable. I have forgotten most of the floggings I got because I believed those floggings to be justified. However, I have never forgotten the one caning that was not justified. I remember every detail, every stroke of the cane. That is the nature of injustice.

Why should this common act of caning, only six strokes, offend me this much? The anger was so extreme that I refused to give in to the headmaster and managed to rack up two more canings before being sent home that day. I am quite sure that it was from then that my understanding of the treatment of the under-privileged and the weak, the slaves as set out in the history books, became so striking.

Lucea, Hanover

I had settled in at school in Montego Bay only 4 years when my father was transferred to Lucea in Hanover as the tax collector there. From that transfer I was fortunate to have attended Ruseas High School, where the exceptional headmaster Eric Frater, a visionary who mastered the art of teaching, led the school through a remarkable run of growth. Mr. Frater oozed fairness that so impacted on me that he became a role model. Here was a brilliant, gutsy, optimistic, selfless man who worked long hours, never giving up. Wherever he pointed us, we trusted him. We accepted his guidance, and the students excelled.

I would be remiss if I omitted here the tremendous impact of this man on Ruseas High School and on the people of Western Jamaica. Jamaica is the ultimate beneficiary of Mr. Frater's vision and leadership. The very high standard of teachers placed in the school through his efforts to lift the school above "O level" [3] grade; many of those teachers, though having varying levels of qualification, seemed to have the gift of imparting – so typical of the man Mr. Frater. Eric Frater himself was a natural teacher who, whenever he filled in for an absent science teacher he would lecture to us so clearly and eloquently that writing notes was unnecessary.

We were motivated in every area we ventured. On our first attempt at the Scientific Exhibition competition in Kingston we placed first. It was no surprise at that time that Ruseas was known to have the best debate team in Jamaica. Eric Frater refused to accept any lack of effort. I always remember the look on his face when he suspected a lack of guts by any student. Even the "rebels" of Ruseas were usually transformed with their spirits intact by the time they left Ruseas. A "gutsy" man, Frater showed great displeasure when students threw in the towel without a fight. A disciplinarian he was, yet no student was afraid of him. We knew and trusted that he would always be fair.

I recall in about 1962 as a cadet we performed dismally in the annual cadet corps inspection. To Mr. Frater this was unacceptable and two army officers were promptly assigned to train the corps. They alternated their training duties as they "drilled" us on the parade grounds in front of the school and tested our toughness in sham battles. It was no surprise that the Ruseas Cadet Corps won the annual inspection the following year. So impressive were we that at a camp in Newcastle I heard comments made by cadets from various schools implying that they had never seen better performances on any parade. Our outstanding performance allowed us to represent the raising of flags of various countries at the Pan American games in Jamaica—a proud moment for me as I raised the Guatemalan flag.

Lucea was a peaceful, quiet town on the Northwest sea coast of Jamaica, and I spent much of my extra time fishing and swimming. My friends and I often "snuck out" with our parents' cars at nights, although we had no drivers' licenses. So few were the cars in that town that it was unlikely that we would have encountered traffic late at night when we pursued our indiscretions. We were however quite aware of the consequences if caught. I suppose 'boys will be boys' and I suppose this kind of thing still happens today - except that the chance of accidents is much more likely now.

Quite prominent in my mind was the raising of the Jamaican Flag on the day we got Independence from Britain on August 6, 1962. I could feel the spirit of the population, the feeling of growing up, maturity, of freedom, as if we had found new life. Life was just beginning and the feeling that much better was to come, captured our hearts and minds.

Violence was practically non-existent in Lucea. The same respect that I had seen as a child in Jackson Town was evident there. As a boy, I was friendly with the sons of the judge in Lucea and was in awe of him. At no time did I ever hear a comment from anyone that was critical of his integrity or judgment. It was as if he was put there by some omniscient authority who knew that he earned that position and was the best person for it. The police, the pastor, the nurse, the teacher, the doctor, the motor vehicle examiner were all held in the same high regard. It was a paradise that was not to last much longer.

CHAPTER 3

WORKING IN A NEWLY INDEPENDENT JAMAICA

After sitting the "Higher School Certificate [1] (A level GCE equivalent) [1] it was time for me to earn my keep. I was in love with studying medicine but back then university courses required full time attendance. My father's earnings could not support me full time in university and so off to work I went. My departure from Ruseas took me to Kingston where I was employed in 1966 by a heavy equipment company called Jamtrac .This was the first step in a line of business which I also enjoyed.

Two years later I was employed by an uncle who was doing well in the same heavy equipment business. There, with my new boss Terrence Causwell ("TC"), I was fortunate to be guided by the same values and principles in which I was brought up. He had returned to Jamaica after serving as a pilot and navigator during World War II and capitalizing on a scholarship granted by the British Government at School of Brixton in England.

My boss's motto was "a square deal to all" and he truly lived by those words.

Many of his contracts were based solely on a handshake. I saw him advise truck owners on what price to charge on various jobs in which he had no business interest, and they kept returning for more free advice whenever they needed.

As I learned how to bid on jobs I became quite fond of calculating the cost of carting earth and from time to time my boss would lecture me on the finer short-cuts and "tricks" in earthmoving. He would almost always finish his lectures with a reminder to be fair and honest at all times.

One of his many lectures came after some truckers had given him a quote for a job he had won by bid and he thought that their price was much cheaper than should be. This was typical because many of the truck owners could not calculate their costs, and some could not read and write well. After he hired the truckers and increased their rate he went to great pains to explain to me why he paid more than they asked. His lecture went something like this: "Never accept a quote too low from someone whom you know will unknowingly lose money, and in particular, someone whom you know has not had the benefit of an education that would help that someone to know better. Pay him what is fair and what guarantees him a profit" he would say. "That way", he explained, "the trucker will have no reason to cheat with the quantity of earth he carries in the truck, nor will he have reason to influence the load counter to falsify the number of trips. Instead, he will tend to always give you a square deal." Such was the integrity and caliber of so many of his generation.

All those he employed were in awe of him. He was a quiet man who was most profound with the few words that he said. When asked to justify a decision, an employee would often find it difficult to respond adequately when confronted by his perceptive and probing queries. An instance of his uncanny logic was demonstrated one morning when, as was customary, we drove to visit a site that was under construction. He explained his habit of travelling as early as 3am or 4 am in the morning by saying, "It is cooler, easier on the car and the body." He often dozed while I drove. On this particular morning a sports car was on my tail and I thought I could outclass the ambitious little sports car without waking my boss. At 19 years old I had to brush aside the challenge from anybody sticking on my bumper. As I stepped up the pace on the very curvy roads, the car behind squealed its tires so loudly that my boss awakened. Typical of the man, he calmly asked me a simple question "What are you going to do with the ten minutes when you get to the site?" That left me speechless. I could only have saved about ten minutes by speeding and we had left at a time to arrive at the site at daybreak. That is a simple example of the type of mind of the man that was seated beside me.

An opportunity to learn was rarely wasted. My time in the heavy equipment business equipped me to handle basic land surveying necessary for setting out projects, mechanics, project management, and believe it or not the actual driving and operation of dozers, scrapers, and other heavy machinery. Much of my progress on sites was gained from the Land Surveyor Richard Myers, also a bit of a 'MacGyver' who passed on a lot to those willing to learn.

The changing Jamaica

By 1969-70 I started to see small changes in the attitude and morals of the civic and political leadership of the country, and it was spreading to the masses. My boss "TC" was disturbed by this creeping dishonesty. As a contractor he found it difficult to outbid those who were willing to bribe for construction jobs. His success in the early 60s was accomplished without passing a single dollar to curry favor.

As dishonesty became increasingly evident my boss opted to get out of heavy equipment businesses rather than pay kickbacks to get work. It had obviously started some years before but was becoming more prevalent. This was to me the start of the dilemma we have in Jamaica today. I recall my boss's abhorrence when a certain Member of Parliament, under cross-examination at the 'DaCosta Commission of inquiry'[2] into corruption during distribution of contracts, admitted giving away government lands free of charge and defiantly repeated that he would do it again if he was again elected to a position of power

With retirement in mind and what he referred to as "a labour of love" he ventured into the Thoroughbred horse business mainly as a breeder. This was one of his fascinations as a child and my early childhood experience in Jackson Town served me well here. In 1969 I was sent by my boss to a millionaire's farm in Ocala, Florida to "learn and observe." Or at least that was what the US authorities said I was doing, since I had no work permit and my time there was without any remuneration. The size of the farm was such that all employees drove from barn to barn. Each barn had sleeping quarters occupied by a farm hand who was familiar with horses and could be called on at nights to assist the resident veterinarian. Watchmen drove from barn to barn observing the horses for problems like colic – a condition which is quite prevalent in horses. I occupied the living quarters at one barn which gave me quick access to assisting the resident veterinarian if he was called on by a watchman.

Young, energetic, anxious to learn, but naïve to some social problems that I would have to endure in Ocala, I plunged headlong into work starting at the bottom cleaning manure from horse stalls, changing bedding hay, grooming, bandaging feet, 'hot walking' horses, and the like. The discipline and versatility that I had acquired previously came in handy. Up at 5 am each and every morning, I lost weight although I ate more than I had ever eaten at any time of my life. The more effort I put in the quicker, I could return to Jamaica, I thought.

By far the most challenging issue I encountered, though, was the rampant racism in America at the time, particularly in the Southern states. At the time black churches and white churches were kept separate, as was the norm throughout the Deep South. In my naivety I found it difficult to understand how this was allowed and why coloreds were not allowed to occupy rooms on the farms. I had experienced a small amount of class segregation in Jamaica, but never color segregation.

My presence there was a novelty and raised some eyebrows. Some whites did not converse with me, but employees who had migrated from northern states were hospitable and went out of their way to accommodate me. An Irishman in charge of the hospital barn was very kind to me and guidance from him was most valuable.

After choosing to hang around the resident veterinarian as he attended his patients at nights, and making the rounds at the various different barns, I felt like I had covered a year of work in the first 3 months. By the time I was ready to leave for Jamaica I felt like I had accomplished 3 years of work in less than 9 months.

On returning, I lost no time questioning my father who was an elder in the Evangelical church why his Christian brethren tolerated the segregation I saw abroad. His answer was not to my satisfaction but was very simple and turned out to be somewhat prophetic: "Time will change that, violence or any other retaliation won't do it any quicker". I didn't agree but the achievements of Martin Luther King strengthened his point.

It didn't take my boss long to find out that the racing industry was not conducive to honesty either. It was not the same as when he was a boy. In fact, in hindsight the entire country was changing around him and he was only seeing what was directly exposed to him. He only found out when he got into a particular business and stumbled onto corruption at each step, so gentle and subtle was the change.

He fought to oppose anything that encouraged corruption and he had the vision to see a problem as well as the way to discourage it. He had a strong belief in a system that would discourage the "pulling" of horses in races. Pulling to lose was used by stakeholders to alter the allotment of weight to be placed on each horse. Losing races allowed horses to unfairly have their weight allotment reduced in order to better their chances and win, often when the punters least expected it. Losing a race did not affect only the horse owner; it also affected thousands of punters who bet on the losers. While he fought for change in the horse racing industry he continued to breed horses of extremely high quality. I watched him fight for years before he withered away some twenty years later, a frustrated, thwarted, and disappointed man. He was one of the last of a once noble and productive era.

Despite the shifting public morals, this was a period of tremendous economic growth and the impact of the changing values in Jamaica were not to be seen as immediate as pulling a switch. Jamaica between 1965 and 1969 was hailed as one of the fastest growing developing nations in the world – at least better or on par with Singapore. Between 1960 and 1969 Jamaica's growth averaged 5.2% per annum. A United Nations Development Programme estimated that based on per capita income, life expectancy and educational attainment, Jamaica ranked first among 79 industrial and developing countries."

Unfortunately, at that time, with that growth came greed, corruption, and an inability or unwillingness on the part of the ruling Jamaica Labour Party (JLP) to stamp it out. It had to be stopped somehow, and many Jamaicans believed that way was through the electorate. Our opportunity came in 1972.

Despite this booming economy under the JLP, the people wanted a change. In 1972 the People's National Party (PNP) under the leadership of Michael Manley took power as the majority of Jamaicans registered their displeasure with the JLP. There was jubilation island-wide; we had, we thought, gotten rid of a corrupt and uncaring government. My boss Terrence Causwell and I had been involved in the campaigning process for the change. The charismatic Manley had everything in his favor and the people adored him. He had the perfect opportunity to build on the economic boom.

Through the first year in office his popularity soared, he continued to hold practically all the people in his hands; we were mesmerized. Then, in 1973, the DaCosta Commission was set up to investigate the corruption under the previous Government. At that time a commission could be trusted to get to the truth and was considered much more reliable for acting with integrity than 40 years after. The Commission was indeed an exposure but I can't recall a message by way of consequence. It seemed like a 'tit for tat' agreement that opened the door to legitimize corruption on both sides. I got the feeling that the opposition party was forgiven and the PNP was owed huge favours in return, as no one was punished after the commission report exposed corruption by JLP politicians. This was clear indication that the PNP intended to benefit using the same methods that were exposed and more.

CHAPTER 4

THE TERRIBLE SEVENTIES

In 1974, Michael Manley declared that Jamaica was embarking on a path of Democratic Socialism. The business class immediately went into shock. The birth of the "handout culture"—distribution of wealth or distribution by pretext of "entitlement"—was on. Rhetoric like "rapacious capitalists", "imperialist colonial masters," and the like was spewed with regularity. This was never part of his campaign for leadership. It came as a complete surprise to those who had supported him, and it set Jamaica on a course from which it has never returned.

The world oil crisis in early 1970s seemed to provide some excuse or reason to escalate the rhetoric. The average person was made to believe that some large factories were 'theirs' to be operated through cooperatives; the apprenticeship programs that had produced top quality workers after serving as apprentice carpenters, masons, mechanics and the like, disappeared after Manley's rhetoric of "no more masters and servants." So too went the high quality of tradesmen generally. No more maids—instead they were called "helpers," helping their employers with their households. The word "maid" was seen as demeaning, even though they performed the same menial tasks as before.

The mentality encouraged entitlement rather than hard work, as if the colonial powers "owed" us for years of exploitation. Such was the perception of the message from the political leadership of Manley's PNP government. His rhetoric intensified into speeches inferring that he would be "walking to the mountaintop" with Fidel Castro. Announcing that idle lands would be handed over to the "people" or taken by the government in exchange for bonds was met with objection from the land owners and financial institutions when it was discovered that the bonds were to be "non-transferrable and non-negotiable" as was done in Cuba. The word "idle" seemed designed to initially legitimize the confiscations, but the pressure from the institutions in particular, brought about the rescinding of the terms "non-transferrable and non-negotiable". Still, the government set about distributing plots for agricultural use under projects like "Project Land Lease".

As entrepreneurs hollered in objection to what was seen as too many moves that were identical to those taken in Cuba's road to Communism, Manley responded to complainants reminding them that there were "five flights per day" leaving Jamaica. In what many saw as arrogance, others saw proof he was going full Communist.

The culture of handouts that Manley brought about was great news for many, as it became an essential part of the power structure. Handouts were subsidized using whatever was accumulated by way of robberies, scams, kickbacks and other unscrupulous acts. But who really picked up the tab for handouts? The taxpayers of course – handouts funded from the kickbacks taken from government contracts were usually distributed in a partisan way. Here the leadership could kill many birds with one stone. They could control and manipulate votes while keeping the people dependent on those in power. The old masters were no more. But little did the people know that those were only being replaced by new masters, new leaders. In a climate of scarce benefits, those who failed to "stay in line" could find food to be scarce and life more difficult unless they remained obedient servants of these new masters who conned them into partisan allegiance. Local activists or 'foot soldiers' who reported to the party 'dons' ensured that the recipients of scarce benefits voted 'correctly' when it was election time. Vote rigging became common as well. Administering of punishment was delivered by local activists on instructions from the dons – certainly not without the knowledge of their masters. These activists were called "Thugs and criminals" when it became necessary for the politician to separate him or herself from such characters.

The name "comrade", a typically communist term, was perceived as a privilege to those in the new political PNP band and gave the perception of equality for all. "Comrade" became the call sign of PNP supporters. Despite the dark history of the word, Manley was not afraid to use it. The terms "Comrade Leader" and "Comrade Minister" or plain "Comrade" remain standard tag-lines of the PNP even today, used commonly as a term of endearment.

Manley's fanaticism to "free up" the people led him to make maverick and detrimental decisions. Some of his actions were obviously not well thought out as he seemed overwhelmed in the fanfare of his huge popularity. The ideas of the Manley government were not all bad, but the way they were presented made entrepreneurs nervous—eventually to the level of panic. In hindsight it is not clear why he had to put on 'the scare', unless he really intended to turn Jamaica into a Communist state. Many of the policies installed by Manley bore similarities to the pre-Communist stages in Cuba. Some actually copied programs that existed in Cuba then.

During this 'wild' period, the Manley government embarked on a drive to make secondary education accessible to more students; a brilliant idea and an act of justice. Yet the program was plagued by lack of vision, inadequate planning, and gross overestimation of the funding that was possible at that time. The announcement of the plan came at the surprise of his ministers including his Minister of Finance. Today we are bearing the full brunt of his recklessness; the fruit that tempts many leaders to maintain popularity despite any negative repercussions: You give the people what they want today, let another leader and generation deal with the impact tomorrow. That was what happened.

But to his credit Manley certainly made it easier for the poor to access all levels of education. His method of doing good was often ad hoc and without any planning whatsoever. Despite this, his education initiative was the best thing he ever did for Jamaica during his reign as Prime Minister. As this drive progressed it became obvious that there weren't enough schools, and not enough new schools were being constructed to cope with the demand. Let's face it: Teachers are not made overnight. As a result schools had to be operated in two shifts each day, a nightmare for working parents, among other problems, and a bit of sharing in order to accommodate all children. Although this could remain a matter of debate there was the general belief that education standard was not keeping pace. It is difficult to expect more when facilities were being shared resulting in fewer hours per student. However there is absolutely no doubt that good values and attitudes were being abandoned in the process despite some good intentions.

With this initiative and others, Manley's heart seemed to be in the right place, but his rhetoric did the country a disservice. The opposite of slavery is not freedom, but rather an opportunity to build oneself. Freedom carries with it huge levels of responsibility. That was a message that Manley failed to impart.

As the flight of money and managerial skills gathered speed, the Manley government upped the hype. Lavish houses dropped in value as those migrating sought to get quick sale and US dollars. Crime increased, and food was in short supply. Many in the middle class travelled to Miami and returned with scarce products like soap, toilet tissue, and rice. Corn flakes became a luxury. Aiming to prevent the flow of foreign currency out of Jamaica, the government put in place a branch of customs called the Financial Investigation Unit (FIU), a fearsome agency that arrested persons leaving the island with more than 55 US dollars or anything in excess of special permits issued for businessmen. Fines of three times the value of the currency and confiscation, along with the possibility of imprisonment, intensified the fear and currency left faster as new and smarter ways were found to transfer foreign currency overseas.

A ban on most imported products soon took a toll as businesses and factories closed, and the government sought to provide work opportunities for the labouring class through a program called the "Crash Program" [1]. Street cleaning and side-walk bushing became the norm in this program as thousands were paid to attend work but not encouraged to perform. Some collected pay without turning up at work.

Unfortunately, this new culture of entitlement became engrained in society and was seen as typical of what happened in communist countries. It served to further encourage the "handout" mentality that has grown exponentially since then and is still a part of the Jamaican culture today.

The communism scare became increasingly apparent as Manley activists labeled "Brigadistas" were being trained in Cuba. Guns were smuggled into Jamaica using military personnel who illegally bypassed immigration and customs. These guns included American Smith & Wesson makes that would not be traced back to Cuba where they came from. Sinister acts of the sort heightened fear and escalated political violence as both parties tried to strengthen their 'armies'. Tribal politics and 'garrison' wars intended to protect and maintain control of partisan areas led to murders exceeding 1,000 per year.

As austerity stepped up and businesses failed, spare parts for power generating stations were hard to afford; power cuts became a nuisance to residents and a costly impediment to production by manufacturers. More businesses failed and even the workers' cooperatives that were owned by "the workers" faced related problems.

In response to the growing crisis, Manley upped the hype again and declared that sinister activity was taking place to overthrow the government. He declared a State of Emergency and decreed that anyone found with ammunition, a gun, or any part of a gun be arrested and detained in the "Gun Court". Many persons deemed to be political activists—particularly those attached to the opposition—were arrested and detained indefinitely without stated reason or trial.

My boss's trust in the Manley government put him in trouble with his bank. It seemed ridiculous and even impossible for a bank loan to be repaid in full yet remain a debt with interest accruing indefinitely. He had been offered a $200,000 USD "Euro Dollar loan" by First National Citibank which he repaid in Jamaican dollars but the Bank was not permitted by the Manley government to convert it into foreign exchange, so the loan remained floating with interest accruing. It wasn't until many years later when the Seaga government took over that the debt—which had by then increased to millions through devaluation—was released to be converted to foreign exchange.

The toll of the turmoil of the 1974-75 period had taken down a model person as his spirit all but folded. He told me once that his spirit while flying in England during World War II was much higher than what he faced in Jamaica then. Yet, he would not run away overseas as many did, leaving the Bank holding the keys for depreciating assets. It would have been an injustice to the bank in his eyes.

With my boss's support I left his employment in 1975 to join an earthmoving company that had been awarded the contract to construct the May Pen Bypass Highway. As Project Manager for two sections of this highway, my responsibilities covered approximately 10 miles. Site violence was the order of each day and survival then was the name of the game. One planned one's life day by day. What was likely to happen "today" was all that occupied my mind. One never looked even 2 or 3 days ahead. The only planning ahead was what was necessary from a 'critical path' perspective of work to be done within allotted time limits. One learned to expect anything; the project might shut down at anytime.

During this time, I routinely witnessed shootings, beatings, threats of killings in the streets. At that age (late twenties) my fear was replaced by a cocktail of stupidity, curiosity, rivalry and some intrigue. Stupidly at times I would call a gunman's bluff and throw his threat back in his face. I recall the adrenaline flow each morning as I headed out to the site from my home in Kingston, anxiously looking forward to the excitement for that day. I would see a picture in detail of having to 'kill' an assailant and the question was not when, but which one? It was to happen at any time on any day. To witness two gunmen shooting at each other from behind bulldozers was not a surprising sight. The silence of guns at times gave an eerie feeling. Every day I expected to have to pull the trigger. I suspected that death at any time was possible, but I reveled in the thrill of cheating death, against the odds. Also, for whatever reason, a gun in the hand of a criminal did not appear then to be as awesome as it does today. I was actually becoming warped. I was actually enjoying working under terrible conditions. Was I in a dream or in shock?

I suppose youth and inexperience often alters judgment and might even trivialize very serious and dangerous events. "Death is only for old people", I often thought.

Meanwhile, on the highway job we were often denied access to lands projected as part of the highway that was supposed to have been purchased by the government from landowners who were living, farming, or occupying the path of the highway. As we would discover later, much of this had already been paid for by the government, but the proceeds had been fraudulently diverted by political goons. This resulted in attacks on our staff as we attempted to build the highway through such areas.

I had one personal experience with the dreaded "Gun Court" constructed by the government to house persons who were caught with illegal guns or ammunition. It was common knowledge that no one was ever given bail when charged and placed in the Gun Court—except of course, those with 'connections'. A group of activists approached a supervisor on the highway site one morning and informed him that his services were no longer required on site and that someone else was selected from among activists to replace him. Just imagine: these were goons determining who was qualified among their group to occupy managerial or supervisor positions. It was so ridiculous that it sounded like a joke, and no effort was made to protect the supervisor. For this reason I don't think the supervisor took it seriously either. The next morning the supervisor was shot. Some weeks later the shooter was arrested and placed in the Gun Court. To our shock the shooter was out on bail within a couple of weeks. Obviously he had good political connections.

Despite the highway project being a government contract funded by international organizations like the World Bank, violence and intimidation dominated the whole endeavor. The PNP politicians governing at the time were not just the cause; they were part and parcel of the problem as 'tribalism' conflict raged between their own activists on site for positions of power. In May Pen and its environs, tribalism and political warfare raged. The ruling PNP government factions dominated the site while competing with each other for positions of power, creating some adrenaline flow for themselves and for our staff. The work site stretched for miles, and monitoring over such an area was only possible through supervisors who over the years had acquired the requisite knowledge and skills for road construction. They were not really equipped to handle threats backed up with violence. With the exception of union skirmishes which some of us encountered in the past, this warfare was very typical in1976. Hardly three hours of work was ever accomplished in a day. When it wasn't a strike in place, it was a supervisor disappearing from the site in an effort to protect his life after threats, or a group of tractor operators abandoning their machines after gunmen fired shots in their presence or in their direction. Labourers demanded pay for work not done, and supervisors—to remain alive and pain free—added absentee workers to the pay bills on instructions from goons.

Fear became the standard driver on this site. I often wondered how the World Bank representatives remained in Jamaica as I saw the fear on their faces every day. One day, a land surveyor connected to the overseeing engineers from the international funding organizations was pounced on at the site office front gate and beaten. That was meant for Richard Myers, our project coordinator, but the goons appointed to do the job beat the wrong 'white' man in error.

On one occasion an ambush was arranged for me at the site gate. I had sensed that the trap was set and the only way they could be sure that I was captured was to close the gate, leaving me outside of the compound long enough for the goons hanging around to assault me. I drove slowly and hung back far enough behind a supervisor who was approaching the gate. Then as the gate was opened for the supervisor I raced down on his rear bumper as the 'gate man,' acting on instructions from some goons, tried to shut me out. When I was safely inside I parked and approached the 'gate man' to let him know how lucky he was that day. "You are so lucky today" I threatened "Big Youth" . . . Yu nearly dead today" I told him. Backing down on that occasion was not an option. He was part of the plot to lock me out of the compound long enough for the restive crowd outside the gate to pounce on me as they did with the foreign surveyor.

While I held the position of project manager, I had instructed my subordinates to not play the hero when faced with danger from activists. They were to look about their self-preservation. But I had psyched myself into a state that prepared me to die rather than give in to them. I had thought about it so often. Leaving Jamaica was an option if I happened to kill anyone, and I was prepared to do so to survive. Somehow I always felt I would come out on top.

Our project director, George Brown, a clever, articulate, and quick-witted professional with an ability to walk between the rain drops and stay out of the line of fire, was the man at the top. His gift of gab was necessary to defend the company during the violent work stoppages even as the World Bank supervision sought to have the project proceed while under fire. His hands were full, what with the tribalism, denial of access because of fraudulent snatching of compensation for land purchased for the highway, union interference, various security problems, area violence and site violence.

Our project coordinator, Richard Myers, was a fearless, unbelievably calm, experienced land surveyor and earthmover; a kind of jack-of-many-trades. I once received a request from a known gunman who had shot a supervisor on the site. He was in hiding and wanted to see Richard Myers. I questioned his reason. Glossy eyed and slurring as if under the influence of 'ganja' he told me "mi haffi kill Missa Myers." He seemed fixed in stare and insisted that he visit Richard's office to carry out the threat. I tried stalling and got a warning off to Richard who simply told me to send him in. I followed him closely, and was prepared to shoot him if he went for his illegal firearm. Richard calmly handled him. He left Richard's office humbled and weeping. I have often thought about what happened in Richard's office and how without disarming this gunman, he took control so calmly.

Eventually the site had to be protected and housed by 16 military trained (Harmon Barracks) police who operated on a 24-7 zero tolerance basis. Many were to die by their hands. This remained so for some months until the project was shut down by strike and lack of access to lands forming part of the highway.

Not far away on a bauxite mud lake site the same was apparently happening, where a contractor had to work under similar conditions of intimidation and fear. Each day I looked through the newspapers for details but saw no reference to any problem on our site. I can only surmise that the newspapers considered this normal and did not think it newsworthy. Or maybe they were afraid to print. In fact mention of our dilemma on site was never a surprise to most. The country was actually changing from the old standard of good values and seemed to be rapidly becoming much more tolerant of bad.

The Making of Delinquents

With open warfare apparent as the order of the day, people did what was necessary to survive. Unreasonable laws were never a surprise and only succeeded in labeling more people as criminals. Those travelling overseas were allowed something like a measly $55 USD per year for a vacation trip and this was being recorded in travelers' passports and enforced by law. We were told that families overseas would have to sponsor those vacations. In fact, apart from those who got special permission to procure extra foreign exchange for occasions like health, business or even for government travel, anyone caught with more than that $55 USD was arrested and charged. So, most people who had always held onto their values with honesty became liars and criminals in order to exercise their right of freedom to travel. If one insisted on wearing a halo, one would have to think about not travelling. The right to travel was being denied without it being explicitly stated.

It reminded me of a quote from Martin Luther King, which was used in a different context but surely applied here:

"One has not only a legal but a moral responsibility to obey just laws. Conversely, one has a moral responsibility to disobey unjust laws."

The people of Jamaica had a moral responsibility to disobey that law. Yet many stood idly by and let it happen.

Similarly, import licenses for goods were issued on a "no funds" basis. Almost everything imported required an import license. Applicants were told that they would be granted a license if their families abroad, or overseas investors were funding the imports. How ridiculous! Who would have family abroad donating to projects here? For whose gain? Which investors would seek to dump funds into a country that was swamped by violence, seen as going communist, and headed for bankruptcy? That too deserved the same treatment of moral responsibility.

The choice was simple; migrate or become part of it. But fighting against the system was not a wise option. One could find oneself on the untenable end of serious persecution or even imprisoned without bail or trial. Most who chose to migrate were not allowed to legally take all their assets with them. Those who risked and succeeded in smuggling some funds overseas were lucky or 'connected.' Those who were willing to risk moving large amounts were either exceptionally lucky or lost most (if not all) to rascals who offered to move it for a fee. Unfortunately, those who were ripped off had to suffer in silence or seek justice their own way. To whom could they complain? Fear and panic ruled among those who had it to risk. The FIU had become the Gestapo of Jamaica, but those who had connections often escaped prison in exchange for seizure of money. Of course, in a case like that the funds would be taken by corrupt police or FIU agents. It was not unusual to hear of funds like $30,000 USD escaping the government coffers and settling in the pockets of enforcement officers. The flight of money was against the law and the enforcers of the law were becoming more corrupt.

By the mid 70s, many wives of the well to do had migrated or had bought houses overseas to hedge against losing all in Jamaica. Fear and panic was so high that the sound of gunshots miles away provided good reason for instant diarrhea, particularly among the wives who had not yet migrated.

A State of Emergency installed in 1976 was indeed the icing on the cake. It gave the police authority to arrest and imprison for prolonged periods without trial and without giving reason. Some people who were affiliated to the opposing party wisely left the country to avoid arrest. Many were arrested and detained without charge. Many who were hanging on, suddenly got up and left, but the problem of family left behind was a constant worry.

All this impacted additionally on the perception of what was right or wrong. Survival was right at practically any price. Breaking the law increasingly became no longer a bad thing. Standards were being altered at increasing pace. Anxiety over incidents that were once seen as shocking became 'not so bad.' Consequently, a business sector in fear, panic, and uncertainty can never truly flourish, and when the economy collapses a country is truly in serious trouble.

My Working Journey Continues

Violence, nonpayment for lands through which the highway passed, and disarray in the government put a hold on the highway construction. I had barely left the highway project after it was shut down when I joined Industrial Chemical Co., a producer of sulfuric acid, salt and alum. It was a calmer environment than the politically charged highway project, so I welcomed the change.

The country seemed to be on the brink of bankruptcy, unable to pay its foreign bills and shunned by its neighbors, including the USA. In the mid and latter 1970s, the Manley government continued to court Fidel Castro, and fear of communism became increasingly evident. Guns continued to blaze leaving hundreds dead yearly. Rumours abounded, some taken to the extreme, sometimes into fantasy. An acquaintance would call and say, "The Cubans are at the airport, you've got to leave now!" Wives would panic and board the next flight. Close friends would migrate without informing anyone, for fear that the FIU would harass them if they found out that they were leaving for good. Houses were being abandoned as owners defaulted on mortgages. Banks were recovering what they could by way of auctions. House owners said goodbye after handing their keys to banks. Yes, we were sure that communism was on the doorstep. Yet somehow I felt I could get out whenever I wanted to go.

A Culture in Rapid Change

By 1977, my former boss seemed a broken man, but despite this he never let go of his values. I now have absolutely no doubt that he could never have survived the Jamaica of the 90s and onward. The change in values of pre-1980s was so drastic and so fast that he never accepted it.

Jamaica, the Paradise of the 50s and 60s, a country with the most resourceful, honest, caring and friendly people on earth, seemed to have given notice that it was abandoning its values. She was on a path that would guarantee her a place among other failed nations. Sharing and caring, honesty and integrity, respect and family values had all been so evident pre-independence and shortly after were going out of style. The 10-year-olds of 1970, who had grown during a period of diminishing values, would be 19-year-old adults by 1979 and they would know nothing else. Much of the educated middle class had migrated or had removed their investment dollars. Many were already settled overseas, bought houses and businesses and were not sure when or whether to ever return. Others would return without their assets only to secure the few assets they had left behind.

Crime grew in to more and more crime. The JLP was no walkover and they had their share of ruthless gunmen. They seemed to be fewer in number but much more feared than their counterparts who were protected by the governing PNP. Criminal gunmen from the PNP and JLP turned loose on each other; murder, rape and savage behavior scared people into the kind of fear that drove inhabitants from one community to another as innocent people took refuge from marauding gunmen. Savagery that manifested itself in acts like babies being thrown into fires by gunmen, street dances "sprayed" with high powered rifles, Members of Parliament involved in shoot-outs, citizens from one political party labeled as "bad men" lured into a desolate area and riddled with bullets by the security forces in planned executions. In a show of power (or as some may say an act of contempt) men allied to Manley's PNP party who were wanted for committing murder in Jamaica slipped into Cuba and were allowed refuge there.

To go into details of pre-election violence would take up volumes. It was violence that begat more violence; a bloody period to say the least. I had supported and campaigned in the drive to replace the JLP in 1972. I regretted it and offered my time campaigning against the Manley Party in the general elections of 1980. Violence raged, guns seemed to bark incessantly and the very mention of the names of feared leftist politicians sent some scampering to the bathroom. Electioneering was on and many volunteered to help in a last ditch effort to save the country.

On the day of election in 1980, along with other volunteers I travelled into various areas around 'South Side', a stronghold of the JLP that was located inside Manley's constituency. High-powered rifles barked continually in the areas around. I recall driving a pickup truck with two men in the back as they shouted instructions indicating where I should turn. They were in familiar territory and I was not. One lane had PNP gunmen and another just yards away had JLP gunmen. The trick was to know where not to go. They shouted "tun right ya so", "tun leff ya so." I made a wrong turn and the two men vanished from the back of the truck. I had mistakenly turned into PNP area where only PNP persons dared. They were hiding behind a wall as I backed up to collect them. "Boss a mad yu mussy mad." One said as he jumped back into the truck and we continued to 'wind' left and right to avoid hostile areas.

That day I saw firsthand the absence of the 'value of life' in underprivileged areas that dwarfed all that I had seen in the previous years of violence. On a particular occasion while standing outside the JLP constituency office at "South Side", I saw two children playing by old wrecked cars that had been placed in the lane to block any movement of vehicles entering from hostile areas. The top of the lane was in a hostile PNP area nicknamed "Tel Aviv," Also located inside Manley's constituency.

Preoccupied with what I was doing, I was ignoring the constant gunfire from this area until I realized that the children playing around the old cars were actually using sticks as tools to remove the bullets that lodged in the cars from the gunfire up the lane. They were enjoying themselves as the occasional spark from the bullet's impact on the car fascinated them. I was shocked when I realized that the adults nearby were unconcerned about the danger. I grabbed the arm of one of the activists nearby and pointed out where the children were playing. "Move from deh Johnny" was the casual unconcerned response, then it was back to what they were doing. This was an experience that remains embedded in my mind. There was no value placed on the lives of those two kids. There, 'life is cheap'. It wasn't even worth the effort to shout at the kids sternly and have them move to safety. It has often passed through my mind what their reaction would have been if one of the kids were shot that day.

Those who had volunteered to help campaign had done so at great risk. We were in an era of change that was moving so rapidly at a pace not previously anticipated and we often wondered what the hell we had to look forward to. A culture in the process of rapid change; new persons with new outlooks on life; a reduced private sector leadership that had stuck it out and had survived in the line of fire, with a clear understanding of risk; a populace who learned to survive despite disastrous odds—this was our future.

For sure, Jamaica then was not short of people with guts. They had so far survived turmoil. They had learned to move funds overseas and to manipulate the system; to falsify whatever was required to get an import permit for raw materials and keep their machinery going. Whatever was required for survival was 'engineered' and made to work.

I had managed to survive those tough times. I had, during the 70s, taken advantage of every opportunity to expand my knowledge. Already exposed in the 60s to operating and repairing heavy equipment, and I had become quite comfortable with it. I even enjoyed personally operating bulldozers while cutting roads. I had acquired some land surveying knowledge from Richard Myers—enough to set out basic construction jobs. By studying at nights, I had successfully pursued and graduated in an electronics correspondence course and I had managed to acquire a private pilot's license all before 1980. I suppose all this was done because I was young, energetic, and keen on further education. If Communism was to take hold in Jamaica, any asset I had would be best stored in me. I had resisted migrating but did not rule out the possibility. If one day I had to migrate without taking along any assets— of which I had very little— I would at least have more options and a wider choice of profession.

My mother had died in 1979 and my father, having worked in the Civil Service during a time when all he had seen in his lifetime was a country which was a model of stability, did not have reason to distrust the Jamaican dollar much less to understand the consequences of devaluation. He retired and he soon discovered that as a retiree relying on a pension, he was unable to survive without help from his church and his children. His monthly pension in the 80s could not keep him alive, and were he alive today he could not survive for a day off a month's pension. That is the nature of rapid change that has taken place since the 1970s. The Jamaican dollar had moved from a value of 77 US cents to a value approaching 15 US cents in the late 1980s. It would only get worse.

Many felt that Manley meant well and had seized on the surest way of extracting from the rich to give the poor. The world had not yet seen that Communism was not workable. Rightly or wrongly, Russia was seen by the average educated Jamaican to be viable only because of some kind of forced labor and control by depriving citizens of their freedom. Jamaica was in a boom period when Manley took over and he might have seen the need for social adjustment as greed and corruption had eaten into some of what should have reached the poor. Why he sought to improve social justice by scaring away the very source of proven employment and growth still puzzles me. It seemed obvious to me that removing opportunity for employment was a death sentence, but he might have intended to replace private employment with state employment.

Many argue that Manley's target was not much different from his successor Edward Seaga's, but the routes they chose were miles apart. His aim of increasing the access to education was a necessary and a most creditable act of social justice. His legitimizing fair and equal opportunity for those born out of wedlock was long overdue (my father was a "bastard" as was the label back then and ought not to be persecuted for his parents' indiscretions). Credit can be given for many of his other policies . . . but at what cost?

Conversely some believe that Manley's message might well have been a political ploy that seduced the masses who were still healing from the scars of slavery. He sold a message that the people wanted to hear. He played the minds of the people. In other words, although the message in and of itself was good, the intention of the messenger made it bad. It was never about the people. The people were a means to an end; he sold them freedom and it resonated with the people. Such hugely conflicting views created uncertainty.

However good Manley's intentions were, he failed dismally in a way that caused further suffering on the poor. That, combined with the fear of Communism, lost him power. It was clear to me that what had happened to Jamaica in the 70s created problems that left a battered nation seriously wounded morally, culturally and economically for a long time, possibly for generations to come.

Manley failed to realize what Evangelical preacher Adrian Rogers rightly identified:

"You cannot legislate the poor into freedom by legislating the wealthy out of freedom". What one person receives without working for, another person must work for without receiving. The government cannot give to anybody anything that the government does not first take from somebody else. When half of the people get the idea that they do not have to work because the other half is going to take care of them, and when the other half gets the idea that it does no good to work because somebody else is going to get what they work for, that my dear friend, is about the end of any nation. You cannot multiply wealth by dividing it."

CHAPTER 5

NEW BEGINNINGS AND THE BIRTH OF EML

In 1978, I along with my wife Lynne formed a company Equipment Maintenance Limited (EML). I was already self-employed and working long hours carrying out heavy equipment appraisals. A stint at the Industrial Chemical Company in charge of equipment maintenance had served me well.

This chemical plant produced sulfuric acid, salt and alum, three of the most corrosive products in Jamaica. The corrosive conditions I witnessed while working there convinced me to enter the motor vehicle rust-proofing business. I had seen rust prevention techniques work, and it looked like a solid investment in a tough business climate.

I approached a cousin, Michael, to partner with Lynne and me in the rust-proofing business. Michael in turn asked that his brother Richard be included.

My total savings was by then about $3,000 ($3700 USD at that time). I agreed that my wife and I would retain 1/3 of the shares with my cousins Michael and Richard would hold 1/3 each. By then Lynne and I were already comfortable with embracing an attitude of sacrifice and hard work. Money was seen only as a measure of success from that effort. I didn't even think about owning a house.

1979 found us working day and night. Lynne slaved at nights without pay writing up the cash books, saving on employing staff that would be paid to do this, while she worked days with a large private company as a computer analyst. Richard and I moved vehicles in and out of the work area, drilled access holes in vehicles, closely supervised the treatment for high quality, and wrote invoices for jobs completed, while two employees taped out sections of vehicles for protection, removed wheels, sprayed undercoating, applied rust-proofing material at high pressure and cleaned up after what always appeared to be a messy job.

We aimed at doing the best job we could. We removed door covers to make sure we saw to good coverage. We sprayed all seams and thoroughly treated enclosed areas, twice if we thought it necessary. EML quickly became known throughout Jamaica as the best in rust-proofing. We looked at what our competitor Ziebart did and did it better.

Richard and I drew very little remuneration in order for the company to grow faster. Lynne drew no salary. We all knew that keeping salaries as low as possible would help the growth of the company. Therefore, the company paid basic personal bills for Richard and me, which were charged to us as salaries at the end of each year. Creating personal savings was not important.

Jamaica was in violent turmoil. This all took place under conditions of extreme violence. Violence was the order of the day outside our work sites. Gun shots rang out from adjoining areas. Goons strolled along the roads with AK-47s and M16 rifles openly displayed, even as police in plain clothes or uniform challenged them.

At times work would be interrupted as employees scampered over the walls of the premises, ignoring the deterrents of razor wire and cemented broken bottles. Our employees would marvel at times how they scaled walls that normally would be impossible without ladders. One employee told me about a time he scaled a wall only to be greeted by gunmen when he landed on the other side, the same gunmen from whom he was attempting to escape. “Mi shit up mi pants” he said.

I carried a licensed pistol; I was prepared to die rather than leave Jamaica. It was easy to think and say such things when youth was in my favor and with that natural feeling of invincibility so typical even at age 31. There were many of the younger generation like that. The older, smarter, less reckless ones opted to leave the country. At that age strength, agility and extensive practice with a pistol created a tremendous confidence that in hindsight drove many like me to take spontaneous and unnecessary risks. So many of us cheated death and really believed that it couldn't happen to us. We had not yet come to terms with our own mortality.

~~~

During this time, challenges faced by the crumbling economy and distrust for the government was exasperated by the brazen conduct of communist leaning governments, particularly that of Cuba. The worrying involvement by Cuba in the political affairs of Jamaica was resisted unyieldingly by many of us in the private sector and although many more scampered to hedge against this by migrating or straddling the USA and Jamaica, brave efforts to thwart a leftist takeover must never be forgotten.

At that time the *Gleaner* newspaper was one on the few lines of defense through print. Some, including me, would argue that it was the last line of defense. The kind of pressure placed on this newspaper by the PNP government could shut it down if a strong stand was not taken. Government control by regulating import licenses exposed print material availability to great risk. This was a frightening thought. The *Gleaner* was then the only non-government news source, and when the paper called for support by way of voluntary purchase of 'bonds' as a means of financing its operation and continued existence, support came in a hurry. I was one of those who quickly put up what I could afford, although very small, it had to be done. It wasn't done as an investment for financial gain; it was one for survival through freedom of speech and free access to honest information.

When Ulysses Estrada, the then Cuban ambassador to Jamaica, famous for his revolutionary collaboration in Africa and South America and a close associate and admirer of the legendary Che Guevara, made public statements that were seen as direct interference in the affairs of Jamaica, candidate Edward Seaga responded fearlessly and aggressively. I was personally frightened when Estrada had the audacity to join Michael Manley in a march on the *Gleaner*. As Manley threatened during his march "next time" ..."next time"- a threat that indicated that he would be more
~~~

assertive next time round - private sector confidence shook and those who planned to stay had to strengthen their resolve.

A Vote against Communism (The Seaga Era)

In October 1980, the Manley government was removed from office after a hard fought campaign. Boston-born Edward Seaga was voted into office as Prime Minister by a large majority of 51 to 9 seats.

Celebration and appreciation were tremendous. You would have believed that it was Independence Day as the country exhaled. Camaraderie returned in abundance. Many who had left started to return, first, without their money, then as confidence returned so did some of their money. The shock that they had experienced sent a strong message to returning Jamaicans, a message that meant "never put all your eggs in one basket". The massive drain of the 70's took a tremendous toll and would never be replenished - certainly not without absolute trust in government. Seaga didn't delay in sending a message to the Cuban government. He immediately ordered Ulysses Estrada to leave Jamaica, declaring him "persona non grata". The thought that Manley could return to power years later seemed unlikely.

This is a period in Jamaica's history destined to be indelibly engrained in the minds of a generation. The Seaga government had a huge task rescuing a country that was broken in pocket and spirit and had already been though severe austerity. Recovery began but we were all aware that although it felt like a switch had been pulled, there could not be progress without more sacrifice and additional pain. The search for new confidence was on. Alas, the attitude towards work by the majority of Jamaicans left behind was already less than desirable, even as the population was in survival mode, do or die. Crime was being trivialized, dishonesty was taken less seriously, the vacancies left by the 70's mass migration were now being filled by the subordinates of many who left and obviously not with the same standard of skills and knowledge that once existed.

Edward Seaga was never one to beat around the bush with sweet rhetoric; he lacked the velvet glove for his iron fist and at this time Jamaica needed tough love to steer her on a path to success. He believed in hard work and production, which was the medicine needed to set this country right at that time. Some saw him as also believing in collective civic duty. I once heard the story about one of Seaga's constituents who visited his office asking for some money to clean the drains in his community. Seaga, the member of Parliament for that constituency, in very few words simply replied that the drains were situated in the constituent's community, blocked with their litter, flooding of which would impact them - and not Seaga directly - and so the complaining constituent should see it as part of his responsibility to have it cleaned. There was no free ride.

Prior to Mr. Seaga being appointed Prime Minister, I had personally done some appraisal work for his personal finance company. Whatever he requested was accepted only if it met the very highest standard and was on time. That was what he demanded. He was a planner and tended to go exactly where he had predetermined.

Mr. Seaga had taken over leadership of a country which was devastated by mismanagement, and his job required him to make unpopular decisions. He had to tighten the belts on a people who were already squeezed from the debacle of the 70s. In order to turn around the economy he had huge tasks, chief of which were to cut expenditure, stabilize the currency, reduce crime and violence, encourage investments and return the business sector to an environment of trust. Daunting tasks they were, and he didn't dither and play politics. In one particular task he laid off some 20,000 civil servants, an act that would later help to usher his party out of government. It was an unpopular decision but he had to do it. No other leader in my lifetime has dared to deliver this type of medicine for the service of country above party.

In 1983 he played a critical role as Jamaican military troops took part in the US invasion of Grenada, and by 1984 Seaga called a general election. Uncontested by the PNP, Seaga was again appointed Prime Minister. This gave him 100% of the seats in Parliament. With 100% support from Parliament he could have thrown his weight around All credit to him, he chose to keep his power base from abusing this position by appointing 'watchdogs' to the Senate, persons from civil society who were not considered to be affiliated to any political party.

Seaga's leadership provided optimism and opportunities to occupy vacancies left behind during the panicked migration period. Suddenly fear and panic seemed to disappear and business opportunities grew. The violence that haunted the country diminished.

The cautious return by those who had left the country in a hurry was to my advantage. We had made a name and were established in the rust-proofing business and had already started importing small quantities of windshields to satisfy a demand created by those tough periods during the 70s. The company expanded from equipment appraisals to include automobile rust proofing and auto glass business. As the company grew it purchased new offices at auction, with the help of a near 90% mortgage.

EML continued to do well. Profits were invested in land that we later developed to produce rental income. By the mid 1980s while operating the rust-proofing and windshield business, I took on satellite dish technology as a hobby, and in a short time capitalized on an electronics course I had done earlier. Work became more demanding as 18 -20 hour work days were routine. Satellite work occupied me, usually between 6pm and 3am the following morning along with Sundays all day and many nights out of each week. This was very hard work, though worth it from the point of view of procuring the best for our unborn children's future.

Every satellite receiving system I installed, fine-tuned or inspected personally required my having to enter homes of customers and converse with— parents, children, employees, rich, poor, humble, honest, shady, cocky— every strata of life right there in their homes. Satellite receivers were more technical and time-consuming than those of today. Most were often located in the most "private" areas of homes and repairs or installations required communication and interaction with occupants in these areas of the home.

My former boss Terrence Causwell was affectionately known to his friends as "TC" and by his employees behind his back as "TC coming". I remained on good terms with him and continued to draw on his awesome experience. In the early 80s, while he resided on his 540 acre property with a spectacle of a house built with walls cut to perfection 12 inches to 18 inches thick, he assisted me in constructing my house and a residence for the caretaker at EML.

He had formally applied to subdivide the 540 acre property into 5 and 10 acre lots, which was suited to Jamaican hillside farming. The panoramic views from the lots would be an extra for purchasers. He started out expecting to be dealing with professionals and soon found out that corruption was not restricted to the construction and heavy equipment business or the horse racing business. It was in subdivision approvals as well and it meant that approval would only be granted after satisfying all of many stages including the Parish Council, the Fire brigade, the Water Commission, Agro 21, Town Planning, and more.

You can imagine what would happen if you failed to get approval after incurring costs up to, or approaching the last stage. At stage one, the plans presented were delayed for months as constant checks provided a wide assortment of excuses like "file mislaid" or "still being worked on". Meanwhile discussions with other applicants indicated that plans submitted by others went along speedily provided bribes were paid at each stage. This was unheard of pre-independence or even up to 1966.

"Poor TC", I often sympathized. He was getting a thorough whipping and he was frustrated as years passed and approval was not granted. His earlier experience with the Manley government made matters worse as a US$200,000 loan had turned into millions of Jamaican dollars through interest and devaluation. The Manley Government had barred the loan repayment causing interest combined with devaluations to accrue.

This caused him to approach me with a proposition to have EML take over a majority of the property at a price including the escalated debt. Approval to subdivide was granted only after he and I ran the gauntlet of multiple stages for more than 5 years.

As a businessman in the 80s I found it easier to plan, to rely on a stable dollar, and to trust information relative to business that emanated from his government. As EML grew and increased our cash flow, we looked for buildings and land within reach of the company's credit ability. I made sure that our cash flow could handle these investments although I was often criticized for being too conservative, too cautious. During the 1980s, although the country was recovering, any instability of the Jamaican dollar or calling of loans by the banks could put us into financial difficulty. For this reason I chose the cautious path. I had seen instability and opted not to assume that it couldn't happen in Jamaica again.

EML grew rapidly as building after building was erected with profits from the windshield business, assisted by carefully managed bank loans. Rental income played an important part in paying these bank loans as well as providing additional cash flow for purchasing additional land for development. We purchased land, which we would later develop to produce enough income to cover their mortgage payments. Between 1986 and 1991 I was optimistic but cautious when borrowing.

"TC" assisted by guiding me with the construction of an 11,000 sq ft. building on a piece of land we had purchased earlier. Building costs were relatively low then compared to those that were to come later in 2001. A $4.5 million building in 1990 would appreciate to about $35 million by 2001 and to over $80 million by 2011. This was typical as the rate of inflation and currency devaluation in Jamaica galloped.

All the while, Michael, who was not a working director for EML, ran his own motor vehicle repair and car rental business. Richard and I continued to draw low salaries, preferring to keep the money in the company for faster growth.

By late 1980s Lynne resigned her job to work full time at EML. Again the company's growth was greatly assisted as she worked without salary from some eight years. She was willing to live on a small salary from the satellite business, supported only by the small salary which I drew. She worked real hard, and at night she also assisted with the books for the satellite business. I often wonder how she did it. She toiled without complaining.

Mr. Seaga's JLP party had taken over a bankrupt country and resuscitated the economy enough to eventually create growth. As an appreciative tractor operator once said to me *"mi can mash down di house in six minute but mi need six month fi build it back"*.

Mr. Seaga was not only a no nonsense man; he knew the business incentives that would create the opportunities for employment and the means for social reform through taxes. Starting from a huge deficit position required the political will to put country before politics. Seaga was a disciplinarian and seemed never tolerant of "bandooluism," [1] as he called it. He would not hesitate to fire or move officials holding high positions if he saw incompetence or corruption. It was said that his friends knew not to ask for special favors of him or his government because they were likely to hear a response like "find yourself a good lawyer". He was seen as abrupt and tough; however behind that 'tough' demeanor he would melt in the arms of a poor 90 year old woman and at the same time be tolerant of the indiscretions of a young child. If you were of working age, healthy and well, he expected you to work and produce.

Seaga's early days as Minister with responsibility for Development and Welfare served him well for his role as Prime Minister. He knew the culture of the people but the importance of votes obviously took second place to what was good for country. His penchant for collecting taxes from elusive businessmen was respected and at times feared. For example, a "compliance certificate" was required to qualify for importing anything. Before imports could be cleared from the wharf or airport, a certificate confirming that all taxes including statutory pay-bill deductions were paid up to date needed to be presented. That single certificate was intended to cause all those in business to voluntarily pay up without government having to chase them down to collect. This worked well at the start, but when he left office corruption soon crept in. Certificates became available for a price, possibly as bribes after some tampering with government computers. The certificate system is still in place, but over time corruption and cronyism has rendered it less effective. This has come to be expected in the

Jamaican situation and no leader can change this until the justice system works for all Jamaicans.

Mr. Seaga was also well known for championing human rights and judicial reforms. His stand at the UN against apartheid in South Africa is well documented. His penchant for development was more than likely a means to an end. With development projects he could see growth and employment; with growth he could see enough profit to provide for taxes and not discourage entrepreneurs from investing; with employment he saw the need for better housing and education; with that and more in place he could see the need for better transport, healthcare and better amenities, more water and electricity supply as well as whatever was required for social justice.

I had special admiration for Mr. Seaga's aversion to corruption. He could see the negative impact of greed on the society and stepped on it to the extent that he was fitted with a reputation for being "hard" even on close friends. Yet, despite his attention to judicial reforms including the installation of the Contractor General and the Public Defender, corruption found ways around these posts when he was no longer in power. Scandals ripped through Jamaica while he was in opposition – an indication that his opposition to corruption needed more than his personal attention. I will often refer to these as "back-to-back" scandals mainly because they were too often, too brazen, and too many to be accurately listed and critiqued in one volume.

Mr. Seaga, however, might have misread his peers in business and on both sides of the political fence. Allies and advisors all around him reached a level of unabashed greed that rendered even the Contractor General ineffective. Jamaica was eventually overtaken by massive corruption, from the 90's to today.

Yes, hindsight is 20/20. Still, good vision and success in running a country is better judged by hindsight. Even looking back, though, there is not a lot to criticize of the Seaga era, but we can visit a few here.

Mr. Seaga failed to capitalize on existing import restrictions. He seemed to have surprised some when he swung the gate for free trade wide open allowing a flood of cars into the country shortly after he took office. Such foreign exchange was better invested in business.

Many felt that the gate had been closed by Manley for so long that the population had grown accustomed to it and that a gradual change might have been better. It is possible that he was doing this to encourage residents to return home and re-enter business, but having seen it shut for so long many expected a gradual opening. Also, he might have realized the terrific shortage of transportation created during the Manley austerity years. Possibly, he saw the foreign exchange as being already moved overseas and its return of any would be a gain.

Another missed opportunity was his failure to take advantage of retooling incentives for manufacturers at a time when all areas of the country had collapsed and most of the equipment in place was aged. Many of the businessmen who had left, along with others who had seen the huge change would have been happy to invest in new equipment for manufacture, had duty free concessions on capital items combined with tax free concessions for guaranteed periods been offered.

Worst on the list of missed opportunities was Mr. Seaga's failure to deal with the justice system more astutely at that time, having been through the terrible injustices of the state of emergency. He was expected to react sternly the moment he took power. However, rumors have suggested that at that time Mr. Seaga had seen the country fight a brutal war, and thousands had died as a result. In addition the suffering resulting from the financial crash under the previous government had created so much anger that he had decided to not prolong the rivalry and disunity with numerous inquiries, commissions and attacks on the system which might be seen as reprisals. On the other hand, some ask whether he could have secured more protection for those in his party, similar to those used by the previous government. Possibly, but it seemed unlikely that both political parties would want to preside over a lame justice system that was becoming increasingly corrupt, unless there was some motive like power or money.

In my own struggles for justice, I have often reminisced on why Mr. Seaga failed to more adequately address those ills in the system. While he acted sternly against even his party's Parliamentarian misconduct, his efforts were not enough to ensure continuity when he was not in power— a huge oversight that haunts us even now. He might have thought that his constant demand for accountability might have directed the culture more positively, therefore negating the need to overhaul the justice system.

Despite his success in rescuing the economy and providing for growth, the improvement in crime rates during his tenure was largely due to improved confidence and employment from increased business. A cleaned up justice system would be phenomenal, even if he was replaced as Prime Minister afterwards, because it would have served the country in a way that transcends politics, then and now. After all, he had 100% of Parliament for some years. He obviously failed to recognize the real damage that had been done to the culture and the extent to which greed would devour the political and business leadership. He should never have assumed that those coming after him would be in anyway akin to angels.

Despite all the pros and cons, many feel that had Mr. Seaga gotten one more term in 1989, Jamaica would have recovered totally and would have been a much better place today. Possibly, the state of the justice system might have been spared its catastrophe had he not lost power in 1989. In comparison to the PNP, his omissions or outright errors were few. Throughout his political career of some 45 years, his contribution to economic and social development was more extensive than any other leader of my generation—possibly any generation in Jamaican history.

Many believe that the target he set out to achieve was no different from Manley's; he just went about it much differently. Under Manley the level of handing out of money and employment without commensurate production literally guaranteed economic failure then, and contributed to a culture that would also impact negatively in the future. To correct this took guts and a 'country-before-party' approach, a quality that has been woefully lacking in Jamaica ever since.

The Second Manley Administration

In the 1989, Michael Manley returned to power. After recovering from bankruptcy and having to accept some economic adjustment measures, the Jamaican people yearned for a easing of austerity measures.

Many people felt the belt was too tight for too long. The 'handout' life was enticing, and the country had recovered to a point where the people once again longed to taste some 'freedom'.

Mr. Seaga had taken over a bankrupt country in 1980 and had to do politically unpopular things— things that no government has had the fortitude to do since then. The return of Manley saw a pensive middle class. The business sector was eerily silent. Could this man be trusted? Personally, I was in shock. Would Manley return to his old leadership style? The population did not accept the necessity for austerity. Although they had suffered through it in the 70s, I sensed they wanted a breather and the culture of handouts was obviously at play here. Those who had no great wish to grow—and who could therefore be satisfied with just enough to get by—needed only to vote themselves wealthy. The future seemed bleak.

At the time, I often compared the leader of the country with a CEO of a company, and I wondered how one could reappoint a CEO of a company after it was driven into bankruptcy under the leadership of that CEO. But Manley of 1989 seemed a different man.

He abandoned his old rhetoric and scare tactics, appearing to shift towards the middle. But much of his old policies remained. His message was essentially, 'We are not going back all the way, but we can go back part way'. A nicer more charming man you could not find. He oozed charisma but I don't think he had a clue about managing anything —certainly not the complexities of an economy.

Obviously, I became more cautious in business and so did many others. I planned for growth, but I did so with more uncertainty. Some who had seen the devastation of the 70s started to "hedge" with one foot in Jamaica and the other overseas.

A Return to Rackets

No government in Jamaica, specifically after 1962, was unaffected by rackets and scandals, and Manley's regime was no stranger to this. After Manley's victory in the 1989 General Election, the country was distracted by scandal after scandal: the Rollins Land Deal, the Zinc Scandal, the Furniture Scandal, and the Motor Vehicle Importation Scandal, just to name a few.

Parliamentarians involved in the Furniture Scandal were made to refund public funds used to purchase personal household stuff. A staff member of Gordon House was actually convicted and sent to serve time—a rare occurrence of punishment that would be unlikely today.

The Shell Waiver Scandal of 1991 saw some casualties, one of whom was PNP chairman, P.J. Patterson. Patterson, who had served then as Minister of Finance, resigned and somehow avoided prosecution. Despite this, by 1992 P J Patterson was appointed Prime Minister. Michael Manley had been having serious health issues and had given up the leadership of the ruling PNP party. The corruption of the past would seem like insignificant compared to what was coming next.

CHAPTER 6

The FINSAC Era—and My Troubles Begin

The change in leadership from Manley to Patterson, whether by poor leadership or incompetence, seemed to signal a further freeing up of corruption. 'Back-to-back' scandals became so prevalent and so unobstructed that it appeared they were the actual policy of those in power. One of the most horrific scandals involved Operation PRIDE (*Programme for Resettlement and Integrated Development Enterprises*), a huge housing program intended to focus on the poor. It was saturated with massive overruns and lost over 7 billion dollars. Although the Minister of Housing, Dr Karl Blythe, was eventually a victim in this scandal by way of demitting office, no one went to jail for it.

P J Patterson's time in office from 1992 to 2006 saw the greatest decline of the country in the history of modern Jamaica. Those of us in business can appreciate what happens if we borrow what we cannot afford and then borrow more to pay the interest. This was indeed the start of an insurmountable debt crisis. It is not mathematics but simple common sense, which every "higgler" [1] in Jamaica knows. One must therefore conclude that this happened either knowingly or just recklessly.

I have been around long enough to clearly see who have been the beneficiaries. This conduct coupled with power and corruption formed a deadly force that was to come: the Financial Sector Adjustment Company, or FINSAC. [2]

~~~

Meanwhile corruption scandals ruled to the point that they became accepted as mere distractions. There hardly seemed time to dwell on the "why's and "who's" of one scandal before another materialized.
~~~

Scandals followed each other so closely that as soon as one was met with horror the next one broke; before good discussion could take place, a newer one replaced it.

The press and electronic media were kept busy. Nearly all of the scandals were rooted in serious corruption, not the type involving 'womanizing' or cheating on a spouse. After all, that type of misbehavior was already accepted as a norm in political circles. For some, it might even be called a pre requisite for promotion to higher office.

Each scandal—from the Foreign Exchange Scandal, the Holland Land Distribution Scandal, the Sand Mining Scandal, the Fat Cat Salary Scandal and more—was rewarded with fancy talk from high circles, gossip on the streets and relentless salvos of ridicule from cartoonists. By and large they were treated with sarcastic humor and facetious commentary. All eventually faded from view, without consequence to those in power.

FINSAC, from a Small Businessman's View

During the 1980s, the JLP Government operated a tight fiscal and monetary policy. In order to get help from the IMF, the Seaga government defied the usual political vote-seeking trend and laid off more than 20,000 civil servant workers. This was an act of fiscal responsibility that is rarely seen in Jamaica. Many of those laid off used their severance payments to start small businesses—a win-win for the country and fiscal responsibility. But those laid off were not to forget.

There was economic contraction in the early stages, but by 1988 the economy was already growing. Then came hurricane Gilbert causing billions in damages.

Jamaica had not had a severe hurricane during the previous 36 years and during that time insurance companies built up huge reserves.

The imported adjusters were very generous and were liberal with the average clauses so that rebuilding and repairing the damage actually stimulated the economy. Despite an excellent job by the then Government, Seaga's JLP lost power in 1989.

Laying off civil servants to attain efficiency was a move that most voters in an educated first-world country might treat as economically responsible, essential, and best for the country. In Jamaica, it was political suicide. The civil service runs this country, not the politicians. They exercise great power and influence. Laying them off in large numbers in times of economic hardship was a sure way to lose political power. And that's exactly what happened to the JLP in 1989.

Shortly after the PNP government took over, they liberalized the exchange rate without having net international reserves to support the sudden demand for US dollars- so the dollar took flight. Within two months of liberalization the Jamaican currency lost half of its value.

Memories of the 70s under the PNP had not disappeared. Those with cash to spare converted to US dollars and moved funds overseas instead of investing in productive ventures like factories, exports, and the like. The sudden depreciation of the currency led to massive price increases and a wave of business failures among those who had US dollar debt and Jamaican dollar sources of income. To support economic activity in local currency at price levels more that 100% higher, the Bank of Jamaica flooded the markets with printed currency.

The result was economic overheating, more inflation and negative international reserves. The Minister of Finance decided to cool the economy by raising interest rates. This would have been the correct thing to do to compensate for the mistake of liberalizing without international reserves, providing it was not done for a long period; certainly not more than a year. No one expected the high interest rate policy that was started in 1993 to continue past one year. Which company can withstand 60% and 80% interest for years and remain competitive?

Unconscionably, this tragic and ridiculous policy lasted some seven years, and as interest rates climbed rapidly the government chose to access foreign funds by way of bonds, treasury bills, and CDs through a program called FINSAC (Financial Sector Adjustment Company). Of course if these were made available at high interest rates, investors would be interested. So this they did, and to make it even more attractive they made it short term. Foreign investors converted their US dollars to Jamaican dollars and jumped in. Local holders of cash also jumped in. After 30, or 60, or 90 days they would jump out and convert back to US dollars then return their US dollars overseas with huge gains. To them this was money for jam, but it came at a huge cost to the Jamaican taxpayer. The government was unable to fork out these large amounts, so they just printed more money.

Some investors who had traditionally slaved to operate factories and employ workers were better off shutting down and laying off workers to instead invest in paper for much better yields. But those who were patriotic enough with plans for a future in production and continued employment were in for some lessons. The more investors played the paper game the larger the burden of debt on Jamaica.

So what of the local businesses? They were accustomed to normal operating conditions that had kept them producing and exporting for years. They had very low interest loans with the financial institutions that suddenly became high interest loans of 60% or 80% and paying these high rates was obviously unsustainable. Some of these were agricultural businesses that had borrowed at government-encouraged incentive rates. They were decimated by these rates, and some of their owners died with their businesses.

No legitimate business in the world can absorb 80% interest rates for years and continue to honour their debts. What do you expect to happen to a business that borrows $1 million at 9% interest and finds that shortly afterwards it owes increased, compounded interest amounting to say $4 million? It will fold of course!

Meanwhile, sadly, the government continued to print money, line the pockets of friends and 'connections,' kill exports, crash businesses, fund their voter population in selective garrison areas, and borrow ever more to keep up this lifestyle. As a result, banks moved in on the assets of these companies and sold them—some for as low as 30% of the outstanding debts. Somehow, and strangely so, many locals were not given the privilege of buying, or buying back their businesses at that rate. Many of these businesses were sold to overseas connections for a mere 30% of the amount owed..

The Jamaican dollar continued to devalue and seemed out of control. Yes, the same dollar that had remained stable for over 4 years under the Seaga-led government in the 1980s suddenly took flight in 1990, declining to half its value in one year.

The destruction of thousands of small, medium and large business told the tale. The lives of hundreds of thousands were negatively affected through job losses, business closures and bank defaults. Some forty thousand entrepreneurs, a huge majority of more than 90% of honest, patriotic, hardworking people, were snuffed out. More than ten large financial institutions failed and were either closed or bailed out by the government.[3] Only a very small number of those who were capitalizing on loans out of greed actually crashed.

The Jamaican people remained silent suckers. Many of our current difficulties have their beginnings in this stupid, shortsighted and in some ways, 'dishonest' policy that carried the label FINSAC Today, Jamaica "ha fi borrow fi pay interest pon di interest". Who will dare to invest here?

Instead of correcting the financial crisis, FINSAC instead provided bailouts for friends and crashed the unconnected.

Lessons from FINSAC

The period between 1992 and 1998 was the most devastating and damaging period for Jamaica in my lifetime. The imposition of FINSAC on the Jamaican people was so horrific that the message learned was that government can be expected at any time to destroy brave or trusting entrepreneurs while supporting their power base and enriching 'connected' friends. There was no room for honest investor optimism left. The message killed the productive spirit, removing from the nation its young and future providers of jobs, growth, and hope. It further devastated trust in government and politicians (what little that might have been left, that is). It literally enriched the informed holders of cash without them having to work or take risk for it, at the expense and ruthless slaughter of those who chose to produce and employ. I cannot think of a more destructive way to kill jobs, growth, and trust that would starve the people of several generations all at the same time. No other occurrence in Jamaica's modern history caused more breakups in families, suicides, depression, proliferation of corruption and fear of investing than happened in the 90's—not even the Communism scare of the 70's is comparable.

A few were fortunate to be 'connected' to the 'establishment' well enough to be "bailed out" or to be part of it through insider information, but most who suffered through it directly and are still alive will never recover; neither will pensioners who have all seen their savings lose purchasing value at a shocking rate. It is so reckless and wasteful that all this devastation was happening in an era when the rest of the world was booming. Sadly, Jamaica's route was to splurge and destroy with no growth.

But let us not forget a handful of businessmen who had tried to capitalize on FINSAC by borrowing funds without plans to invest, employ, or grow. Those planned to reap by speculation and without laboring for profit. They got their due. They used funds to buy real estate hoping to benefit when it appreciated and became casualties of the FINSAC debacle. Their real estate was unable to keep pace with the interest and penalties levied on them, first by their creditors and then by the FINSAC 'axe-men'. To buy real estate with near 100% loans and to sit without generating a cash flow to service the loans is a reckless, stupid, and selfish business strategy and I have no sympathy for those who lost their shirts pursuing it. Some of these dishonestly raided the assets of companies and partners to steal a bailout for themselves. In contrast, investors who put their loans to good use with hard work, good ideas and honest intentions, did not deserve to be raped and pillaged.

By 2006, FINSAC continued to pile up debts that were unsustainable. Assets were being seized, and some debtors were uninformed or unaware of their correct outstanding balances. Ruined entrepreneurs were denied the opportunity to purchase their assets at low prices offered to overseas purchasers. As the assets of investors were plundered, foreign pirates were rewarded with the chance to revel in the spoils. That was FINSAC, and the effects of this disastrous policy can still be felt.

Where is the Leadership?

The PNP government of the 90s clearly demonstrated that they were absolutely unfamiliar with the complexities of managing an economy.

They were prepared to ignore the simplicities and were not prepared to act against corruption.

Yet, it was during the same period that Prime Minister PJ Patterson led the massive call for a change in values and attitudes. It was a campaign that was run in every sphere of the local popular media. It saturated workshop seminars and retreats. Ironically, he presided over by far the most corrupt and unstable period of post-independent Jamaica. Despite the numerous scandals that darkened his cabinet, the show of desire for values and attitudes seemingly did not extend to his own administration. One wonders if it was all a facade to convince the people that they were concerned with the problems plaguing their government and were doing something about it.

The law was no longer a shackle; crime and violence spiraled. Money launderers masked themselves in 'legitimate' businesses causing authentic businesses to fail because of unfair competition. Lawlessness scoffed and taunted the church. Young men proudly declared themselves as "gangsta fi life," and popular culture legitimized criminality.

Politicians grew fat from the harvest and playfully slapped at crime and violence to keep the watchdogs off their backs. The nation wallowed in moral decay and all kinds of permissiveness. The campaign for values and attitudes became enshrouded by salacious crimes.

Who was really thinking about the interest of the nation? Did anyone think for a minute that it was their share of the pie that was part of bringing the country to its knees? I watched this happen all around me, but never did I think this culture of "me first" would infect my own family—or my business.

The First Signs of Trouble

Despite the turmoil all around us, the core business of EML remained auto glass sales, and growth was good. Competition was almost non-existent because we properly managed breakage, kept prices extremely competitive, and maintained high standards of quality. Prudent timing of construction projects kept the auto glass business free of financial pressure even as we stocked a wider variety of glass.

Lack of growth in the private sector was evident. As FINSAC ate away at investors, I stayed away from large bank loans that required guaranteed cash flows or projections that required high-risk speculation. I certainly shied away from living recklessly. My risk-taking days had passed, and in any case, they were not usually financial in nature. I relied less on risk and worked hard to compensate.

Although the dollar was devaluing at unpredictable rates, and could cause real estate purchases to appreciate in future, to borrow for this and speculate that gains could be made later was greedy. It meant that those 60% or 80% interest charges, when applied and compounded, would wipe out any potential gains from the appreciation of the real estate and create insurmountable debts. Also, the fact that the FINSAC crunch caused fewer buyers of real estate meant that whoever bought then should be able to wait for potential buyers later. It therefore suited those who were willing to use idle cash and willing to wait; or those with the 'connections' to arrange a bailout at taxpayers' expense. This was plain common sense, so I stayed away from the high risks.

In about 1996, EML had its first "flirtation" with the used car business. Interest rates were at an astonishing 40% and upwards. To attempt to enter this business meant borrowing funds at horrendous rates, scaling down on windshield stocks, and cutting back on our development projects. Nevertheless, my cousin and business partner Michael aggressively recommended we go into the used car business. Richard and I reluctantly went along with him. This was the start of trouble.

I knew that our core business was doing well. EML owed very little to the banks, either on the projects that were completed or those under construction. We had to continue to provide good service and good stocks to maintain market share in the auto-glass business. Up to that time we had little or no competition.

I embarked on a method of providing easy accountability by setting up a separate bank account for the used car business. This would clearly show if the used car business could service its loans without burdening the auto glass business. Prior to venturing into the used car business, we did not need to have very formal meetings but with the advent of this new business I insisted on meetings to ensure accountability and transparency.

The business showed early and obvious signs of failure. The business had clearly peaked, and some who were in the business before us were getting out. Our timing was poor, and I also suspected that many of our competitors in the used car business were funded by laundered money. It was impossible to compete with persons willing to chop prices by 20% and more off cost in order to clean up money. It wasn't long before I had to reject an offer for this kind of funding although it could guarantee up to 20% gains before cars landed in Jamaica.

I kept pointing to our losses resulting from lack of sales and even suggested to Michael that we switch to the body parts business instead. At one stage EML sold as few as two cars in a month. With interest rates in the region of 45% and higher, this was trouble. In meetings held specifically to monitor used car sales, I consistently warned of losses, lack of sales, cars priced too high by Michael, and stated that some of the other established competitors were getting out of the business. In one meeting I indicated projection of losses in the region of $12 million dollars within a year. Michael scoffed at that, but the separate bank account set up for the used car business took little time to show that the business could not service its loans without drawing on the auto glass business for loans.

By 1997, the car business became a burden on EML's core business, and we were forced to stock less glass in order to meet debts created by the purchasing of the cars sometimes exceeding $20 million in purchases and in overdraft. With terrible income from the sale of cars, I was at a loss to understand why it was not clear to Michael that more serious losses were inevitable. Richard remained indifferent and made no effort to convince Michael to change course. Although older, he seemed to be fearful of his brother Michael.

For the life of me, it couldn't be clearer. In a time when the Jamaican dollar was unstable and weakening, interest rates were among the highest in the world and sales were slow, all at the same time, we ought not to be borrowing money.

With no action taken, things got worse. At one time Michael applied for and received an import license for some two hundred 1988 model Toyota Corollas. The application was made just before the end of a year to allow an 'over-age' car into Jamaica, even if those cars had exceeded the regulation age in January of the New Year. This was a way to legally beat the system.

Fortunately, the bank would not guarantee the letter of credit without advanced payment into the account. As it turned out, that model was not in demand the following year and would have put the company into serious trouble, possibly bankruptcy. We had escaped a potentially huge failure.

To add insult Michael started suggesting that we omit "GCT" on car sales as others in competition were doing so. I objected; this exposed me as Managing Director to criminal liability. Michael was taking crazy risks, yet Richard avoided commenting. I steadfastly refused to comply. Then, a used car supplier named Kappa inadvertently shipped cars for a Jamaican company that did not possess an import permit. They had landed in Jamaica, without license, illegally. Apparently Kappa was not aware of the seriousness of landing cars in Jamaica without import licenses. In good faith they had shipped cars on credit to the Jamaican company. Michael heard about it and offered to negotiate with the suppliers and to assist them by negotiating with Jamaican customs, paying the penalties and taking over the cars at an agreed US dollar price.

Kappa had a hand in the lion's mouth and had little choice but to accept a verbal agreement from Michael that we would clear the cars, pay the duties, and pay Kappa a total figure of just over US $30,000.00—but only in installments as the cars were sold. This would save Kappa from a total confiscation by customs and a total loss on the cars.

It appeared to be a very compassionate act of kindness by Michael to a foreigner whom we did not know. The entire transaction with Kappa, with the exception of a fax or two, was done on our word. This was also necessary since we could not guarantee that the cars would all be sold at reasonable prices.

Having agreed to buy the cars at a set lump sum price, the cars were taken over, duty with negotiated penalties paid and sales started.

On the first attempt to pay Kappa an installment, Michael suggested that we simply not pay them. I objected, bypassed him, and paid what we owed using Richard's and my signatures on the payment cheque. (Two signatures were needed to pay.) We continued to make payments by similar installments, as we had agreed to.

Months later, an attempt was made by our parts manager to have Michael endorse a cheque to pay Kappa another installment after more cars were sold. Again he objected and, without notifying Michael, I paid this final amount.

Michael's obsession with going into used car business at the wrong time was worrying, and the treatment of those with whom we did business was more troubling. Richard, though indifferent, was behaving 'above board' and that somewhat calmed my concerns.

The used car business was taking its toll on the company's building projects, the auto glass stock, and on me personally. I finally got all to agree that we get out of that business. But I sensed a change in values around me. Still, I had finally managed to extricate us from a business that had continued to sap the capital and would certainly have put us in bankruptcy.

However, our used car import license had not yet expired and remained valid. EML had always been able to get licenses, because we kept all our statutory and government commitments paid up to date and clean. Or so we thought.

The New Zealanders

Sometime later, a group of New Zealanders from Robinson Motors apparently heard of us through Kappa—which was obviously happy that they were paid in full as we had verbally agreed, and had no inkling of Michael's plan to stiff them—and wanted to do business with us. This meant going back into a business from which we recently extricated ourselves, so I politely declined the offer.

Shortly after declining the Robinson offer, I was stunned to discover from a fax that about 16 cars consigned to EML were shipped without my knowledge. Richard was also unaware of this. My inquiries revealed that Michael had "done this for himself" using EML's 'used car importing' credibility and licensing privilege. He had decided to import the cars for his personal business and benefit, using EML as consignees.

If the cars landed in Jamaica without import licenses, EML would be exposed to sanctions and as Managing Director I was responsible. This seemed like desperation on his part, and it placed EML at risk. Richard, though quiet, must have realized that this was all going wrong.

I pondered the problem day and night. Could I allow the cars to land without a license and hope they avoided scrutiny? No, the company would almost certainly face sanctions and fines. Instructing the parts manager to apply for licenses was the only choice.

We had to rush to the Licensing Authorities for import licenses before the cars landed. As Managing Director, I was not about to be held accountable by customs for illegal imports, and I believe Michael knew this. If I reported Michael's indiscretions to the customs authorities, the partnership would have crumbled immediately. I wasn't getting strong support from Richard, although he seemed a little concerned about what was going on. If I couldn't stop Michael I had to, at a very minimum, manage what was happening in a way that saw to some transparency. I needed to enforce legality, but I could sense trouble on its way.

As cars arrived, through one of Michael's companies called Auto Auction Limited, Michael, armed only with a verbal agreement with Doug Robinson, proceeded to sell the cars using EML invoices. Since the cars were imported in the name of EML, such invoices were required by law to legally transfer the cars to whoever bought them, irrespective of who funded or claimed ownership.

Auto Auction Limited was a company formed by Michael specifically to sell imported cars at auction. I soon realized that the proceeds from the auctions were not being deposited in the account of EML and were also not being paid over to the New Zealanders from Robinsons Motors. They had shipped the cars on credit, sending funds in advance to EML to cover duties and other landing costs. EML had received and logged those funds on behalf of the New Zealanders and Michael.

As the auctions progressed, my concern about other problems grew. I had a difficulty with the sale of cars by auction which resulted in an "as is, where is" sale situation that contravened government regulations. Government regulations required used car dealers to give a warranty on cars. The auction route appeared to remove this responsibility, but this turned out to be minor bother compared to surprises that were on the way.

This kind of disregard for the law and for regulations was becoming more prevalent in Jamaica and many were comfortable with this as it was not seen as bad. The standard in pre-independence days had changed to that extent. Beating the system like this was now seen as smart business. The high-risk life the 70s had dwarfed the standards expected of the rule of law, causing some wrongs to be seen as OK. Was it that my upbringing was outdated, or was I stupidly not adjusting to the times that had so drastically changed?

Soon the New Zealanders started calling me for payments because Michael was not paying over to them for the cars sold. Michael claimed he did not owe Robinsons, but rather Robinsons owed him. I had a problem understanding this since the cars were supplied on credit and cash was provided by Robinsons to cover duties and other expenses.

Suddenly, EML found itself in the middle of two parties who were about to argue, and none of the cars were supposed to be the financial business of EML. In an effort to get Robinsons to release EML from any responsibility for the car payments, I wrote to Robinsons asking them to confirm that their accounting records should show EML as owing "nil", and the amount due from Michael his company Auto Auction Limited should read according to their agreement with Michael. But by then Robinsons Motors realized the only way to collect what was owed to them was to hold the consignee – EML - responsible.

Shortly thereafter, Doug Robinson replied that their accountants required a full statement of accounts – already requested from their "agent" Michael of Auto Auction Limited – but that he had not received a statement. Thus he could not confirm that EML's balance was covered.

Doug Robinson asked for my assistance in this matter, and I had little alternative. I had to remove EML from the problem, and this could only be done by preparing a detailed costing for the importation of all the cars. This would require all the transactions passed through EML as a licensed used car dealer as well as full cooperation from Auto Auction Limited, Robinsons Motors, and Michael.

Added stress was to come when I discovered that more cars were already on the way; that the deal with Michael involved a total of about 60 cars; and that some of the cars that were already on the seas were due to land here before a license could be procured for them.

How much worse could this get? We were barely recovering from a drain on the auto-glass restocking funds when were suddenly saddled with the responsibility to manage a business affair that was not owned by the company.

Doug Robinson and his partner came to Jamaica in about January 1998 and made subsequent trips to sort out the accounts. They complained that they kept travelling to Jamaica, and Michael most times would not meet with them. I continued to impress on them in writing reminding them that their deal was with Michael and not with EML. But they understandably used the fact that cars were consigned to EML, and therefore the only legal way to collect was via the consignee.

In May 1998, Robinsons Motors wrote a letter to EML saying they were disappointed with the lack of accountability from Michael, who seemed reluctant to present them with an accounting for cars sold or with a profit and loss position. They said it was impossible to continue in this way and insisted they were holding EML responsible. EML was also requested to hold funds from future sales of cars left in stock until the accounts were sorted out. This we started to do with the support of Michael's brother Richard who was obviously aware of what was happening. Michael who continued to avoid meeting with us, would not give an input on the costing and took to malice.

While all this was happening more cars had already been on the way from Japan without my knowledge. No surprise, they arrived in Jamaica illegally, without a license and consigned to EML—a very serious offence that attracted fines and seizures, would scar my reputation, and that of EML. I became extremely concerned when it appeared that curious efforts were being made to clear these vehicles.

This was becoming a more serious conflict. There was no easy legal way to clear those cars. My attempts to monitor the clearing of the cars became frustrating and stressful. A broker who was said to be responsible for clearing the cars seemed evasive and declared to me that he only took orders from Michael.

There were two obvious ways to clear the cars: Paying a hefty fine after admitting to an illegal act, or 'spiriting' them off the wharf. Neither was acceptable to me. It was years later that I was informed that the broker refused to attempt clearing them.

Surprises seemed to follow closely on each other and more were in incubation.

At one stage, while attempting to sort out the accounts, Robinsons informed us that the prices on the invoices were not the real prices but were lowered at Michael's request. On Michael's instructions, they had been shipping the cars to EML with invoices written for reduced values. These values were provided by Michael.

So in order to settle with them the invoice figures that should be used to tabulate the real costs were not the ones used for paying duties and clearing customs. This resulted in the parts manager hastily searching for and destroying some invoices to avoid being charged with a criminal offence. The under-invoicing of imports had become common business behavior in Jamaica, each business seeking to gain an advantage on the other. As Managing Director I was also exposed to arrest for this offence.

I was in a mine field, in panic, making a desperate effort to protect my reputation and stay out of prison. I had already hurriedly written Robinson Motors instructing them that at all times they should invoice only for what they intended to collect for the cars but resolving this problem became increasingly unlikely.

Later that year, after consulting with Richard, we decided to take EML out of the used car business completely and for good. I declined to renew our used car permit in order to prevent Michael from continuing his stubborn intent on importing his cars in EML's name. This made Michael livid.

The friction increased tremendously after I arranged for EML to collect all sale proceeds from cars that were still in stock, and pay them over to the New Zealanders. In the end EML purchased some of the cars in order to complete the transfer of cars as quickly as possible. Richard cooperated with this by co-signing letters of request for bank drafts payable to Robinsons.

At the end of the day the accounts showed over US$14,000 still owing to Robinson Motors. In fact that balance over US$14,000 was very conservative when I discovered further that some sales invoices were less than the amounts receipted at the auctions.

It is hard to fathom so much misconduct over so short a period, all relating to a single, seemingly innocuous business: the importation of used cars.

Later, Michael accused me of telling Robinson Motors that he "stole" $5 million of their money. "Stole" was in Michael's choice of words and was obviously taken from the fact that he had sold over $5 million in cars and had not paid any of that money to EML or Robinson. Although I had not used the word "stole", I had accurately given Robinson the total sales figure from our invoices.

There is no doubt that the New Zealanders came to Jamaica to do business, and their approach was one of great trust. They got a lesson that should guarantee that they stay far away from any temptation to invest again in Jamaica. They left Jamaica licking their wounds after heavy losses, and no doubt passed on the word to all they could. No telling what a small fruitful investment would have meant to them and towards influencing them in making much larger investments. A win/win opportunity for both Jamaica and an investor went out the window. Had their experience been good, they might well have thought of building a factory to employ Jamaicans and utilize products indigenous to Jamaica that would benefit even more people than would be directly employed by them.

My efforts to see them treated fairly failed. Indeed, it could be strong notice to anyone thinking of investing in Jamaica. And, sadly, there was more to come.

CHAPTER 7

BROKEN TRUST

As Managing Director of EML, I had a job to do. I had to see the company on the straight path. I had to preserve my reputation, protect our employees' reputations, and importantly, I had to lead by example. The whispers that emanated from among the staff about Michael's behavior were embarrassing, but I believed that staff confidence would hold up with fair and honest leadership on my part.

As difficult as it was to do business in a terribly corrupt country with an inept government, that my own partners were piling on additional stress was hard to accept. But I didn't see the next problem coming until it hit. Before the New Zealanders used car debacle began, Michael had asked me to help source low interest funds for him because he had become heavily indebted and was paying huge interest on these debts. He was in deep financial trouble.

At this time Jamaican interest was above 40% but somehow one could negotiate for as low as 12% if taken in US currency. The only risk was that if the Jamaican dollar devalued by huge margins, finding the Jamaican funds to repay the US loan would be painful. However, with the wide disparity between paying 12% and 40% interest, it seemed well worth the risk.

I had not asked Michael the extent of his debt, and he didn't volunteer to tell me. I had called a senior official at Caribbean Trust Company and asked him to meet and speak with Michael. That official is a trusted person whom I knew would give Michael a fair deal. He met with Michael and did his best to help. Michael received the loan in US currency he was seeking from Caribbean Trust, and I made no attempt to monitor the loan because it was Michael's personal business and not the business of EML.

One day Michael called me asking to have EML take over or guarantee responsibility of a bond or loan of US$130,000 for a friend in New York whom we all knew. He explained that he had exceeded his borrowing limit and needed a source with strong collateral to accommodate helping his friend. I resisted this but Michael asked that I do this "for him" as a personal favor. I sensed something fishy about this and was reluctant, but to get him off my back I took the chance.

The loan was guaranteed by EML and payments on that account started out fine. Soon after, we started getting calls from Caribbean Trust complaining that the payments were not always met on time and were more in arrears than not. We at EML had no alternative but to make the payments when they were not honored by Michael or his friend. We kept proper records of these transactions but I had more reason to worry.

As the used car matter worsened the Caribbean Trust problem intensified. Eventually, payments from Michael's friend ceased completely. EML had to take over the burden of paying the principal balance and interest on the US amount using Jamaican overdraft funds at a rate of over 40%. This further cranked up the interest. EML was therefore left holding this outstanding debt of more than J$2 million, which was never paid back.

It was later that I discovered that this US$130,000 was actually paid into Michael's account at Caribbean Trust to pay off one of his loans that was 'called' by the lender. The beneficiary of the US$130,000 therefore seemed to have been Michael and not his friend. So, in effect, Michael had not only borrowed from Caribbean Trust once; he had borrowed again to pay the interest on the first loan, with EML as guarantor. That loan balance was climbing rapidly on his total loan obligations because of devaluations and huge compounded interest. Money had to come from somewhere to save his private assets from seizure and auctioning.

The economy was not a happy one. It was in FINSAC mode, as we used to say; socio-economic conditions worsened, financial instability reigned, the consumer price index was skyrocketing, and the mood of the country was restive. Gas price hikes led to widespread rioting and island-wide roadblocks after a 31% gas tax hike. The resulting crippling of the education system and public transportation was the tip of the iceberg. Loss from wanton burning of public and personal vehicles, and major dislocation of business resulted. Island-wide pillaging, plundering, shootings, killings, and the like were par for the course.

At that time Jamaican investments in the US stock market were minimal, so the dot-com bubble bursting had little effect on the Jamaican economy. The pressures in the Jamaican economy were created by Jamaica's own leadership. I personally was not paying much attention to the rioting for that was not unusual; that was expected. I had known of damage done to folks who got trapped in similar road blocks, including a friend who had to shoot his way out of one; I had seen worse and we learned how to handle it; I learned where to not go. If I got trapped after securing my family and assets, then I would do whatever was necessary at that time to stay alive. To me, my personal problems took priority.

Isn't it shocking that anyone would choose taking a chance with rioting individuals over trusting the system that was in place to protect life and property? Where else in the world could that apply? That was the mood in my country at the time.

It should not be surprising that from about 1999 disagreements further intensified between the partners in EML, particularly over the abuse and diversion of company's funds, the use of EML's name to import cars on behalf of Michael or his company, the under-invoicing of these cars, and the manipulation of the accounts of the EML group by the auditors of the company's books to the huge benefit of Michael—among other things. Our board meetings were replete with allegations and counter-allegations; through all this the company was heading for a cessation of growth although it had a net bank account credit of over Ja$7 million in addition to a net real estate value at approximately Ja$300 Million (or US$6.6 million then).

Simply, the company had no debts against its assets, had large stocks, equipment and an additional $7 million in the bank. At a time when the infamous FINSAC was on its destructive path, this was an enviable financial position to occupy. Of course, the partners were embroiled in conflict, but I expected Richard to stay with the straight and narrow. I was mistaken. Given the choice between right and his blood brother, Richard took sides with his brother.

Our auto-glass competitors continued to take advantage of EML's lapse of attention to the auto glass business and I had reason to believe Michael was planning to remove both Lynne and myself from the company. All that was necessary now was a way to justify our removal.

Michael finally got his brother Richard on board to commence the process of pushing us out. Richard, though reserved somewhat, had been fair and honest throughout the stressful used car problems. He had agreed with me that deals made should be honored and had signed cheques to honor these commitments, but I saw him wavering as he faced the choice of right or wrong. He had reached the point where he had to choose between what is right and what his blood brother wanted. As was becoming more and more typical in Jamaica, what was wrong became more acceptable the further along that we were past Independence. Richard chose to side with his brother "for better or for worse".

Meanwhile, Michael's indebtedness was apparently increasing even more because he was not meeting his commitments, and he urgently needed funds after one of his assets was auctioned by a finance company. Although I knew Michael had borrowed from Caribbean Trust to reduce his interest burden, I was not aware of the full extent of Michael's indebtedness. Friends informed me later that Michael had visited them and was under great stress because he owed so much and was not seeing a way out. But he never mentioned to me the actual extent of his troubles. I figured that if it was bad enough he would put aside his pride and at least try to 'pinch' me for more.

The friction intensified. Fabricated accounting engineered by our auditor at JB Causwell & Co. became more apparent. J B Causwell, a company once completely owned by the father of Richard and Michael, had been our auditor since the business started, and I had no reason not to trust them. Their father was a man of unquestioned integrity. He had died before the formation of EML, but his company was kept in operation by an employee, Basil Cunningham. I quickly learned that Basil was not the honorable man Richard and Michael's father was. He knew much more about the accounts than I did. His knowledge of financial statements, preparing them and reading them, was way ahead of me. Frankly, I hate financial statements and avoided them like the plague. The auditor knew that his rigging of the books would weaken my position, and he knew too that I would not challenge his integrity.

I was forced to satisfy my curiosity about the handling of the company's books. I had always trusted our auditors and had always accepted their accounting. Analyzing the financial statements would be difficult for me since EML owned two other companies that would also need analyzing, and "consolidating" the accounts of three companies (the term used by the experts and not within my area of expertise) could only be done by seeking help from someone capable outside of JB Causwell & Co.

Meanwhile Basil Cunningham admitted in a meeting of the directors in July of 2001 that Michael had been in financial trouble and that after my objections, he diverted some $18 million to Michael and his company Econocar Rentals. I thought that this was tantamount to a bailout. I gathered from him that he made temporary adjustments and hinted that this was used only to permit the books for Michael as a poor performer to look better when seeking loans. Basil Cunningham when pressured by me in a meeting, agreed to correct his "creative accounting." The reversal was never done, though, and at a later date Michael attempted to claim this manipulation was a legitimate transaction while Cunningham opted to cheat the company of those funds by not reversing the transactions.

Making these transactions look legitimate was a difficult task for the wily Auditor. Only full disclosure could satisfy my curiosity. The courts would see to this . . . or so I thought. In hindsight I believe that Cunningham originally intended this book transaction to be temporary, as he felt duty bound to help the son of his longtime boss.

Distrust grew in the wake of these contentious meetings. Richard arrived in a meeting armed with a tape recorder. I followed suit with one myself at the next meeting. Soon all directors would have access to recordings of the meetings. I saw signs of manipulating of the minutes of meetings and my recordings became an obstruction to Richard and Michael. Eventually they wrote to me banning recorders in the meetings except for the recording secretary—who just happened to be a private person appointed by them.

In about September 2001, I spoke with Richard and requested that he and his brother buy our shares. His response was clear: They were not interested. Knowing the incompetence of his loan-burdened brother and Richard's poor management skills, I would have to be an idiot to leave it there. My suggestion that we take the matter to Christopher Bovel for mediation was rejected. They did not want to buy or sell. Dunn Cox the law firm that advised me at EML from time to time on matters, mainly minor, and had been the firm that Lynne and I employed to form Lynne's and my company EML in 1978. In fact, Janice, Michael's wife and a partner in Dunn Cox acted on Lynne's and my behalf forming other personal companies, handling our personal private affairs, including our wills. All this was seen by us as personal and confidential. I was also aware that Mr. Bovell had previously acted as mediator in a matter between Michael and a housing scheme investor in Runaway Bay,

So why was this rejected? Surely, Chris, the head of the law firm of which Michael's wife is a lawyer and partner was in a position that would protect them from any injustice they might expect from me. I was the one putting trust in the hands of a man who was Head of the firm of which Michael's wife is a partner.

New Millenium . . . More of the Same?

As my personal problems were beginning, it was business as usual in Jamaica. More scandals and more corruption were the order of the day. The beasts in the stampede were at full gallop.

Every Jamaican was so embroiled in the immediate issue affecting them that they hardly had taken notice of the path to devastation in which we were all headed; those involved in scandals were busy trying to worm their way out. The poor were finding creative ways to make a hustle, and I was too stunned by the conduct of my partners and the possibility of losing all that I had worked so hard for.

Amazingly, the voting population seemed in tune with this changing culture. Successive elections had returned the PNP Government to power as the JLP Party more often than not seemed divided and unable to woo the voters. The JLP Party, seen as more middle of the road liberal conservative and capitalistic in policy, did not appeal to the new handout culture. The PNP Party, seen as socialist and very entitlement minded since the Manley era, was superb at telling the people what they like to hear and getting them to believe. They accomplished this by appearing to be more caring and by diverting kickbacks, contract loans, and proceeds from sources of corruption scandals into areas allowing them to own and control those who had benefited.

I knew that this perceived free ride could not go on forever. There is a price to be paid for the entitlement way of life. The penalty had to be 'no growth' followed by its significant implications.

Time to Part Ways

In October 2001, Lynne and I filed a petition to wind up EML. Either the partners could buy our shares, or the company would dissolve. After more than 20 years of sweat, sacrifice, hard work, sleepless nights, exposure to violence and all the stress that came with it, the time had come for separation. I figured it would be a simple matter of a fair valuation.

While sitting at my desk one day Richard approached me with a cheque for JA$3 million drawn on an EML account to Michael. He explained that Michael had lost one of his properties in an auction by one of his creditors, and he needed the funds urgently to stop further bleeding. I could see the intent was not good and the rush was enough to indicate that worse was to come. I refused to sign it, so both Richard and Michael signed it themselves. I wrote to the auditor and to Richard and Michael objecting.

I saw the writing on the wall at this point. I had seen the trend for some time but it felt as if I were dreaming. A dissipation process was in motion and it was being done with impunity. These actions were not compatible with those of the Michael or the Richard I had known in years gone by. Michael had to be very desperate for money to behave this way; Richard had to be weak and spineless at the very best to support this behavior.

Was this why Michael acted so aggressively during our stint in the used car business? I wondered.

I had noticed years previously that he had been purchasing real estate. The way his business operated, it appeared that it was impossible to generate adequate cash flow to satisfy loans matching the purchases. But I was not in a position to know if his purchases included inputs from any other partners or his wife and, if so, to what extent. However, it wasn't difficult to see that a profit could not be generated from his business actions, and solvency could not be sustained unless there was some sizable input in cash that was not yet obvious to me.

After our petition, directors meetings became even more contentious. There were lies, denials, and more lies. Meetings were pre-arranged with the stage set to justify our removal, usurping my authority as managing director, and bypassing Lynne. Poor treatment of staff (such as sudden salary reductions) became commonplace.

Abuse became so bad that one evening after work both Lynne and I were stopped at the gate on the company's premises by Richard and his two sons. They closed the gate, effectively holding us hostage. His sons stood guard while our vehicle was searched as staff looked on. One of Richard's sons was armed as he sat in his vehicle. Staff members looking on were aware of this and conspicuously showed their anger. Unable to find something to incriminate us, I watched them carefully to avoid them planting anything. Although it was embarrassing, the presence of the staff might have been a blessing. This harassment and intimidation was obviously planned. More effort was being made to justify our removal or force our resignation.

As I left the premises that evening a member of staff, visibly angered, approached me and said "Boss mek mi get a man fi done dem fi yu" [1]. I did my best to calm him by assuring him that justice would be done. I assured him that I had called my attorney and he had instructed me to not resist or retaliate because it would make matters worse for me.

The following day I spoke with the employee again and tried to calm his concerns. He stared at me in a cold angry way; his demeanor appeared to be asking *"wa wrong wid yu boss . . . .yu na go deal wid dem?*[2] as he hissed his teeth and writhed his body and arms. I could read his lips . . . *"Boss, yu must be tun eediat"*[3] he said.

Many minutes passed before he toned down a bit, but he continued to stare at me with piercing eyes, unconvinced that I was making the right decision. I was not surprised at his offer to "done dem" That is the standard method, especially among the working class who believe that it is the only way to get justice. I was surprised by the person making the offer, though. He was a peaceful, passive, non-confrontational, happy-go-lucky, semi-literate person who had lived in Jamaica from birth. But he knew very well that were anything as demeaning done to him he would have no alternative but arrange a hit. He knew that for him, there was only one route to justice. The average Jamaican knows that they could not rely on the top for justice.

When persons in leadership positions are so flagrantly corrupt, where they control all the conduits of justice, where they have the fiscal power to enable them, what choice does the man at the bottom have but to create his own courthouse?

The abuse by the partners continued, but more aggressively. Electronically recorded directors' meetings continued to be commonplace, and corporate decisions continued to be pre-arranged. Allegations became more overt. Justifying our removal became a very aggressive effort. They needed us out in a hurry. What could the motive be? What is it that required their urgent unchecked access to the company?

Lynne was repeatedly and falsely accused of not having worked at EML at all and of not being a director—a ridiculous claim that was easily dispelled. Her position as a director had been repeatedly endorsed by Richard on returns made to government, and her signature was on many of the company's official documents. The ridiculous allegations indicated the level of desperation. Seeing this level of aggressive falsification, it came as no surprise when they eventually removed her as a director.

Frustrated, Lynne resigned as an employee of EML on January 8, 2002. On January 25, Michael and Richard did what would give them access to the assets of the company: They voted and removed me as Managing Director.

From this point on, they had absolute and complete access to the books, and more importantly, the funds of the company. I had already seen to the recovery of the company from the debts created by Michael's pet project, the used car business. Despite being battered by the used car debacles, I saw to it that; the company still had more auto-glass stocks than any other competing company in Jamaica, and the buildings and real estate formed assets valued more than US $6 million dollars. In short EML was cash-rich and debt-free. This was an indication of the strength of a company that had stood up to blows and had remained strong. In hindsight the company was an attractive source of money; had it been in serious debt, it is unlikely that anyone would have great interest in it. But to allow it to be dissipated was not an option for me. I had simply worked too hard and too long.

CHAPTER 8
THE JOURNEY FOR JUSTICE BEGINS

Our petition was filed in the Supreme Court of Jamaica to wind up the company. This was not challenged and eventually after several trips to the Supreme Court our partners—now respondents—Michael and Richard advised through their attorney that they would buy our shares rather than wind up the company. A consent order was prepared and signed by all parties. In its spirit the consent order intended a valuation of our shares to be completed in 90 days and payment for our shares would be completed in a year. It seemed straightforward.

With the company so strong in assets it is common sense that the assets ought to be protected until our shares were paid for. Michael's behavior and the change that I was seeing in his values convinced me that the assets of the company were exposed to dissipation. In addition, his obvious ineptness at managing any type of business practically guaranteed this, one way or another. Apart from his more recent questionable behavior, why would anyone want to see someone put in charge of any business after their conduct had directly caused that company's predicament?

I had placed a lot of trust in him for more than twenty years, but that was when we all had very little to lose. Now we had gathered some wealth through EML but not enough to bail out a hugely indebted person or company without seriously diminishing the company's assets.

The Consent Order

Parting ways seemed so logical and simple. Dividing value into three seemed like common sense. A consent order was all that was required. Simplified, the order said that a professional auditing firm would carry out a valuation within a specific time line (90 days) and that the company would continue to do business as was normally done— renting premises, importing and installing auto glass—but would not sell any fixed assets. Knowing the state of the Jamaican dollar and the extent and frequency of devaluations, it was clear that delays would penalize us unjustly. Also, knowing the contentious nature of partnership, the auditor (valuer), a company called KPMG, was to take into consideration all the companies which were part of the assets of EML and "take into account any assets or funds of the Company which have been diverted, utilised or paid by or to any of the shareholders". The purpose was obviously for determining a value and to penalize by way of interest and principal, any funds diverted by any of the shareholders. This required that the operators of the company hand over all information from the books of the company and its subsidiaries. The subsidiaries obviously represented part of the value of EML. During this time, the fixed assets, none of which had ever been sold previously in the lifetime of EML, were not to be sold or dissipated by the operators of the business. To permit the sale of any such asset would diminish the value of EML.

It all seemed so straightforward.

The court accepted that KPMG could, and would complete a valuation in 90 days. The court-approved agreement also mandated that the values would be in Jamaican dollars tied to 2001. It was therefore in my interest to cooperate fully with KPMG. All that was required was a justice system that ensured completion in a timely manner and to protect against anything that could diminish the value of our shares pending completion of the valuation. Unfortunately, the partners saw delays as a financial benefit to themselves.

It did not occur to me for one second that justice might not be available, although there was every reason to suspect so. But what would have been the alternative? For me, surely not the route the majority in Jamaica prefer to take!

So confidently, on May 29, 2002, after more trips to the Supreme Court, with our trust placed in the Justice system, Lynne and I accepted the valuation conditions set out in the court-endorsed consent order and felt comfortable with a valuation of shares to be completed in 90 days. After all, it was while we were in attendance at the Supreme

Court that KPMG informed both attorneys by phone that this 90-day period could be comfortably accomplished.

We all knew that stalling would have huge benefits to one party only. Most importantly, KPMG knew this. We had seen the impact of FINSAC, the most devastating occurrence in Jamaica in my lifetime, and we had heard stories from various victims about the conditions in the courts, but we figured that it could not be so bad or so brazen as to be blatantly unjust, particularly while in the hands of the professionals at internationally-renowned KPMG.

Naively, we believed that 90 days meant 90 days, and outside of a catastrophe of nature the Supreme Court would see to justice. Additionally we expected KPMG, as an international professional auditing firm, to be absolutely fair and not permit unjust behavior by any party. KPMG would also expect to have a smooth journey as all the books of accounts were in the possession of the company and out of the reach of Lynne and myself.

KPMG, as expected, prepared a letter of engagement setting out what information they required to meet the conditions of the consent order. After some delays by Richard and Michael, it was signed by all parties on August 23, 2002.

But shortly after signing onto these commitments, it appeared that Richard and Michael had no intention of cooperating with the valuation process. They were in full control of the operation of EML, all of the $7 million in the bank and all else that it owned, including its sizeable real estate assets, stock, goodwill, and, most importantly, all the books of accounts.

Since the trigger for interest payments as agreed in the consent order commenced at completion of a valuation, then if there were no valuation by KPMG they could, if they chose, continue to operate the company without ever having the valuation completed.

Surely KPMG would not permit this. Surely the Supreme Court would not support this either. Surely this would be strongly opposed on all fronts . . . or so I thought.

This must be a strong message and lesson to investors seeking to do business with countries known for their unstable currencies, particularly those with a reputation for corruption. Jamaica easily falls within this category. There is no need for investors to study the type or methodology of the corruption.

Here, I was the seller, selling shares to be valued in 2001 with more than 80 % of its value in the form of real estate holdings. The longer the delays are, the more the injustice applied to one party—exponentially so. But the obvious blatant stalling, to the extent of such unfair losses to one party would be very difficult and unlikely without some protection of the perpetrators by individuals within the Justice system. Also, professionals by themselves cannot get away with this conduct unless some protection was available from inside the justice system. In fact a delay extended from 90 days to say four years seems impossible in any democratic country with a working justice system. But to get away with delay by stalling is a strong indication of the enormity of the power wielded by way of connections.

I was so certain that the worst could not happen, that although many cases were suffering the same fate—delays, for months and years— I was not tuned in to the details of these and only heard snippets which I brushed aside as rumours.

One needed to understand the shape of the culture. I was learning quickly. The Jamaican justice system has so many departments—Police, Attorney General, Solicitor General, DPP, Resident Magistrate Court, Supreme Court, Appeal Court — that to navigate the pitfalls one had to endure many painful delay tactics. Ease of access to fairness would require immense influence and access to the heart of power inside and outside of the system. The majority are not connected well enough to enjoy this privilege. Those who are too exhausted to bear the frustration simply give up, and it is therefore common place to hear someone say, "*mi drap di case yaw mon, mi jus can badda...is betta mi pay a man.*"

Paul Cole's Jamaican Lessons Commence

Mr. Paul Cole of KPMG was designated to determine the valuation of the shares. In his first interview with Lynne and me, he was quite aware that we had no access to the books of the company. He acknowledged this and asked us to point him toward the area of the records that would uncover the most data possible. I gave him all the information that I had and promised more if I ever got my hands on any.

Shortly after Cole's very first visit to EML, the stall began. Michael and Richard withheld information, even as the real estate holdings appreciated to compensate for devaluations and even as these devaluations ate up what would be our 2001 share valuation. Our former partners realized that the longer they held onto our shares the more they would gain and the more we would lose. If they could simply not cooperate and wait to hand over the requisite documents as late as say 2011, they could enjoy a cool 700% gain. If the valuation process was stalled until 2015 then they could gain 1000% or more. As sellers of our shares, we would feel the pain of a greater or corresponding loss.

Again we assumed that a professional company like KPMG would not sit by and permit this. Surely, after a reasonable time without cooperation, they would report this to the Supreme Court and preserve their reputation. They were guided by the consent agreement and **they** had set the period for completing the valuation. Surely KPMG must have meant what they said when they suggested 90 days.

As KPMG tolerated delay after delay, they knew what devaluations were doing because they saw it as routine in Jamaica. They knew that when the Jamaican dollar devalued 100 % the value of real estate would eventually double from that occurrence alone. They knew that after such a valuation we, the seller of our shares, would be sucking up that loss. They knew what time cost in Jamaica. They knew why they should not be permitting or accepting the delays that they were experiencing. Yet they did.

I had a gut feeling that Mr. Cole wanted to do what was right, but I also had a feeling that he was not completely free to do so. I sincerely hope that in credit to him, my gut feeling was right.

After 90 days had expired without any cooperation from the partners, we went back to court in an effort to remove the delays. On November 20, 2002, Supreme Court Justice Anderson ruled amending the May 29, 2002 order by 31 days to September 23, 2002. This was the first legal step by the Supreme Court to address the injustice resulting from delays. However, in keeping with their behavior to date, the partners appealed this and predictably, the appeal created another profitable delay for them.

Here again is a lesson for investors. With the right connections, appeals can be very effective in Jamaica. Our former partners' appeal was heard between May 2003 and July 2003. And a ruling on the appeal was made about eight months later on February 18, 2004. This again allowed a 90 day commitment to vanish and a huge delay to benefit the partners.

The Jamaican economy was in its customary decline, and while we waited I did whatever I could to watch out for the possibility of dissipation by the partners. During this time we continued to pressure KPMG through our attorneys to expedite the valuation. By then I had already discovered about $60million of liabilities unaccounted for in the EML financial statements. We realized that the auditor had used his accounting skills to create a large debt or debts in favour of unknown entities. But to whose benefit? It was certainly not to mine or Lynne's.

I began to believe that some was credited to Michael or his company, but I was informed that missing amounts could only be accurately ascertained by consolidating the accounts of the EML group. I had written to Basil Cunningham questioning this approximately $60 million of 'net current liabilities', but I got no response from him.

Both Lynne and I were now in a precarious position, and subsequent events were to further test the integrity of the justice system. Richard and Michael changed attorneys to Dunn Cox & Orrett—the firm where Michael's wife worked—in late 2003 when their starting attorney Priya Levers took up a post in Cayman as a judge. By then, nothing that happened was viewed without suspicion.

Lynne and I were already uncomfortable with the presence of Janice, Michael's wife, attending the judge's chambers as a lawyer who was not representing them. Understandably, we became more uncomfortable with our former partners moving to Dunn Cox, the very law firm which formed EML many years prior and subsequent personal companies for Lynne and me, transferred real estate for us, and even prepared my will.

We had to stomach a combination of auditor and law firm both blood-related to one side of the case. Janice had openly and possibly officially switched alliances to represent Richard and her husband. It is unthinkable that Dunn Cox—having represented Lynne and myself for most of our adult lives—could decide to represent our partners to inflict this kind of injustice on us.

As Janice frequented the Supreme Court in their defense, I reminisced on the irony. I had previously contemplated and suggested seeking mediation by way of her boss, but the partners had rejected this. I had been guided by attorneys at Dunn Cox for more than 20 years, had an excellent relationship of trust with them and had done a lot of legal business with them. Suddenly I was in the courts opposed by companies I had employed to defend me for decades. It said something about trusting professionals in Jamaica. It said something about ethics that is freely tolerated in the new Jamaica, something truly symptomatic of the state of the country. It said something about leadership in those companies. It was once very unusual for the respected head of a large professional company to allow this, particularly for an unrelenting period of near 10 years. How things had changed.

It is amazing that what we see and what is, can be so vastly different. I was reinforcing that the greatest lessons are learned from experiences during hard times. I am now absolutely convinced that one's true character is never obvious during good times. Observe one's conduct when one is in debt and what you see is a true reflection of one's character. The impact that this has on trust is so devastating that integrity of the systems in governance has to be overly effective for investment and growth to take place in any country. The system must always protect investors from the evil that suddenly comes forth from investors who fall on hard times. That in turn is an incentive to invest. I cannot overemphasize the importance here of integrity and an affinity for proper ethics in leadership, particularly in every justice system.

While I watched the defection of my allies, rapid devaluation of the Jamaican dollar continued in early 2003, hitting rock bottom for by mid-year and causing more pain to businesses, particularly those with debt. Projections for improvements in the justice system only attracted attention in international news media. Jamaicans correctly paid absolutely no attention. Widespread taxation and public servant layoffs left Jamaicans uncertain, fearful and nervous in the face of economic policies.

By the end of the year gun violence claimed the lives of scores of people and included large numbers of police shot and wounded. The business sector, reeling from the murders called for a state of emergency, while tourism suffered from overseas blacklisting. Civilians reverted to their common call of "We want justice!" as the courts prepared to place on trial six police officers for charges of murder.

By November 2003, severely frustrated, we changed attorneys. Between 2002 and 2005 we wrote to our attorneys many times requesting that they seek ways to expedite the valuation. They in turn wrote to KPMG and to the partners' attorneys Priya Levers and Dunn Cox without any success.

Voluminous correspondence continued to pass between all concerned and by June 2004 we were back before Justice Anderson in an effort to answer questions relating to the cause of delays. Paul Cole of KPMG, along with us and the partners, attended the Supreme Court about 5 times between June 2004 and January 2005 and got absolutely nowhere.

Finally, in January 2005, Paul Cole informed the Supreme Court :

> ". . . due to the continued failure of EML to provide KPMG with the requisite information, it would not be possible for me to complete the valuation exercise in accordance with the Court orders. . ."

Why had it taken so long for KPMG to say this? Why did an international auditing firm allow themselves to be placed in this situation, unable to carry out their duties and not objecting? I spent many sleepless nights turning over the questions in my mind. Why did KPMG suggest 90 days yet show no urgency when they knew the repercussions on us if it exceeded that period?

I had to rule out the possibility of incompetence on their part. I had to, if only because of their international name. But it begged questions: Who else were at play here? Why was the late return to the court by KPMG not impacting more positively on the handing over of information? Could it be that external influence was at play—the type of influence that is taken for granted in a corrupted Jamaica? And if so, who could have the power to influence a KPMG? And, was Mr. Cole free of duress?

If 'connections' were in play, they were strong. Lynne and I seemed to be the only ones concerned enough to press the matter. The more we pressed the more vague and elusive the results.

Take for example the glaring and brazen conduct which was eventually exposed here: EML financials that KPMG requested from 2001 were hidden away by the partners for more than 3 years without as much as a hint of consequence. In 2005 those financials were still in hiding. How was this exposed? An attorney for the partners wrote in 2005 saying that 2001 audited financials did "not exist" but that "audited" 2002 was available. She later provided a copy of these as "audited" financials.

Amazing! How could audited 2002 financials be prepared without having 2001 financials?

After we had these 2002 financials examined by a chartered accountant they turned out to be unaudited and tampered with. In countries where justice prevails, this is called "fraud" and the consequence is a clear deterrent to those who might think of trying it. In Jamaica, the law calls it "fraud" and the court applies consequence depending on who did it and who the "connections" are.

Being labeled as "audited," could pass as an error. But the "doctoring" of the 2002 financial statement by making modifications under the signature of the professional who prepared it, seemed fraudulent. Those who knew and engineered it didn't seem to care

Did I expect differently? Yes. Was I shocked? No. Not after more than three years of stalling. Disappointed in KPMG? Disappointed in the system? Yes. It was too blatant; it showed no fear of consequence. Such a flaunt in the face of justice! And there was no one available to even entertain a complaint.

In fact, as we would see later, the pressure I applied by bypassing any 'connections' in the system caused a careless response. By July 2006 one of the opposing attorneys wrote to us attaching a copy of 2001 financial statements—the very financials said to not exist! They were dated in 2002 and signed by the partners, Richard and Michael, solid proof that they existed from back in 2002.

The brazenness and impunity with which lies and manipulations were taking place was insulting to the system and to the professionals who tolerated it. So brazen, so flippant were they about the possibility of consequence as if sure of protection.

Our continued exchange of correspondence between both parties, J B Causwell & Co. and KPMG about the numerous delays started to feel like a waste of effort. We kept writing to KPMG questioning reasons for more delays and we became increasingly concerned that the stalling was causing more serious losses by way of inflation, devaluations of the Jamaican dollar, and the loss of opportunities to use the proceeds of our shares to invest in solid assets or another business. It became much clearer that recovering any amount of value would become worthless if and when it happened.

We were haunted by these thoughts relentlessly and concern grew as the partners added to the fight in the court by trying to get access to assets of the company which were converted to cash and that were so obviously protected by our consent order agreement. This became our added battle to protect and secure the assets of the company. I was sure then that this was the future for investors and the state of the economy would be guided by the conduct of the justice system that I was experiencing. At that point I was seeing the future economy of Jamaica as a failure but I didn't want to believe it; but I felt more resolve to make an effort to change it.

By this point, I was even more aware that Michael wanted funds to settle personal debts. We had been warned that the assets of an EML subsidiary were being dissipated or sold and that accountability would be a problem. Surely the Supreme Court would never permit this, or so I assured my friends and acquaintances who inquired of the progress of the valuation matter. In turn, they would tell me how much EML was shrinking. Some even suggested that by the time we got our settlement, there would be nothing left– a thought that drove me deeper into disappointment and depression.

Numerous adjournments continued to be the order of hearing dates. Documents regularly disappeared from the Registry, Judges adjourned cases nonchalantly and without care for the costs involved. Friends in the field of law would assure me that justice was coming, but I was increasingly unconvinced.

More shocking to me was that this was known by most at my level who had been to the courts. It was common knowledge that this was widespread occurrence in the system. It was par for the course.

I never understood this. *"Why do you lawyers permit this to happen?"* I would ask many attorneys. *"Why don't you take a stand? Why do you tolerate the adjournments that push back cases for years? Have you reported these problems to the Chief Justice?"*

The typical response was one of surprise that I could ask such a silly question. *"Are you crazy? From time to time we have to go before the very people we would be reporting!"*

What a sad indictment of the integrity of officers of the Court. That statement is a stark admission that persecution of officers of the court is expected if one dared to take a stand against any injustice inside the courts. It is an untenable admission of injustice.

That Poor Old Lady . . .

Some time in about 2005, I was beginning to see things clearer. On one of my more than 70 visits to the Supreme Court, I saw an elderly lady in obvious discomfort. She was wiping her face and sweating as I approached her.

During my many visits I had felt some discomfort from the heat in the Supreme Court building and always wished for windy days. I had found a spot by an arch where the coolest air passed on the hot days. As I got closer to her and suggested where she could stand to get the benefit of this airflow, I realized that she was weeping. I asked if there was anything that I could do to help. She explained in a shaky, tired voice that she had finally won a case that had commenced some ten years earlier. She had finally won an order to wind up a business venture in which she held shares or partnership.

"Unfortunately, the assets are all gone," she said. "There is nothing left."

So sad. Her assets had dissipated during the long wait, and she knew what would happen if she sought compensation.

I thought for a while that she was unlucky or had poor representation. Surely this was not to happen to us, I thought. Surely if she had kept an eye on the assets, the court would have protected her.

Despite the previous four years of exposure and obvious discrimination that I saw inside the courts, and despite my feeling that my encounter might have been somewhat worse than her experience, I just could not accept that the same fate was headed our way. I was to discover later that this was standard in Jamaica. Never mind that competent judges ought to understand the impact of time on business. Yet the general reaction is to never complain because that too would have its consequences. There were times when I could not shake the eerie feeling that I was being punished simply for taking this matter to court.

Depressed and frustrated with the incompetence and corruption so evident in the system, I struggled to strengthen my resolve to continue to take a stand. Even if it failed us I figured it would benefit others one day.

On March 18, 2005, we were advised that attempts were being made to settle. As a result another hearing date was adjourned without resolution. This was a strange and unexpected occurrence. It appeared (to us) to be an initiative on the part of all the attorneys involved and more likely than possibly, including the judge. We knew nothing about it beforehand, however later on the reasons and strategy involved would become clear. Was this really initiated by the judge? And why would a judge already sitting on this matter involve himself in negotiating a settlement in the matter? Why not leave that to someone else who was independent or unconnected?

We had little alternative but follow the instructions of our attorneys, not knowing if they were coerced into going this route. As negotiations commenced between the attorneys and as Justice Anderson intervened, we recognized that the suggested settlement could have huge tax implications. We would risk being held legally accountable for dishonest manipulations by the EML's auditor Basil Cunningham. Despite our not being beneficiaries of that huge manipulated sum, to not be indemnified could cause us to be implicated. At least $18million of false payables was manipulated in favour of Michael or his company.

As unprepared as we were for this kind of negotiation Lynne and I heard what the Judge had to say. Michael and Richard also heard what Justice Anderson had to say. The proposed settlement would not have required a valuation of the company. However, the matter of $60 million that was unaccounted for remained a concern. This figure had apparently contributed to the income tax department making an assessment against EML and an indemnity would be needed to protect us.

We insisted on indemnity. We requested that they accept responsibility for their gains made through those false manipulations. After all, we had never been told where this sum of money went. On the other hand a negotiation outside of the consent order could allow the partners an opportunity to improperly legitimize the false payables on the books but this would leave them open to possible exposure by me. I however, would never accept liability for something wrong done by them.

The refusal by Michael and Richard to indemnify us against tax and any other liability resulted in a failed settlement attempt. The sum for settlement was not an issue, and if there was nothing to hide, why not agree to indemnify? Also, surely I could have been sworn to silence if we signed accepting a settlement that included improper manipulations. And why was Justice Anderson so expressively angry in our presence when we insisted on the indemnity? As he saw the settlement slipping away, and as he writhed around, groping at his head in an obvious impatient fit of temper, I couldn't help but think how unbecoming it was for a Supreme Court Justice to behave this way. It seemed to impact more on him than on the partners. They knew a road to travel and he too must have needed our submission badly.

This also presented us with an additional concern. Justice Anderson had been part of the negotiations. Why? There was no need for the judge to become involved in this way. Now he could not continue to sit on this case. How convenient! Why was he suddenly in a great hurry to end this case? Was he in the process of clearing his desk of all his cases? I will not speculate as to the circumstances which caused his withdrawal but it caused great damage to our case and has done nothing to boost my confidence in the administrative competence of the Jamaican Judiciary.

In a small Island like Jamaica practically nothing is a secret and rumours persisted as to his reasons but I refuse to repeat them here. Before he took leave of the case, Justice Anderson, not to be outdone by his previous tirade of antics displaying disgust of our insisting on indemnity, played a parting shot by removing the injunction protecting the proceeds from one of EML's real estate assets, effective within one month. This was an act that would force us to keep going to court to extend it; this was an act that would cost us millions in time and legal fees. This felt like an act of reprisal, an act that would lead to the improper removal of over J$80 million in cash from an interest bearing US dollar account. This was an act that could be proven to be unjustified all the way through the Appeal Court and to the Privy Council, the highest courts available. This was an act carried out by a judge who supposedly specialized in commercial cases; a judge whose job it was to sit on numerous such cases in Jamaica. If only few judges knew of the need for indemnity against improper movement of funds, it should include Justice Anderson.

Like a Stuck Record

After more than 1600 murders in Jamaica during 2005, the country braced for a violent 2006. Throughout 2006, crimes connected to thousands of criminals deported from overseas jumped to parishes outside Kingston in various forms, like extortion and drugs. Crime everywhere; even inside churches.

Highlighted by the murder conviction of Donald 'Zekes' Phipps, a don known to be a PNP supporter who controlled a PNP garrison where the gun ruled, several other dons were indicted in a special effort by the police to put a dent in the out of control gun crime.

Putting away dons who control garrisons is quite unusual in Jamaica; especially if these dons control garrisons which are dominated by the ruling party. Many felt that the special effort to put away 'Zekes' for murder was only because he was becoming out of control. I am inclined to agree. In fact Zeke's power was so evident that when he was first apprehended by the police his supporters were so aggressive towards the police that he was allowed to calm the crowd using a police speaker-phone. Amazing! The man in handcuffs had to to protect the lives of the police who arrested him?

Throughout the history of garrison politics in Jamaica, dons were protected by politicians who used them to control votes. But when they got too big for their pants, they were removed one way or another, often violently. Zekes' removal need not have been by the gun since it was made easier using a witness's evidence of homosexuality about oral sex performed on Zekes by a man whom he is convicted of killing. That would never be supported by average Jamaicans inside and outside of the garrison, the large majority of whom are known to be homophobic.

During this time of continued unrest, from November 2005 to January 2007 we had to visit the Supreme Court more than 10 times for the sole purpose of renewing the injunction that protected these proceeds of an asset that was first left exposed by Justice Anderson. Our former partners and officers of the court seemed all too comfortable as a mockery was made of the justice system. Our letters to KPMG inquiring about the delays were usually answered with the circular logic of "when we get the information from EML, we will do the valuation." Such a reply suggested they could do the valuation in 12, 15, 20 or 50 years if necessary.

It had to be a dream. The behaviour of officers of the court was so unabashed, so blatant. For hours I would dazedly marvel at how the population went about their daily business ignoring the happenings in the justice system clearly and openly indicating that they already knew what the outcome on practically any issue would be . . . nothing!

The court ignored the multiple scandals and adjusted as best they could to the maneuverings – legal or illegal - that guaranteed their survival. Many from every strata of society who heard of my predicament would chastise me for being so stupid as to go to court. They would say, "Man would a dead long time cause mi nah go a court, only idiot go a court. . . boss yu no read newspaper, yu no si how tings get seckle?"

My upbringing had too great an impact on me to go down that road. This had become the standard way of dealing with issues in Jamaica. The majority had already learned to conform to this culture. The corruption had reached a level that had permeated every nook and cranny in Jamaica; only an idiot would assume that the departments of Government responsible for seeing to addressing and removing this corruption were excluded.

With the snubbing from some corners in the courts and with no progress from the seemingly overly-tolerant KPMG's efforts, we had exhausted every avenue to procure the information withheld from KPMG. There had to be a government department that could uncover the manipulations by EML's auditor.

I felt some relief when my inquiries led to the Public Accountancy Board. We filed a complaint with the Public Accountancy Board (PAB), a body that in layman's terms has a duty to keep licensed accountants in line with standards applicable to laws in Jamaica, and I sought help by letter dated April 12th 2005 followed by another dated April 22nd 2005.

Gun shy from my experiences in the system, I didn't know what to expect of the PAB and I admit that I made the complaint to the PAB with much cynicism. My attorneys had not shown great interest in the Public Accounts route, so I undertook the responsibility to single handedly make and pursue the complaint to the PAB.

Without as much as consulting my attorneys, I gathered the information that I had handed over to KPMG and relied on the PAB to access the information that was being withheld for so long. In 2006 the correspondence between the Registrar of the PAB and the auditor Basil Cunningham bore fruit. Suddenly the same attorneys who had been denying the existence of financial statements for 2001, managed to find those documents.

How miraculous! The very financials that KPMG had requested in 2002, deliberately withheld from as early as 2002. You can imagine the relief I felt. I was seeing light at the end of the tunnel and there was some sign of jitters on the part of the Partners. They had hurriedly found the "nonexistent" 2001 financials. The manipulations on the financials that had been exposed in a directors meeting was now in a position to be seen. We had a friend look at it. The manipulations were not reversed as was promised by Cunningham.

But my hope was that this would be exposed during the investigation by the PAB. I was naturally cynical about the PAB. It was a body of government and the endemic problems of 'connections' remained my concern. But this investigation came about unexpectedly and did not involve the court in its early stages. I believe the fact that the PAB was contacted by Lynne and me only and that the courts had nothing to do with it, improved our chances of seeing justice from that Board. I believe that had our call for investigation been known by the partners, the possibility of an injunction or some other court involved act would have denied us the chance of exposing the manipulations.

KPMG's Paul Cole Throws in the Towel

While we were awaiting the intervention by the PAB, Paul Cole of KPMG filed an affidavit in the Supreme Court clearly indicating his frustration, and in his summing up stated to the effect 'that even if at this time, were he to receive the requested information from EML or the partners he did not think a fair valuation would be possible because it would require EML's full cooperation'.

Cole is clearly indicating here that he has never had their cooperation.

The verbatim text of the final paragraphs of Paul Cole's Affidavit stated:

> "Over the three year period since August 2002 when the valuation assignment commenced, KPMG has experienced

> considerable difficulties in obtaining from EML the requisite documentation and in some cases in a form that is conducive for us to carry out a proper valuation exercise in accordance with the Court Orders. To date, some of the requisite information remains outstanding without reasonable explanation.
>
> Based on the knowledge gained from the interviews with the Petitioners and Respondents, there are a number of accounting related matters that, given the lack of co-operation and documentation provided to date, would prevent me from ascertaining with any degree of accuracy, the equity value of EML as at December 31, 2001
>
> These experiences have led me to conclude that, even with full documentary disclosure I cannot, from a practical perspective, provide a proper valuation, since I need management's cooperation to understand the activity documented."

This affidavit was addressed to Justice Anderson and filed on December 5, 2005, along with impressive attachments in support. Cole's affidavit provided solid additional evidence that withholding of information was deliberate and that he was obviously throwing in the towel. Additionally, bear in mind here, tremendous damage was already done to us as minority shareholders. Without saying it literally, Cole was actually confirming that "over the three year period since August 2002", the partners had used time to enrich themselves by holding onto real estate and other assets belonging to the minority shareholders as the Jamaican dollar devalued effectively diminishing any potential gains that were due to these shareholders.

Cole was a soft-spoken man and his accent bore British intonation. From interviews I had with him he was a consummate professional who seemed to know what he was doing. He appeared to be honest and fair, and appeared to have read up his homework, asked the critical questions, and understood what was happening.

Cole left KPMG shortly after he wrote his affidavit. Ever since his unexpected departure I have wondered why he allowed himself to become part of the delay process. Knowing the level of corruption in Jamaica, I have often wondered if Cole was under any kind of duress from interfering 'connections' within or outside KPMG, to conform with the status quo. Was he guided or influenced by his superiors during this valuation process or, for that matter, during any other project? Was he unhappy about not writing this affidavit earlier?

His final effort was more like the Cole who first interviewed Lynne and me, and I just can't help often wondering what really happened. Waiting over 3 years past the 90 day period in the eyes of any professional cannot be reasonable and he must have known that by permitting this delay KPMG would be contributing to us being denied the fair value of our shares.

The Public Accountancy Board Outshines the Supreme Court

Pressure from Cole's affidavit and from the PAB's asking of the auditors the kind of questions for which we got no answers had stirred some activity; activity that would help the PAB to garner some response.

We knew that the auditor would have a problem telling the truth but we hoped that he would come clean to recover some integrity. We also expected that he might be intimidated and pressured to keep hiding his $60 million manipulation, already among other skeletons in his closet. He had previously sneakily and skillfully hidden other 'written-off' debts but digging into those without access to the company's 'accounts-receivable' statements of accounts would be more challenging. Finding and exposing the bigger manipulations would be less time consuming.

Eventually the PAB was able to get some of the information that was deliberately withheld for years, albeit with some difficulty. Information that the justice system should have long caused to be extracted in the process of delivering justice, was finally exposed to scrutiny, although only in part.

What an indictment on the Supreme Court for us to have bypassed them and gone to the Public Accounts Board for justice! And what is the message here to investors?

With the PAB investigating EML's Auditor, and with Paul Cole's affidavit threatening to expose and punish them for delaying, there suddenly seemed to be some late desire by our former partners to either cooperate with KPMG or hustle to engineer more 'maneuverings'. Even if elusive 'maneuverings' was the intent, they had to show now some intension to hand over data. Their auditor, who had manipulated figures and had avoided my letters, had to answer questions before the PAB.

Michael and Richard had already made huge financial gains from devaluation and inflation and they feared the consent order would no longer be valid if KPMG backed out. They also had the benefit of diverted funds and manipulated figures that the PAB might expose. They knew this would likely lead to winding up of the company so this was good reason to be in a hurry to get KPMG back on the job to do a 2001 valuation based on 2001 Jamaican dollars (not US dollars), more than 3 years late and effectively handing us huge losses. A working justice system would not have permitted these losses to be passed on to us!

At this stage there was only one route from here to justice and that would be to wind up the company, hold the partners accountable for any misappropriated funds, and for the interest on those funds.

Our application to this route was put in place, but the partners sought to hold onto their gains from the delays and to have a 2001 valuation done. This they hoped to achieve if the requisite information that was once hidden could be made to suddenly appear. This would bring about a huge victory for them. Imagine having assets with 2006 values in hand, while paying out 2001 values which have been used by them and diminished.

KPMG was aware that doing a 2001 valuation was unprofessional, yet even after Cole's damning KPMG affidavit they seemed to be siding with the partners. Surprisingly their Mr. Heron bypassed my attorneys and called me directly. He tried to influence me to visit his office without my attorneys' knowledge or permission. This is not just simply improper; it is dishonest and unprofessional.

Even as I lectured Mr. Heron about delays and his unprofessionalism he shied from the topic of delays. By then we were not prepared to accept anything but an up to date and fair valuation. I am not surprised that Mr. Heron separated from KPMG soon after.

Although I thought that corruption was not yet commonplace in the auditing professional when compared with what happens in other professions and in general society, from my Jamaican experiences one need not be surprised by much that happens. The average professional has to operate in an increasingly corrupt environment and faces simple choices in order to remain in business. They have to keep 'the powers that be' happy, or go elsewhere, and as masters of their trade they are likely to be good at covering their tracks. They can fit in with the culture of the environment and at the very minimum, do whatever they think they need to do, providing they have protection. So, out goes integrity.

It is sad that companies with big international names will stoop to pleasing those 'powers that be' and in so doing contribute to the protection and proliferation of corruption in leadership positions. The system relies on the opinions of professionals to administer verdicts of right or wrong, guilty or not guilty. International standards get the attention of officers of justice throughout the world and to have professionals bypass these standards negates their usefulness. In Jamaica, although well disguised, it is now standard, expected and culturally correct for them to wear the garb of sheep even as they run with the wolves.

EML's Auditor Investigated by the PAB

Following the damning Cole affidavit, the partners filed an affidavit dated June 7, 2006 supported by an opinion from Mr. Philmore Ogle, a chartered accountant. Hurriedly, they presented this opinion which was met with a countering opinion from Paul Saulter, also a chartered accountant. Paul Saulter's opinion of Aug 2006 was a specific response to Mr. Ogle's letter. Specific reference was made to Cole's affidavit by both opinions but it seemed obvious from Saulter's report that other vital information had not been made available to Ogle. Paul

Saulter's report put a spotlight on the lie about the 2001 financials being unavailable and on the financial implications resulting from information being withheld from KPMG. It highlighted the intention of the consent order, based on a specific state of mind that called for the purchase of shares to be completed within 90 to 120 days, not four years as had passed since the order. Again, KPMG was aware of the resulting negative consequences to us.

Such action was not surprising. It is in keeping with the route our adversaries had taken from the start. Their route chosen was to continue to use the court system to their advantage; a system known to be contaminated. Again, as shocking as it seems, in Jamaica the engrained culture of corruption is increasingly worn without embarrassment on the part of Lawyers, Judges or staff in the courts.

Meanwhile, our efforts to prevent the plundering of assets outside of the ordinary course of business, continued. We were fighting on many fronts and our chief enemies were tools of incompetence and corruption.

The reporting of irregularities to the PAB did not mean that all else was on hold. At no time could we give up on pressing from every angle. We had to seek accountability from every government entity possible if we were to prevent the dissipation of assets and a collapse of the group.

In early 2006, while the PAB was investigating EML's auditor, our attorneys wrote to the Minister of Energy, Mining, Science and Technology seeking accountability regarding the operation of the EML group as required under the Companies Act. We got a hands-off response.

Correspondence to the Registrar of Companies sought information on new companies formed by the partners. Which were used to bypass EML as they traded as competing entities got little or no support.

Our attorneys wrote to the DPP since the respondents were in breach and continued to be in breach of the Companies Act. Again, we got no response.

It galloped through my mind constantly that there was no hope for the people of Jamaica —especially the poor—if someone didn't take a stand. What was happening here was stunning. It strengthened my resolve and increasingly I became determined not to give in. If the agents of justice were seen to be so corrupt it couldn't remain in hiding forever; one day there would have to be exposure and consequence. This embedded culture of corruption, well and ably protected through connections, was far too strong for me to single-handedly put a dent in it, but change had to start somewhere.

A change in the country's Leadership

In February 2006, Prime Minister PJ Patterson stepped aside handing over leadership to Portia Simpson Miller, the first female Prime Minister to be appointed in Jamaica. She was a seasoned politician with huge support, particularly among the poor.

Prime Minister Portia Simpson-Miller was handed a country in serious financial trouble. Despite successive economic failures under the PNP its socialist policies continued to attract strong support.

It was very clear to me and many in high places that many of the sources from which the poor have been funded, corruptly or through irresponsible borrowing, cannot be without end. Lenders are hardly stupid; they will not lend if there is high risk of default. Yet the management of the country continued on its usual path. The decline in production and growth rapidly dissipated much of the assets of the country as businesses fell to purchasers from other countries and debt approached a level that seemed headed for default.

Crime and corruption continued their climb in society, already well engrained and accepted as normal 'runnins' [1]. The government too, continued on its way, same policies, same type of corruption. The funding of handouts became more difficult as the country's debt increased and as the 'need' for handouts ballooned.

Scandals grew. The Trafigura Scandal [2] and the Cuban Light Bulb Scandal, [3] both broke after originating from foreign funding. The Trafigura Scandal [2] was not just brazen, it brought into focus the level of corruption that international companies are willing to be part of, and it leaves to question how many of these have been part of the economic landscape of Jamaica since Independence? Many, no doubt.

This was par for the course, for international companies must successfully bid or negotiate for contracts in Jamaica. They must compete against others who are willing to play ball with Jamaica. For Jamaica's survival to be dependent on tolerance of this, speaks to the state of the justice system and the realization that worse is likely to come.

Trafigura Beheer, [2] a Dutch company, had paid over some J$30 million which ended up in a private account connected to the governing PNP. Interestingly, Colin Campbell, the then–Information Minister and General Secretary of the ruling PNP, took the rap for the Trafigura Scandal.

At that time in 2006 when the scandal broke and after he tendered his resignation, I predicted that irrespective of what followed he would very likely later be in line for reward in some way; he would likely return to take up some senior responsibility in the government. My friends reacted vehemently. They thought that the government could not survive that scandal. It took over seven years to prove me right. In 2013, Colin Campbell was appointed to head up the Public Transport Company. Public outcry was practically nonexistent despite extensive exposure in the media. This is one of hundreds of highly questionable decisions that shows flagrant disregard for transparency in public office.

The fact that the PNP refused to cooperate with the Dutch request to give statements or evidence to the Dutch authorities is seen as "no big ting" in Jamaica. There is no public outcry about that either. The response from the Prime Minister when questioned by a Journalist regarding her governing PNP receiving over J$30 million from Trafigura Beheer supports this; *"don't ask me, ask the PNP"* was her response. Yes, the same PNP that she heads up. What an insult to the intelligence of the Jamaican people!

Through the lack of cooperation by corrupt individuals in Jamaica the failure of the Dutch government to exact justice has to be seen as encouragement for others to do shady business with Jamaica.

Such is the level to which our culture has fallen. Indeed I am disappointed that the Dutch government has treated this refusal so casually. It seems that the plan on both sides could be to 'go nowhere'. Is this what the Dutch want? Will this mean that the Dutch will get to do more business in Jamaica? I wonder.

The Cuban Light Bulb Scandal that followed was little different in conclusion. The 'Light Bulb' racket actually started while the PNP were in power and the scandal broke when they lost power in 2007. It might well have remained a secret had the election results been different. The key person in the scandal, Kern Spencer remained as a member of parliament for the North East St. Elizabeth parish even after the 2007 election. The scandal along with allegations of fraud had little impact on him keeping his position as Member of Parliament.

As huge as these scandals were, I saw them as minor distractions from my matter. I knew what would happen about them. In a word: Nothing.

The Public Accountancy Board inquiry had commenced in November 2006 and it was not until after extensive investigations and hearings that on or about September 7, 2007 Basil Cunningham was found guilty of gross negligence in preparing the 2001 and 2000 financial statements for EML. He was suspended from practicing for six months and fined J$1 million.

Although I viewed this as too mild a punishment, I was for the first time in nearly 6 years seeing justice being truly handed down in at least a part of this matter – and it was not from inside the Supreme Court, because in hindsight I am sure it would never have got anywhere via the courts.

It is my understanding that some leniency was shown as a result of a plea from the Auditor's attorney, citing mitigating circumstances like 'his age'. I cannot agree with that leniency because his age and experience was in his favour to make him a good and honest auditor. He should have known better.

The PAB in its findings applied sanctions to the auditor and made reference to improper transactions involving millions of dollars in the financials of EML that were made in favour of Michael or his company. They stopped short of stating or exposing the exact amounts involved because I believe they would have required forensic auditors to confirm those. The findings bluntly exposed the corrupt actions of the auditor and the negligent treatment of the New Zealanders' account. The hearing also exposed the fact that Michael's son deliberately altered the 2001 comparison figures in the 2001 financial statement. In doing so it affected the progress of the valuation and proved that the hidden audited financials for 2001 was always available; but shamefully, it also proved that conduct of the sort could escape consequence.

The sudden presenting of 'doctored' and once hidden financial statements was an effort to have KPMG proceed in 2006 to do a rushed valuation using 2001 values and without using all the information requested by KPMG's letter of engagement. If allowed to happen this would deprive us of tens of millions of dollars. For KPMG to proceed using old figures which had no meaning in value relative to 2006 would obviously be unjust and certainly not in keeping with the professionalism expected of them.

Why would the partners only then be interested in handing over information they had in their possession since 2001? Well, they had already created large gains for themselves by holding onto appreciating assets, part of which rightly belonged to us; for which they would prefer to pay based on an old depreciated value. A wind-up of the company would therefore challenge those gains as well as expose and sanction them for the improper diversion of funds.

CHAPTER 9

A HINT OF CHANGE TO COME

In 2007, both political parties faced the polls for leadership in an election with less than the usual election violence. The people seemed sick of the economic struggles, crime and corruption. The political scene of 2007 was one of confusion. The love affair that the people had with the PNP policies had cooled after some 18 years of mostly disappointment with the economy; one that failed in almost every respect. The sins of this period were setting in. The debt seemed insurmountable to me, as a businessman who was not in the 'big league.' But I knew that the majority did not understand. This is why politicians can fool them repeatedly, and a good reason for politicians to keep the folks undereducated. How else can they control them and hold on to power?

Bruce Golding, a former favorite and deputy of Seaga returned like the prodigal son to join the JLP after forming and leading the National Democratic Movement. I sensed that the business community urgently wanted change. I also sensed that the people still wanted to have their cake and eat it too. Oh, what handouts and corruption can do! Although there was a spirit of change I found an adage by Robert Orben fitting:

"Most people would like to be delivered from temptation, but would like to be in touch."

Prime Minister Bruce Golding was sworn into office after a hard fought general election in September 2007. He would head up leadership of a country that was in social and economic distress. He had a huge challenge ahead to correct the massive destruction that was wreaked on the economy. It was a daunting task – and in some ways insurmountable – to realign the culture that would see a revolution in the public and private sector with greater levels of transparency and accountability.

His inaugural speech set the mood that there was a wind of change. Knowing that the change begins with how justice is handled, I personally believed that Golding would finally address the collapsing justice system. His inauguration speech is the most substantive and well laid out that I have heard from any Prime Minister, particularly because of the dire need for good leadership at that time. His promises were welcome as he recognized that "corruption was too risk-free".

Many were concerned . . . how would he rein in the corruption that was so embedded when he had only a two-seat majority? Unbridled corruption had infected so many of his own Parliamentarians as well.

But Bruce Golding had that one particular problem that made any quick cleaning up job difficult, if not impossible. All that was required to remove him from office was for two members of Parliament on his side to step across the aisle and join the opposition PNP - a fear that lurked in rumours and threats. Additionally, bearing in mind the very partisan and 'tribalistic' culture that existed, getting a two-thirds majority vote in the House would be almost impossible. So, getting a majority vote on anything that would remove corruption would be practically impossible since it would require PNP members crossing the aisle. Such bipartisanship was hardly ever done; it was usually Party first at all cost.

It is not in the interest of either political party to limit their "access" to funds by any means. So as genuine and well intentioned as Golding might have been, he knew that removing corruption, although great for Jamaica would cut off some 'handout' funds to both parties. In addition, access to the "trough"—in which politicians and their friends had firmly placed their snouts—would be severely hindered. I can see the difficulty in him getting Parliamentarians and Senators on both sides to come up with the necessary votes for change. Bruce Golding would have had to sacrifice self and Party at the certain risk of losing power.

In a culture so distorted by endemic corruption, how does one get the power brokers in both political parties to support an initiative that will cut off the very funds that keep them in power? It should have become obvious to Golding that the task was not possible the old way. He would never get the votes in the House to carry it off.

Former Prime Minister Seaga had long before, while in opposition, made a proposal to introduce an impeachment plan to be applied to the leader of the opposition, cabinet ministers, Parliamentarians and other persons holding high office, where the interest of the country was subverted. From back in the 1990s the Constitutional Reform Commission had accepted this proposal, "save only for the composition of the parliamentary committee that would recommend impeachment of public officials."

Not surprisingly, it seemed to have gone nowhere since the 1990s. In fairness to Mr. Seaga he was not in power to pilot it, but he had again broached the matter during his presentation to the 2003-2004 Budget Debate for impeachment as a penalty for officials.

"The central consideration is to hinge impeachment on failure to perform specific criteria of good governance," Mr. Seaga is quoted as saying. According to Seaga, "while Cabinet Ministers were bound by duty to carry out just administration, protect human rights and safeguard revenues, there were no legal sanctions if they failed to carry out their functions. . . There is need to replace this relic of obsolescence with an oath of office which will bind every Prime Minister of Jamaica and the Cabinet to be accountable for the principles of good governance."

Even More Delays

I wasn't expecting a huge overnight change in justice after the election, but I did expect a change in effort and resolve on the part of the new government.

The Public Accountancy Board (PAB) findings were damaging to the partners' case, but they found a way to further delay. They moved out of unfamiliar territory to their favorite playground asking the Supreme Court to keep the PAB and Saulter's evidence from the ears of any judge in the Supreme Court, while at the same time auditor Basil Cunningham appealed his PAB sentence. Knowing the relationship between the auditor and the partners, I was not surprised. It is obvious that it suited them to continue cooperating with each other.

By then we had visited the Supreme Court more than 30 times. On January 25, 2007, we were again in the Supreme Court to again extend the injunction protecting the proceeds of assets sitting in a US dollar interest bearing account. I assumed that renewal of the injunction would be just a formality as had been routine in the past.

Instead, a most bizarre thing happened. In this Supreme Court hearing specifically to continue protecting these funds— the same funds that were exposed by Justice Anderson and protected subsequently by other Supreme Court Judges—suddenly became exposed, this time by Justice Marsh. His ruling would send a message to the partners that the consent order was meaningless and they were free to use the funds. We have never been able to fathom the reasoning behind this blatant act. His action improperly removed the protection from cash sitting in an interest bearing account, the very funds that we fought so long to keep earning interest and to protect from being plundered.

In any country where justice is readily available this would never happen, not without a subsequent investigation. In fact there should not have been a need to repeatedly go to the courts to renew the protection in the first place. That is not only justice; it is basic common sense. From the instant Justice Anderson 'cleared his desk,' we knew that we had to pay close attention to the security of these funds, but we didn't think that so blatant a ruling could occur.

What really happened then? Strange, we have never been able to get an explanation that we could understand. Looking from every imaginable honest angle I could not accept this as having a hint of legal or moral fairness. But I did believe someone had an urgent need for this ruling at that time; an urgent need for a large amount of money for the personal use of at least one of the partners.

We knew by then that FINSAC had taken over the Caribbean Trust Company and the personal loan indebtedness to them by Michael from before 2001 would have been exposed to massive penalties and interest, more than likely exceeding J$150 million. It was no surprise that funds were needed in a real hurry to avoid FINSAC's agent auctioning another of his properties.

Our former partners moved in on the proceeds by making loans to themselves. Although this would later be ruled as improper, this, in Jamaica, means nothing more to one than a ruling on paper, particularly if one is "connected."

The judge's decision allowed the partners to use the funds as though they were needed in the normal course of EML's business.

As it turned out, some J$80,000,000 evaporated by way of personal loans and other hidden means. To whom do we complain? Whom can we trust? The courts had failed to provide fairness and had already earned that reputation throughout Jamaica as a place the public preferred to avoid. The Ministries of Government we approached went silent or walked between the raindrops, and I had sworn that I would never attempt to influence anyone by seeking a "connection" or by bribe.

Our concerns about continued lack of accountability for plundering of the remaining assets of EML and its subsidiaries increased, and we took further steps to ensure their protection. With a new government in power (JLP) but with ample cynicism, we again wrote to the Ministry of Industry, Technology, Energy, and Commerce as minority shareholders, seeking protection against abuse and fraud. The Ministry in turn sought guidance from the Attorney General's Department. We waited on a response from either department, but the last I heard of it was by way of correspondence seeking confirmation from our attorneys on the matter. Nothing followed that confirmation.

In August 2007, we filed a motion seeking to follow up on the strange ruling by Justice Marsh as to interpretation of "ordinary course" of the company's business which the partners were using to justify the spending of proceeds of sale from company assets. For anyone to have endorsed this, especially knowing that an order was in place forbidding this, implied motive.

Justice Marsh's action was ridiculous if not dishonest and I am quite sure that the partners knew this. His action not only created further delay, it also created a situation that could drive the company into serious financial problems, including bankruptcy. As usual, our filing was not made easy. We got the "run around" while trying to fix a date for the hearing.

At this point I still held on to a smidgen of hope that change was coming by way of Bruce Golding. The more recent scandals were fresh in the nation's mind, but spiraling crime took front seat early in Golding's leadership. The expected fall in crime seemed only a thought as nearly twenty police officers lost their lives in the line of duty and over 1500 murders were recorded for 2007. This ushered in retired military head Rear Admiral Hardley Lewin as Police Commissioner.

For that year Jamaica's crime problems were interspersed with Hurricanes Dean and Noel causing damage to homes and flooding in some areas. This has historically affected the economy from time to time and should therefore be anticipated for budgetary purposes. Year after year as the Jamaican economy is battered, damage from natural catastrophes never seemed to be part of budgets. Instead, reliance on developed countries to help with bailouts seems to be the tendency.

Some good news is rare but the entire population went on a high when athletes including the world famous Usain Bolt began his run to Olympic gold. During these times sports played a huge role for the pressured populace as refuge from stress. Since my youthful days, sports and music have been tranquilizers for pain. The nation always looked forward to big events in sports and music, and this had not changed. A company is so much different from a country in that regard. Companies gain nothing from distraction. Debt simply has to be paid.

Golding's promise of free tuition for secondary schools was put in place and provided some social relief, but with a dead economy it looked more like a platform promise than reality. The old adage "Nothing is free" certainly applied.

Bruce Golding was however destined to have a rough course as even the leader of the opposition promised to be his "worst nightmare". At the same time, I was smack dab in the middle of my own personal nightmare, escape from which seemed further and further away. So, on September 14, 2007, I took matters into my own hands and wrote directly to the Chief Justice. How dare I, you ask? What choice did I have?

I have never heard of any attorney writing to a Chief Justice to complain about anyone operating in the Supreme Court. It was just not done. Any attorney who dared to do so expected to feel the full force of persecution. I kept wondering why it was tolerated in the system when that clearly showed that they, as officers of the court, cannot expect impartial treatment even in a house of justice. Such is the level to which our justice system has declined.

Despite my complaint to the Chief Justice, I was not surprised when the matter regarding interpretation of "ordinary course of business" was placed before Justice Anderson on October 25, 2007 by the registry. The court staff clearly knew that he had long before disqualified himself from this case. Indeed this is typical of the type of stalling tricks to expect from a division so saturated with interference. I also wasn't surprised when we attended court to discover that the partners were not present in court. The matter was before a judge who would definitely recuse himself. Were they privy to that information? Was some influence used to cause this or was it just plain coincidence and incompetence on the part of the court's registry?

This not only caused more delay but costs of the lawyers' time and costs cannot be recovered after this type of adjournment. Numerous adjournments have had the effect of draining our pockets while the partners used the funds of the company as they wished—the funds of a company that had been cash-rich and debt-free in 2002 when they removed us.

The complaint to the Chief Justice yielded a response from the registry by providing a new date of November 8, 2007 for us to come to court. On that date we were told by Justice Beswick that the registry's bundle of documents was again missing. Again I wrote to inform the Chief Justice and was given a date of December 3, 2007. This time a suspicious scheduling error by the Registry forced another adjournment. This was done so blatantly and without care of consequence. What new ploy could I possibly see?

At that stage I was not surprised, but I was disappointed because it appeared that the Chief Justice commanded absolutely no respect and she obviously made no impact by way of her position of authority. As a successful manager of profitable businesses in the past, I saw this as untenable. So, on December 8, 2007, I wrote to the Chief Justice for the third time. However, this time I expressed outrage and anger. I suggested to her that Jamaicans take matters into their own hands because of this type of incompetence and corruption. I again withheld this correspondence from my attorneys in order to spare them the persecution that attorneys in Jamaica so avoid.

I could however sense the anger from one of the partners' attorneys. Some friends had previously commented to me that "Jamaican suss" said the matter seemed to be more between me and one of their attorneys rather than the partners themselves. I had dared to report matters to the Chief Justice, and this would affect the usual maneuverings within areas of the court system.

A running start for Golding

In January 2008 - early in Golding's tenure and what was a great start for Golding - at the annual National Leadership Prayer Breakfast, dignitaries gathered as is customary. Guest speaker Rev. Dr. Roy Notice, pastor of the Mandeville New Testament Church of God, delivered his message in a most emphatic tone, charging the nation and its leaders to address divisions in the country. Dr. Notice was merely delivering at an opportune time what the majority of Jamaicans begged for, but had no volunteers to convey it.

This was a great opportunity for someone honest and frank enough to use the platform in the presence of the Prime Minister and representatives of the opposition for serious impact. Dr Notice in a most outspoken, impressive and stirring message spoke:

> "No matter how much we spruce up the neighborhood, if the soul of the neighbor is still contaminated by, self-hate, self contempt and the need for vengeance, the neighborhood will remain dirty and bloody."

The assembly he was addressing included Prime Minister Bruce Golding, former opposition Transport and Works Minister Robert Pickersgill, who represented the Opposition Leader, Governor-General Sir Kenneth Hall, and a large cross section of government officials, clergymen and leaders. He added that, 'going back to biblical principles, which would ultimately heal the nation, would involve Jamaicans listening to their neighbours before they blocked the roads or bellowed the familiar cry of *"We want justice!"* He appealed to leaders to listen, not only when tourism was threatened, but because the Jamaican neighborhood itself was threatened. He advised the leaders to be in tune with the people.

"We must hear them before they block the roads, before they strike, before the cries for 'we want justice' become entertaining drama on our media", referring to the only trusted route available to the public to voice their serious concerns.

Dr. Notice drew applause throughout his sermon. He was not afraid to speak out when he stated that 'personal greed had captured the hearts of too many in the island, from Parliament to the pulpit.' *"We too tief... pastor man a tief, politician a tief, policeman a tief and we expect to prosper,"* as he tore into the level of corruption in the country:

> "We must expose evil, not in order to gain mileage, but because we desire that all in the neighborhood reap the benefits of the good life. Wherever we see evil and corruption, we must expose it in the workplace, in the Church, in government, in the security forces, in the judiciary."

A strong sermon that was punctuated throughout by applause and ended with a standing ovation, the Reverend was in tune with the people. So moving and so telling was his message that columnist Jean Lowrie-Chin,[1] who was at the Prayer Breakfast, wrote of his sermon:

> "There we were, wearing our Sunday best last Thursday morning, leaping to our feet to applaud a young preacher

after he had roundly berated us. It must be true that virtually every human being hungers for virtue. I have read those response cards left at the tables after the Breakfast, people saying, 'I feel like I have had a refreshing bath,' 'please visit and pray with me' and hundreds of simple 'thank yous'."

Under those tailored suits and silk blouses beat courageous hearts, because it is only a brave man or woman who would strive for leadership in this hard-to-please country. We would have damned our leaders if they had not turned up to pray, and some are damning them because they did. Among the loudest critics are those with selective memories who will quote from Genesis to Revelation but will forget the words of Jesus, "Let him that is without sin, cast the first stone."

We could not help thinking of the frightened women of Tivoli, as Notice reminded us that we did not really belong to uptown or downtown, but were all members of the Jamaican neighborhood. "If one community is excluded from the neighborhood, then the whole neighborhood is under threat. 'I am because we are and since we are therefore I am'," said Notice, quoting African scholar John Mbiti.

More terrible than the cries of the women are the silent stares of the children. Their tender little lives should be lightened by nursery rhymes, not darkened by barking guns. These are not just the guns of the police, as we cannot deny that there have been frightening hauls of powerful weapons and ammunition during operations not just in Tivoli, but also in communities all across Jamaica.

None of us know enough of what transpired that Sunday morning, to pass judgement on police or citizen. What we do know is that too many of our Jamaican neighbours, both police and inner-city dwellers, are subject to criminal activity. This will not end until we start to "speak the truth and shame the devil". The illegal guns being recovered by police all over Jamaica were not brought here to shoot birds. They were brought here to kill us - to paraphrase Mbiti - "he and she are us and therefore we are them." We Jamaicans have the unenviable distinction of having at least one close relative or friend heartlessly murdered. Our police force has the even more unenviable task of capturing the criminals before they kill more of us.

Can we Jamaica, help the police by preventing the spawning of more criminals? Up to last week, police officers and teachers were relating to me that they were really surrogate parents. Parents are ducking their responsibility, and were it not for the safety nets of a police youth club here and a caring teacher there, many more of our children would be easy pickings for the gangs.

A corporate donor was relating his experience at an inner-city Christmas treat last month: they had to feed two generations of children: yes, there were little ones, but the parents were actually children, many in their early teens. This is why Rev Notice was trying to shake us up last week, when he explained that "loving our neighbour also means renewing our commitment to exposing evil in the neighborhood called Jamaica". The absent men who impregnated these young girls must be exposed and required to support their children. "We must all become whistle blowers," said Notice.

Here is the hard part: Notice warns us that "if we see the evil and excuse ourselves claiming that we are clean because we are not involved, we are only fooling ourselves". Then he quoted Buju: "Yes, you can hide from man, but not from your conscience."

Notice gave us one of the best reasons for entrepreneurship and philanthropy: "Loving your neighbor means that we must all lead the process of rebuilding communities of justice and creating neighborhoods that are characterized

> by hospitality. The building of human capacity and the strengthening of Jamaica's spiritual and social capital must always be at the forefront of what we are about as leaders."

Bruce Golding had a good 'push start'. The ball was in his court.

Golding's promises and his challenges

Golding's pre-election promise of free health care and free education came about unexpectedly. People had grown to not expect to see pre-election promises delivered, but he delivered . . . at least for awhile. It might have been sustainable had Golding sought to address the links in the chain that would guarantee reduction in crime and violence, unemployment, unstable currency, and all the rest. None of these are sustainable without justice.

I am of the opinion that Golding found himself in pretty much the same situation that Mr. Seaga was in, back in 1980. In order to recue this country he would have to make tough and unpopular decisions at the risk of his tenure in government. Jamaica has not reached the level of social and economic consciousness to be able to recognize and accept what is best for the country in the long term. We have been made into great students of the short term. Children of the "handout" culture think of immediate gratification, 'feast today famine tomorrow', let the next generation take care of itself. So the politician faces the dilemma . . . 'do I take the unpopular route or do I yield for the sake of political power?'

So what was there for me to expect; what else could be in store for me? Pessimism was not an option. I kept thinking that the justice system couldn't possibly have any more surprises in store, but it always did. I thought it couldn't get any worse, but I had no idea. Other than the PAB, which operated with integrity, there had to be at least one other department of government that we could trust. The Attorney General's Department seemed the likeliest place for justice.

Our attorneys wrote to the Attorney General on December 12, 2007, requesting a copy of the notice and grounds of appeal by Basil Cunningham, the EML auditor, which had been the cause of the most recent delay. A hearing was set for January 2008. Then as often happens in Jamaica, I was approached by an anonymous source that all was not normal with the route this appeal was expected to take. I was warned to expect "a weak defense" which would guarantee a reversal of the PAB findings.

Jamaica is a small island. News doesn't have to travel far and it doesn't take long to return to its source, much less its target. I couldn't disregard the age old warning: *"If yu hear supm an it nuh guh suh den it nearly guh suh."* It was therefore in our interest to pay close attention to this appeal hearing. My further probing confirmed that something was indeed amiss with this matter in the Attorney General's Department.

I pondered how to handle this. I was sick of the interference, the "connection" culture. Yes, I was sick to the gills of the corruption. The Attorney General's Department had a duty to act with honesty and resolve on behalf of the Public Accountancy Board in the event of an appeal like this. This duty extended to fairly defending any appeal against a PAB ruling. The findings of the PAB were handed down only because of my complaint of impropriety. The Attorney General's Department was therefore supposed to be sitting with the PAB, and by extension, with us the complainants.

It was already clear that the PAB, in an effort to hold the auditor accountable for breaches, stated the consequences for negligence and that the negligence findings would expose the fact that the auditor's action had improperly put funds into Michael's pocket. This exposure would not be good for the partners; it would contribute to seeing to real justice for a change. But they were the only persons to gain from a reversal by appeal.

I sought an opinion from a Queens Council [2] who suggested that we apply to the Supreme Court to join in and to be part of the appeal hearing.

I wasn't surprised when my application was turned down by the Supreme Court. By then I had learned to expect this type of justice – but worse came. The Attorney General's Department itself objected to us joining. The objection was brazen but not a surprise. Unknown to them, I had contacted the registrar of the PAB to find out why the PAB objected, only to hear that he was unaware of it and I was reassured that the PAB gave no such instruction. "*Connections run tings in Jamaica, anyting can happen*" I would muse when these 'strange' things happened. There can be no reasonable explanation for a lawyer to switch sides for a short time —long enough to attempt shooting the messenger, then switching back to defend the surviving messenger.

The AG's Department did this without their client's approval. They had to have been influenced by someone outside. Why should there be any attempt by designated defenders of the PAB to injure and offend the PAB? Why try to prevent the persons who made the complaint from observing an appeal that as the AG's Department you had a duty to defend? Who had influenced this and what could the AG's department have to hide? It could not have been an idea that popped into the head of some junior attorney in the Attorney General's Department. It had to have been put in place from higher up and by persons with motive and "connections".

We were therefore forced to appeal this Supreme Court ruling that had supported the refusal to let us in. So off we went to the Appeal Court.

During this appeal it was painful to sit in the court and witness Mr. Cochran of the Attorney General's Department join Basil Cunningham's attorney in arguing against our "joining in". It could not have been more painful. It was shocking, and tested what little faith we had left for justice in Jamaica.

Fortunately, though costly, the appeal was ruled in our favor by the Jamaican Appeal Court, the only other area of the justice system that had consistently showed any old time integrity. Finally, we were allowed to "join in", but more damage had been done and the delay added to our costs and to the injustice we were already experiencing.

I remember hearing one of three Appeal Court Judges asking Mr. Cochran something to the effect, "What damage would be done if the Clackens joined in?"

The answer came hesitantly and sheepishly, "*None, mi Lord*".

Why then was the objection made?

In effect, this was proof that the Appeal Court of Jamaica had up to then escaped the level of interference, 'connections' and injustice, so typical of the Supreme Court. Justice Panton did not sit on this appeal. I know the caliber of Justice Panton, the President of the Court of Appeal. He is a man of absolute honesty and integrity; an extremely bright student at the school I attended, his brilliance took second place to honesty and integrity. Here is where good leadership is proven to be indispensible. A corrupt Appeal Court Registry would not be tolerated by Justice Panton. Neither would he tolerate any influence from outside and any case to affect decisions in the Appeal Court. I say this not because I hear this, but because this was the caliber of leader that I saw in him at school and throughout his life. This is a man who declined sitting on any matter that involved me because, irrespective of his intention to be fair, it would not be seen to be fair... Disqualifying himself, I am sure, was automatic; there would be no need for anyone to request it.

The Appeal Court has been blessed to date only because of its leadership. A more selective appointment of judges at that level has also been a blessing. But for how long will we be so blessed? It is important to note that judges at that level tend to be drawn from the best of the level below; that is, the Supreme Court. As the Supreme Court becomes more corrupted in future, so will the Appeal Court, and that makes it more difficult to guarantee good leadership in future.

However, the higher level of trust presently afforded the Appeal Court is too often negated by the costs to get through that court and the questionable costs granted after judgments. Persons seeking justice too often have their funds exhausted through corruption, incompetence and delays before reaching Appeal Court level. So after traversing the Supreme Court, the decision to go to the Appeal Court is often abandoned. This in turn has a disastrous domino effect of creating precedents from unjust rulings that are eventually used in other cases, leading to further unjust rulings.

Had the Appeal Court been behaving like the Supreme Court, it would have suited us to hurriedly abandon our shares and get away as far as possible from Jamaica. But although we are being battered by a corrupted justice system all is not lost; we at least have hope, a little consolation, that the Appeal Court is still worthy of trust.

More Hurdles?

We had overcome another hurdle at great painful financial and emotional expense, and this was permission to 'join in'. This was only permission to pay close attention to the behavior of the Attorney General's Department. Additionally, we still had to fund and 'sit out' the appeal by the auditor against the PAB findings. Again, more delay and more cost.

Basil Cunningham of JB Causwell & Co. lost his appeal. The million dollar fine, plus the suspension in the findings, stood. Was the appeal really a move by Cunningham or was it orchestrated by the partners? We had a strong hunch it was the latter.

The fight became of less importance as a fight seeking justice for me but, rather, seeking justice for the people of Jamaica who without doubt had no chance of securing real justice in any matter inside Jamaica. Justice was a gamble at winning a chance to a privilege. It wasn't a right. To give in to this, just to ease my pain, would make me a contributor to the continuation of the raping and pillaging of the people of Jamaica - a contribution I was not sure that I could live with.

Premonition insisted that I could be fighting for the impossible because I was swimming against the current. But every thought I had of capitulating and running was shot down by my conscience as cowardly, like water off a duck's back. The more privileged in society knew the conditions and the 'politics'. They would say that we can live here at a much higher status level than overseas. They could enjoy a higher level of affluence. They knew the culture within the country inside out. They knew how to fit in with the corruption. Many already had skeletons in their closets and thought that it was not good strategy to throw stones. They preferred to keep quiet and secure in their glass houses.

With the thought of harassment from government agents in the Tax Department, the GCT Department, the National Insurance Department, the National Housing Trust Department, the Customs

Department . . . it was better to avoid persecution. With or without skeletons in the closet, the harassment would be stressful and could extend even to family members and friends.

Reliance on Professionals

Our matter had by then seen more than six years of delay. KPMG had long before signaled that they could not do a professional job of valuing the shares after the numerous manipulations and delays, but they made no serious effort to bring the matter to an end.

On April 23, 2008, after tolerating some 6 years of obfuscation and stalling, KPMG applied to the Supreme Court to be released as the valuator. It seemed as if they had finally taken a stand, but why now? From a professional perspective, what was it that was happening -between 2002 and 2007 that was different from 2008? Was it access to clean accounts? Was it the cost of reporting to the courts?

While we awaited KPMG's action, the partners had been enjoying the delay process, by asking the Supreme Court to **not** allow Paul Saulter's report or the PAB findings into the records. But this was rejected outright in the Supreme Court before Justice Pusey, who was one of the few judges who would not entertain an adjournment and seemed very well read on this matter. Justice Pusey was possessed of a calm demeanor and who cut off all excuses and escape routes to an adjournment without showing any anger at the wasting of the court's time. He countered every argument for adjournment that was put forward by the Attorneys for the 'Partners' including reminding him of a matter he was slated to hear in the 'Gun Court' the following day. That kind of resolve from a judge resulted in the matter being heard immediately and with no real delay to the Gun Court matter.

From his utterances it was clear that this judge had read all the materials regarding the matter and was obviously not prepared to waste anybody's time by stalling. In his preparation he might very well have noticed the numerous adjournments previously and was not prepared to do likewise. I had found this urgency a rarity in the Supreme Court.

I began to better understand what was happening and why adjournments were so easy to get from some judges, and difficult from others. I was wising up to the system, and I knew then that we would never be allowed before Justice Pusey again. We had also been before a Justice Campbell some time previously when he had renewed the injunction placed against using proceeds from the sale of an asset and had held his ground despite an appeal threat. I had also guessed correctly that we would never be put before him again. Those who live or do business in Jamaica clearly understand these "*runnins*" [3].

It was no surprise that Justice Pusey's ruling was appealed by the partners. Their application was heard by the Appeal Court and dismissed in October 2008. Yes, more delay, more costs, more time to dissipate assets, more losses due to inflation and devaluations. Predicting what would happen next was becoming much easier.

We were running the gauntlet indeed and it appeared that matters before certain judges were placed very deliberately and selectively. Whenever on the rare occasion we got before the "wrong judge," missing bundles, short time allotment, last minute affidavits, and the like would be made good reason for adjournment.

This is not to say that there was a shortage of integrity among Supreme Court judges. We certainly saw and knew of some professionals with integrity who sat on the bench or worked in the courts. The beef I have with judges is that they continue to be too silent and too tolerant of the blatant incompetence and corruption inside the court system. They are letting a noble profession be dragged into the muck that pervades Jamaican society.

After being adjourned before many other judges for various reasons ranging from "missing bundle" to "not enough time allotted", in September 2008 the core issue of the consent order finally came up before Justice Sykes. The partners had stretched the initial 90 days into more than 6 years and sought to justify removing proceeds from the sale of an asset despite knowing that sale of the asset would be a breach of the consent order. A protected real estate asset which was converted to cash obviously had to enjoy the same level of protection against dissipation that all the other real estate assets enjoyed. That is basic common sense.

The intent at the time of signing the consent order was to protect the assets from dissipation (willfully or not). Selling the assets could mean an intention to lower the value of our shares considerably or completely. So the excuse used to get at and remove the proceeds from the asset was that the sale of the asset was "in the ordinary course of business". If that were true then there would not have been any reason to state in the consent order that assets should not be sold. To argue the point of "interpretation of the ordinary course of business" achieved a further delay and created additional opportunity to reduce the value of the company and of our shares.

At this stage, any Judge worth his salt should be asking himself "Why is this matter over 6 years and not within 90 days?" Selling assets specifically to fund operation of a company is not normal nor is it smart business. Combined with more than 6 years of delay, attempting to sell protected assets can only imply motive.

Lynne and I attended court before Justice Sykes, a judge who we had not had any previous experience with. I was not overly worried because I could not imagine things getting worse. In fact, I had begun to feel that light was at the end of the tunnel since this hearing was only a time wasting move with added cost-pressures, not a move to separate right from wrong. I could not have been more mistaken.

A shocking result

In October 2008 Justice Sykes delivered a shocking ruling. It basically disregarded the fact that an order was in place to protect from dissipation and he treated the company as if there was no consent order. It gave the partners in control the right to use any or all of the company's assets as they saw fit. The result was dissipation. The light I was seeing at the end of the tunnel was a train. I have never been able to fathom how anyone inside or outside could act as ridiculously as this.

The fiscal situation in Jamaica at this time was obviously impacted by a deadly world financial crisis. From this, further hardship was wreaked on the Jamaican people. We have a saying in Jamaica that when America sneezes, we catch cold. Well, America went past sneezing; they caught pneumonia. This kind of occurrence is far reaching. Remittances normally paid into the Jamaican economy by relatives overseas were affected by this crisis. As need increased so did corruption. During this time scammers enjoyed the absence of a working justice system. The natural resilience of the Jamaican people was needed to survive the pressures from the world financial disaster, resulting crime, and natural disasters. Even as Jamaican athletes performed well in the Beijing Olympics and even as the people found solace in their tremendous achievements, I found little consolation.

Having to go through another appeal is unfair, but it had to be done. We kept wondering how many people in Jamaica could afford to travel this maze we'd found ourselves in? Probably one percent, maybe less. How many would, for so long, continue trying to find justice this way? Very few indeed.

In 2009 we were again in Court appealing Justice Sykes' ridiculous ruling. After arguments before the Appeal Court were completed by both sides Lynne and I went home and returned to Court when the ruling was to be made. When the Judge reading the ruling stated that he had received an Affidavit late the evening before from the Attorneys for the 'partners' I felt the hair on the back of my neck raise. That affidavit was apparently delivered at the last moment just before presentation of the ruling and without our prior knowledge. What was this about? I wondered. What new stunt was this?

This affidavit basically implied that funds in the region of J$80 million had been spent from the proceeds of the fixed asset that were under discussion in this appeal hearing and that it was spent for the benefit of the company. That was obviously intended to mislead the judges.

As I expected Justice Sykes' ruling was reversed, and permission for the partners to appeal to the Privy Council was also refused by the Appeal Court. They nevertheless appealed to the Privy Council directly. The judge in his delivery of the ruling was obviously correct to divulge this information and seemed frank in saying that the late affidavit did not affect the ruling.

The act of placing a late affidavit in front of the Appeal Court after the presentations had been completed by both sides seemed unfair to me, and I wondered if this was normal behaviour. This was normal conduct in the Supreme Court, but the Appeal Court showed what they were not willing to accept. I had seen this type of slick behaviour escape consequence many times in the Supreme Court even at additional cost to us. What if the affidavit carried lies or incriminating information that would require our response? Was it meant to cause us to have to rebut lies as I had seen in the Supreme Court on occasions? Was it disrespectful of the Officers of the court? Was this just a delaying ploy as we say in Jamaica, "*trying a ting*"?

After the rulings of the Jamaican Appeal Court, the British-based Privy Council's decision backing the Appeal Court seemed only a formality. It was clear that a minimum of $80 million had been removed from the EML group despite being forbidden by the Court-endorsed consent order. These funds were in place and had been gaining interest and keeping up with the US dollar by being held in a US dollar account.

What did this mean? It meant the company, Lynne, and I had been denied interest and devaluation benefits of tens of millions of dollars from its US dollar deposits - all this was falsely labeled as a benefit to the company, proof of which was always deliberately withheld.

The Armadale Tragedy

Bruce Golding came to power at a most unfortunate time. He inherited a country with its economy plummeting in freefall after being destroyed by previous administrations and with crime in full gallop. Ponzi schemes ran amok, unregulated by government, fleecing Jamaicans of millions. More unfortunate - he came to power just in time to face the worst global recession the world had seen since 1929, some 80 years ago. That made governance even more difficult. Somehow his administration kept the country in survival mode, stabilizing the Jamaican currency for over 2 years. It was a difficult period indeed.

Adding to Prime Minister Bruce Golding's quandary, on May 22, 2009 the dreadful Armadale fire took the lives of seven girls and inflicted injury mentally and physically to most of the over 60 girls housed at the juvenile correctional facility. It was a tragedy that should never have happened. Many of the girls no doubt were placed there for reasons that had nothing to do with violent behavior. It is not unusual for children, some of them abandoned or lacking good parental presence, to be placed in correctional facilities because there is nowhere else to put them. The good children then learn to survive amongst delinquents. They are forced to travel a rough passage that shapes their future, often to an adulthood of crime. The failure of the state over decades of neglect and uncaring for the needs of children has sentenced many of them to a life of crime that eventually leads to death at the hands of gangs or the Police.

The Armadale Commission of Enquiry was set up to investigate the tragedy. Yes, one of those commissions of enquiry that normally leads to nowhere. Their ruling laid blame squarely, and to the best of my recollection, a first in the near 50 years since Independence that a ruling of negligence was delivered free of politics, with accompanying recommendations made to prevent a repeat of that type of disaster. Despite the extent of the tragedy, the pain of the survivors and the claustrophobic panic that must have prevailed during the fire as the girls tried to escape death from the secured facility, must have been horrifying. I felt relieved and emboldened that a ruling which appeared fair had been achieved. Indeed it seemed fair and the country waited for action.

The Golding government was pushed by the Opposition to respond to the enquiry findings urgently. By March 2, 2010, the report of the Commission was tabled in the House. Mr Golding explained in the House that it was referred promptly to:

> "the Director of Public Prosecutions, the Acting Commissioner of Police and the Public Service Commission for such action as they consider appropriate in relation to those persons whose conduct has been called into question by the findings of the Commission" . . . . "While public officers must be held accountable for the discharge of their

> duties, the government must accept ultimate responsibility for the circumstances that led to the Armadale tragedy and for the inadequate facilities provided to care for children who are placed in juvenile correctional . . . . or remand facilities. . . . The awful tragedy that occurred at Armadale should not have been allowed to happen. We must ensure that no such tragedy ever again occurs. Some wards of our juvenile correctional institutions have turned out to be exceptionally good and successful adults. We must strive to ensure that they are not the exception but become the norm."

By March 12, 2010, rights groups were protesting outside the Police Officers' Club demanding that the Prime Minister act urgently to address their concerns. These were groups, few in number, who dared to stand up on behalf of people seeking justice. Organizations like "Jamaicans For Justice," "Hear the Children's Cry" . . . lonely voices that refuse to give up.

"We are calling on the Prime Minister to act with urgency, to protect the children in the care of the State, to end the abuse of children in State care. That is what we want," said Dr Carolyn Gomes, executive director of Jamaicans for Justice.

"We are sending a message to the government that we will be standing up for the children, we are going to be watchdogs for the children, and we are asking all of Jamaica to join with us, to support us," urged Betty Ann Blaine from the "Hear The Children's Cry" group. Again the country waited for action.

Prime Minister Golding responded asking the Public Service Commission (PSC) to decide what disciplinary action should be taken against civil servants whose negligence led to the deadly fire at the Armadale Juvenile Correctional Facility.

This kind of pressure should not have to come from human rights groups. As long as offenders know that the justice system does nothing, organizations like those will continue to see repeats, and they will often toil frustratingly in vain.

The Fight Continues

I was not alone in a fight for justice, and what happened at Armadale was a symptom of what was systemic.

On July 30, 2010, KPMG revisited their application of April 23, 2008 for release from this case as valuator. KPMG had by then already waited over 2 years and made no reasonable attempt during those 2 years to set a date for hearing. Their original 90-day appointment had stretched over eight years.

This bothered me. They had filed an Affidavit knowing that they would not carry out an unfair valuation and at the same time they did nothing about it for that two-year period. Why? What were they waiting on? Was KPMG being influenced too? They had good reason to file for removal but they had no good and just reason to not act for over 2 years after filing. Were they waiting on something else to happen?

Then, more than 2 years after KPMG filed their first application, they added an additional Affidavit from their more recent managing partner Mr. Tarun Handa.

This was brought before Justice Rattray who ruled that their application for release would be shifted to be heard by Justice Sykes—the same judge that had ruled incorrectly on the matter of "ordinary course of business" as confirmed by the Jamaican Appeal Court and the British Privy Council. Was this what KPMG was awaiting? It is amazing how matters were moved around and appeared to be so coincidental. A 90 day matter stretches into some 8 years part of which sits for over 2 years before being placed before a Judge who has sat on this case, has ruled incorrectly, his ruling has been thrown out by the Appeal Court, and again by the Privy Council. Again I ask a question: why is our matter back before this Judge who has been 'spanked' by the Appeal Court and the Privy Council in the same matter? What kind of justice is this?

As if this was not strange enough, a separate trial date to request setting aside the consent order which could automatically relieve KPMG of having to do the 2001 valuation was arranged for hearing after the delayed KPMG hearing and placed before the same Justice Sykes.

If the consent order was not set aside, KPMG would then be expected to act contrary to international standards and do the unprofessional thing. So having the KPMG application heard after the request to set aside the consent order provided an out and allowed the judge room to rule in a way that could cause KPMG to feel threatened.

Justice Sykes was already aware of the happenings in this case. There is very little that I could do except watch what would happen next. My efforts to expose irregularities had not changed things; it made matters worse. It angered many persons and their connections, including some whose competence I might have questioned or exposed in writing to the Chief Justice and some whom might have been embarrassed by appeal rulings. How dare I!

Going to trial to have the Consent Order removed gave me no encouragement. I was already pessimistic because of the way events had moved. I kept asking my attorneys to make sure to include Paul Cole's affidavit in whatever form, which was critical to hearing the whole truth. They said that his affidavit could not be included because he was no longer with KPMG and not available to be questioned. Meanwhile, it seemed to be important to the partners that KPMG's "2 year old" application stay out of the court until after the hearing to set aside the consent order. It would allow Justice Sykes the option to try forcing KPMG to do a 2001 valuation; a valuation that KPMG knew to be too delayed, unfair, and in breach of standards, but a ruling nevertheless that would please the partners. It would also leave KPMG with the option to do what many in Jamaica did: Give in to 'connections' pressure and escape consequence.

CHAPTER 10

THE TIVOLI INCURSION

The Tivoli incursion refers to a raid by security forces into a political stronghold known as Tivoli Gardens.

As my case was plodding along amid the usual delays, events in Jamaica heated up. The year 2010 was another period in history we Jamaicans should never forget.

The United States of America had requested the extradition of Christopher 'Dudus' Coke the 'Don of Dons' in Tivoli Gardens, the constituency of Prime Minister Bruce Golding. Golding was already beginning to sow some unpopular seeds among those who had grown accustomed to the gains from '*runnins*' [1]. In Jamaica, cutting off access to 'eat a food' [2] is a hard act to defend. It is part of the 'hand-out' culture that commenced in the 70s and has become embedded.

'Don' Christopher 'Dudus' Coke was wanted by the US government on drug and gunrunning charges. After heated exchanges between the US and the Jamaican governments, Golding gave in and Coke would be extradited. This led to a joint police and military operation into Tivoli Gardens which became labeled as the 'Tivoli Incursion'. Successive governments have by example created and allowed conditions to remain in place that would in effect seem to justify extrajudicial killings, murder, extortion and the like.

The Tivoli incursion of 2010 wiped out some 76 persons in less than a week, many of whom seemed innocent. Some still claim that over 200 were killed. The killings occurred in a raid designed to capture one man. It seemed Don Dudus was not in Tivoli at the time but was eventually apprehended and taken by US law enforcement to America where he pleaded guilty to various crimes and is now serving time in a US prison.

I find it amazing that "Dudus" was considered by many inside and outside of Jamaican law enforcement as a ruthless criminal, yet he was never ever charged for any offence whatsoever in Jamaica nor had he ever travelled outside of Jamaica. He was never in hiding previous to the US request to extradite him; so much so, that crime within his 'area' was almost non-existent. What is it that drove people away from the system to find refuge from the likes of Dudus? Why did it take a force external to Jamaica to indict one of the worst criminals in the western hemisphere?

What does that say of the justice system in Jamaica?

Strangely, this was a man to whom the people in his area looked for food, schooling, security and justice. Why had they not looked to the system?

I strongly abhor the crimes committed by Dons like "Dudus" but I am sure that the people he 'represented' felt more secure against injustice under his leadership than under the justice system as it existed in Jamaica. I too have good reason to distrust the entire justice system and many of those who preside over it. This is a clear illustration of why the Jamaican people have consistently sought justice through Dons and have avoided the system that seems only to pretend it is there to preserve their rights.

After 'Dudus' was removed, I heard much optimistic talk in Jamaica that the country was about to see the end of crime since the 'Don of Dons' and others had been put away. I openly disagreed and warned friends that Dons were only a symptom of the problems. The absence of justice was the real problem. Bragging predictions that crime would be solved suddenly became a joke in less than a year as goons elevated crime to a level approaching that of the 'Dudus' era. The initial fall after Dudus's removal proved only temporary. Murder, rape, scams, and theft returned to elevated levels as the Security Minister stated clearly that he was at a loss for what to do.

In fact, I believe that the only reason for the initial drop in crime immediately after the removal of 'Dudus' was the ruthless terror message unleashed on some people, followed by the brazen slaughter of a man in front of his family.

In the hunt for 'Dudus,' an uptown house in the hills of Kingston, occupied by a middle class family, was surrounded and sections of his residence torn up with what appeared to be hundreds of bullets. Keith Clarke, a male occupant was himself gunned down in that house with more than 20 bullets while his wife and daughter looked on. 'Dudus' was not there. They seemed to have raided the wrong house and an innocent man was killed, shot multiple times in his back. Was this attack similar to what happened in Tivoli? Was it carried out by those who also spearheaded the Tivoli Incursion and in the same frame of mind?

The killing of Keith Clarke sent shockwaves and fear through many in middle class communities. The ruthlessness of the attack carried a strong message. It gave the perception - particularly from Dons who were in hiding after the incursion- that the Clarke killing showed the right of the security forces to kill anybody they wished. Not even 'uptown' was off limits. The perception was also that, as usual, nothing would come of it. It surely sent the message to the Dons who were still alive that the security forces had license to kill them as they wished. No surprise when dons throughout the island abandoned their titles and responded immediately when called in by the Police. Relatives called in for questioning by way of the media were also prompt and extremely cooperative, something we had never seen previously.

They saw what happened, they knew that many had been killed, including an innocent middle class man and they knew that they would be killed if they didn't respond quickly.

Clarke's killing was a shocker to the middle and upper classes and the apparent error became veranda talk. Upper class persons realized that it could easily have happened to them. The Jamaicans for Justice group challenged the action of the security forces and 2 or 3 soldiers were eventually charged for the murder of Clarke. They were common soldiers; but who commanded them? Need I ask anyone to hazard a guess of what will likely happen next?

The removal of 'Dudus' and the Tivoli slaughter was made to look like it would solve the crime problem, or, put another way 'Dudus was the cause of crime. But 'Dudus' was a don created by the same system that protected him from ever being charged for a single offence over decades of his reign.

We manufactured dons for decades, then we periodically went on hunting binges killing them whenever we think they had accumulated too much power, or when the USA sought to bring them to justice. The disease started and remains evident at the top, and 'Dudus' is only one of the symptoms.

When are we going to stop manufacturing these people? When are we going to change what we have been doing for decades and bring to account the persons in leadership who have been responsible? Why do we continue to accept the same explanations and excuses knowing that it can go nowhere? Why should I be surprised at the kind of justice available in the Supreme Court? What happened in Tivoli is hardly different from what was happening to me-only the type of ammunition used.

Why Dons Still 'run tings'

As long as the root of the problem remains, the removal of a Don only gives rise to smarter replacement dons.

In the late 60s when 'Garrisons' were in their early stages, politicians had full control of the community leaders and controlled the distribution of funds for employment or handouts. They lost control as community leaders learned to fend for themselves by controlling the drugs and firearms business. This way, they had their own funds and no longer needed to take orders from politicians. The politicians in turn continued to align themselves to Dons who could influence their communities' support through votes. 'Dudus' was certainly seen as smarter than his father, himself a Don who died in a strange prison cell fire while awaiting extradition to the USA.

Inner city community leaders once had no better use to politicians than to control the voter population in their area by distribution of scarce benefits for the purpose of maintaining power. The don at that time needed the politicians to maintain his power. But as the population of these communities grew, the load on finances became more onerous and the funding from politically provided scarce benefits became less. Community leaders (the dons themselves) had in their pockets the ill gained riches, from drugs, extortion and guns which became welcome and useful to subsidize the meager scarce benefits from the politicians. The dons therefore no longer had to "*run tings*" as an 'employee' of the politician. The shoe moved to the other foot.

The don became boss and the politicians needed the don to assist them. Control moved to the hands of the don. That is one reason why only extradition requests from countries like the USA could remove them.

Government's responsibility to provide a climate that would generate jobs; deliver basic amenities and rights, dissipated even as increasing greed and corruption invaded the systems of government.

It is understandable that the people will seek out what they need to survive including the justice that is not within their reach from their government, but always available through the dons at a more palatable 'price'. It is when the power of the dons get too overwhelming and too out of the control of politicians that the urgency to remove them becomes obvious. This is why the removal process has always been seen in spurts.

In Jamaica the killing of 76 persons in a single operation over a period of days was one of these many spurts over the last 40 years and we cannot expect change until the reasons for embracing dons are removed.

By late 2011, the aftermath of the Tivoli Incursion and other civil unrest had taken its toll. Bruce Golding, after a battering from civic society and clear disappointment from the general populace over his lack of good leadership, handed Prime Ministership over to a young Andrew Holness. The Dudus imbroglio threatened to take down the entire JLP administration. In my opinion, it was a disgraceful revelation of how corrupt we are as a nation, from every angle.

It appears that Golding allowed his fear of losing power to keep him from doing what was best for Jamaica. Instead of ignoring the fear that his parliamentarians might cross the floor, he walked between the raindrops and juggled; Jamaica paid the price. The way I see it, he should have sacrificed party and self for the good of the country.

I believe that had he done so he would not be in power for long but he would have strengthened the resolve for others to stand with him and history would judge him favourably. Golding was Jamaica's last hope. Many said that if Bruce Golding couldn't lead this country out of the rut, no one else could.

Stalemate

On October 4, 2010, the trial to set aside the Consent Order came before Justice Sykes- yes, again, the same Judge that ruled incorrectly on the matter of "ordinary course of business".

Yes, corruption is everywhere:

> To proceed with the trial a summons was to be served on partner Michael. The server, one Mr. Mohamed, a server licensed by Government, reported that on September 1, 2010 he served Michael a summons. How coincidental it was that Michael produced evidence that he left the island the day before… thereby refuting "service". What really happened there? Did Michael get wind that he was going to be served and then left the Island for Florida? And if so why did Mr. Mohamed report that he had served him? Was he coerced to give him time? And did Mr. Mohamed benefit in some way? Was any Attorney involved in any way?
>
> By then these were stupid questions. This is the new Jamaica and lies are without sanction - in public, in the Courts, in Parliament. So keeping in touch with some 'connections' gives all the protection one needs. Mr. Mohamed knew quite well that for me to take action against him would cost millions and would not likely end in the court before my time to depart this world.

This kind of delay is a strategy that allows enough time for maneuvering inside the Court Registry and for selecting the right judge. It is quite typical within the systems and the failure to serve Michael provided a great opportunity for this. Which Judge was to hear this matter?

It is difficult to explain a trial setting that travels down a path that bypasses critical evidence sworn to by affidavit. It is difficult to understand why an affidavit from a chartered accountant who is employed to an international company like KPMG could be kept out of reach at the trial because he was no longer employed to KPMG. Did the system allow the courts to ignore the affidavit from a person most familiar with the frustrations and obstacles that prevented the valuation process to be completed within the stipulated time?

It was a sickening experience. At times I could not differentiate between the judge and the attorneys on the opposing side. I got the message; I could see the ruling long before the end. I was disgusted by the strange occurrences like the sudden appearance in that court, of some books of accounts that had been withheld from KPMG, in effect helping to hinder the valuation for more than 8 years. . . Some of the very books that KPMG's Paul Cole in an interview with us said he had not seen, suddenly appeared. Other books not belonging to EML found place in the Court – posing as if they were for EML.

I was presented all these at the trial for identification and I was skeptical. Had they been altered in any way as was the case of the Financials exposed at the PAB hearing?

And why were some of the books that were definitely not the company's books, presented aggressively as if they were genuinely those of the company? Books built and covered in ancient-like canvas-type material that were never ever the property of the company and never ever purchased for use by the company were made to appear as if they were the company's books.

Were they the property of the auditor – Basil Cunningham of JB Causwell & Co? Yes. I later confirmed that they were indeed the property of J B Causwell & Company, the auditors of the EML group- the same auditor who manipulated the books of the company and was found guilty of Gross Negligence and who had also been suspended from practicing and fined J$1 million for the manipulations…the same auditor who was found guilty of improperly transferring funds from the company for Michael's personal benefit.

During the trial a series of disappointments stood out such as evidence from a professional valuator who had done the valuation of real estate as at 2001, gave evidence that he had done one some 4 years later showing a mere 5% increase. This was an experienced valuator who not much later gave an opinion showing a doubling of values in real estate. As a professional, he was aware of the massive devaluations that had taken place and that it was impossible to find real estate advertised in any of the newspapers or with real estate agents that would show a ridiculous 5% increase over 4 years.

Such is the situation in Jamaica. Professionals garner little trust inside and outside the courts but are part of a system that is perceived as unwilling to deliver justice and we all know why.

The Jamaican economy is quite different from others that are not plagued by devaluations. Between 2001 and 2012 real estate in some areas tripled while the Jamaican dollar devalued over 100%. During this period, inflation was running wild but interest on borrowed money was lower than inflation rates. That fact made it attractive to borrow to buy real estate, which traditionally held its value in real terms. During this period Jamaica's overvalued currency kept adjusting through devaluations. Government dealt with the resulting overheating by creating high interest rates, sometimes to insane levels and sometimes for equally insane periods. The combined result was higher inflation and a contracting economy, as desperate individuals lowered prices to rock bottom.

But as the interest rates were kept high for prolonged periods, real estate prices tumbled. Heavily leveraged persons tried to sell real estate to liquidate high interest rate debt. The bottom line is that interest rates moved well above the inflation rate causing a crash in real estate prices. That created more opportunity for cash rich persons. Some of these cash rich persons held off even longer, waiting for even better prices. With few buyers and lots of sellers cash rich persons were able to scrape up the real estate bargains. By the time the

Jamaican exchange rate adjusted to truer rates and interest rates normalized, real estate values skyrocketed. The true value of real estate, including interest accumulated along with inflation, in effect jumped higher than the devaluation component. So real estate can easily climb 300% while the Jamaican dollar devalues say 100%.

However, real estate values are not difficult to determine with reasonable accuracy in a small country like Jamaica. Real estate agents as well as the newspapers provide a reasonable guide. Despite this being traceable, valuators are often approached to lower or increase valuations depending on for whom the advantage is sought. If it is for transfer tax purposes for instance, much effort is made to get a low value. If it is for collateral use a high valuation is favorable to the loan seeker.

The level of integrity that was seen as normal 50 years ago has not remained unchanged, and that might be so worldwide. I cannot overstate, however, that in Jamaica, so sure are professionals that they will not be held accountable, that most adopt a 'thick skin stance' which allows them to act without shame or regard for integrity. Their wrongs are usually carried out brazenly. Since a high volume of work comes from lawyers who arrange transfers of property, it is not unusual to expect that valuators will seek to satisfy those clients rather than the ordinary man.

The stage seemed set

At the end of the trial Justice Sykes said he would rule on December 20th 2010—after the other hearing regarding KPMG's request for release. I guessed that it would not happen. Had this been heard earlier as was expected when the application was first made by KPMG, a ruling in agreement with KPMG then would have made it difficult to not set aside the consent order as the trial was seeking to do. This gave the distinct appearance that the delaying of KPMG's request for a hearing over two years previously could well have been deliberate.

If Justice Sykes ruled later against setting aside the consent order, he would be sending a message to KPMG that they had better proceed and act unprofessionally, outside of "international standards". So it was no surprise when Justice Sykes pulled the date for ruling forward by more than a month.

I wasn't surprised when Justice Sykes ruled that the consent order would not be set aside. This ruling was made even while KPMG's affidavits were in the hands of the court from over two years before. I figured Justice Sykes had to know all this. It's also bewildering that a judge can try to tell a professional to do what is clearly wrong and opposed by the professional.

There were too many strange things happening in the courts in this single case for 'coincidences' to be accepted as reasonable explanations. After more than 8 years, absolutely no progress had been made. We were where we were at day one and I got the feeling that many within the system knew this. I was told that there were some raised eyebrows, and I heard remarks that suggested that many would bend a bit to save their fellow professionals from embarrassment in this matter.

My resolve for personal justice waned, yet my will and effort to see to justice in all of Jamaica strengthened. I felt pity for the average person. Justice is not readily available to the ordinary Jamaican and they had absolutely no one to go to.

Having also taken a stand through call-in radio programs, blogs, government boards, and in daily conversations discussing the untenable state of corruption in the country, I could not subscribe to the hypocrisy of giving in to this mockery of the system that I was personally experiencing, not just reading about.

As unprofessional as KPMG appeared to be acting, I expected them to eventually live up to the standards that they spoke of in their affidavits and that make them respected international auditors. If they chose not to, then they ought to explain why they delayed and why they relied on tainted material to complete a valuation. But for them to be fair, I knew that they had no alternative but remove themselves as valuators. This was left to be seen.

Meanwhile, the assets left exposed needed my attention, as it was clear that dissipation was continuing. The fact that the Appeal Court had disagreed with the removal of funds meant nothing in the

Jamaican context; it did not seem to matter to anybody but us. In fact, the shameless disregard for the rulings of the court is no surprise anywhere in Jamaica. It was 'connections' and power at work. Really, it was business as usual.

For us to challenge any additional dissipation from the sale of assets listed by KPMG as part of the valuation of the shares, we would be exposed to the same influence and behaviour from the justice system that we saw from day one. It would open another series of court hearings that would be subjected to the same conditions already experienced.

But with the Appeal Court and Privy Council positive rulings in hand, the funds which were improperly removed had to be accounted for and made good— inclusive of interest. The funds were initially and correctly sitting in a fixed deposit account in US$ currency, earning interest at compounded rates. In fact the USD equivalent of about J$35 million Jamaican dollars had grown to about J$85 million equivalent between 2002 and 2008. So the company was deprived of a huge amount of interest when the principal amount was removed from the fixed deposit account. It is obvious that this should have been returned long before along with the interest it would have earned. If not, what would be the use of an Appeal Court and Privy Council ruling?

Appeal Court and Privy Council earns no respect

Off to the Supreme Court we went again. We filed for contempt, expecting that at a very minimum this would cause the partners to return all the funds with the interest that the account was accustomed to accruing. This was heard before Justice Paulette Williams in January 2011.

Just as I had suspected all along, the partners admitted in another affidavit that huge amounts were borrowed from the account for personal loans. This was directly in conflict with their 'last minute' Affidavit presented to the Jamaican Appeal Court which had implied that the funds were removed for use in company business. This was clearly pointed out to Justice Williams and that it had failed to mislead 'the more highly thought of' 'Appeal Court into ruling in their favor. But despite those Appeal Court and Privy Council rulings, Justice

Williams ruled in favour of the partners. The opinions of the Appeal Court and Privy Council obviously have no impact on the Supreme Court in Jamaica.

I had already learned that in Jamaica, particularly if one is 'connected', there is no risk in misleading or lying. This is most often brushed aside and treated as though it is expected. Here, and for the previous nine years, I was seeing it live for myself. Despite the rulings of the higher courts in 2009 and 2010 the partners were, in the eyes of a judge in the 'lower' Supreme Court, not in contempt and therefore had every reason to continue breaching the consent order.

What were the messages sent by the Supreme Court here? Simply, that shareholding directors may rape, pillage, and plunder the assets of a company as they wish, without consequence. That, in Jamaica no investment is guaranteed protection from dissipation and removal or accountability for either. That the Supreme Court supports this to the extent that it is willing to risk showing disdain for the rulings of the Appeal Court and the Privy Council. That Jamaican high court judges lack integrity or common sense or both. And most of all, that investors should expect this level of injustice to continue.

So brazen is the conduct in the Jamaican courts where judges are seen as gods in the system that removing them from positions of power is nearly impossible. These are persons many of whom are put in place by connections (however subtle) inside a political system that itself has proven to be made up mainly of "untouchables".

A final message to investment

At that stage I was wiser. Appealing this ruling from Justice Williams was a waste of time and money. Waiting another five or ten years, spend millions— having already done so and having got no further than where we started nearly 12 years earlier— did not seem smart.

The system is deliberately kept that way. The print media, the radio waves, the streets, everywhere is replete with complaints and to no avail. In this situation we realized that fighting the 'untouchables' would be stupid, but I couldn't walk away without taking a stand at some level and at a very minimum, documenting it.

The less privileged take to the streets bearing placards *"we want Justice"* even as the promises seem without end. Such demonstrations are so prevalent but no attention is grabbed from it. Hundreds of these in a single term only make it to the newsrooms and no further.

So many in positions of influence have seen and felt this scourge but kept silent. I had to remain in touch with my conscience and continue to take a stand. We were now seeing more clearly why there is so much pain in Jamaica and who is contributing to it. The Courts aid and abet in the deprivation and 'control' process and the majority seem jittery but silent nevertheless.

No honest investor with any knowledge of what normally happens here would risk putting money in Jamaica, and if tempted to do so as a gamble, would be wise to think very short term. No wonder some 'gamblers' repeatedly jump in with money and jump out shortly after 'making a killing'. No astute investor puts his money or assets where there can be no chance of fair resolution if the need arose.

Immediately after this ruling by Justice Williams, as we were leaving the Court building I requested of my attorneys that we be given a copy of the verbatim notes which we saw being taken by a stenographer and a copy of the detailed explanation of the ruling from Justice Williams. I needed it for our records while the ordeal was fresh in my mind. Frankly, I had no doubt that the ruling would be at best controversial. By then I quite understood exactly what was happening and the only unknown at that stage was how it would have been done and who would do it. I suspected that my request for that documentation would be frustrated while information would be out of reach. As aware as I was of the level of corruption inside the courts as well as the unlikelihood of any attorney successfully pursuing what is not supposed to be made publically available, I ignored the temptation to abandon the matter and pursued getting and documenting the details as part of my stand.

I was already also aware that the Chief Justice was treated as no more than a figurehead. She was said to be bright, honest, and worthy of sitting on the bench, and I have no reason to disbelieve that, but she showed no propensity for good leadership since the high level of corruption she inherited continued unabated, and in my opinion increased under her leadership. Complaining to her again could serve no gainful purpose except on principled grounds, as previous efforts only increased the aggression aimed at me for 'daring' to report on members of the 'establishment'.

It became increasingly imperative that I document as much as possible. So I regularly reminded our Attorneys to procure the explanation of the ruling and the verbatim notes that were taken. Honestly, I knew that I was just going through the motions.

Jamaica is a small country and information travels at amazing speed, often only with a motive for gossip. Again the general rule for gossip in Jamaica is, "*if it nuh guh suh, den it nearly guh suh*". Information getting to us indicated that sums in the amounts of tens of millions of dollars were removed to' bail out' a partner's personal FINSAC debts while the company's fixed assets were deteriorating, the roofs of buildings with minor hurricane damage many years earlier deteriorated as they were ignored and left exposed to the elements, stocks were being used without replenishment, personal companies were being formed by the 'partners' and used in direct competition with the EML group; but worst of all, there was no accountability. The offenders were being rewarded. This is what investors can expect.

For this, the government bears huge responsibility as movers, shakers and overseers of the various agents who are supposed to monitor the behaviour of companies and individuals through Financial Statements and other returns of accountability. Without this, how would those in any business make tax returns that would satisfy government guidelines? Government sets policies that should not only guide investors, but protect investors. At best there is selective protection on a fairly large scale and there are 'untouchables' through strong connections. Seeking redress is selectively discouraged - usually by arranged delays.

'Time' in Jamaica is a killer as the plummeting of its currency is the norm. Fifteen years in the courts is a huge deterrent to seeking fair redress. Offenders capitalize on this with surety to benefit from it. This is so obvious that taking action against fraud is done only to send a message with the hope that others will avoid the embarrassment that may be seen in the news print, not because of any potential consequence.

Going through futile reminders ….for the records.

In the months that followed, I routinely pestered my attorneys for the verbatim court records. My follow-up emails all seemed ignored, hidden away inside Jamaica's dark justice system.

Meanwhile, my attorneys seemed timid to write to KPMG, so I wrote to them myself. I already had a target on my back, and I was convinced that any attorney who dared to interfere with predetermined intensions inside the system by appearing to push KPMG would have problems surviving comfortably inside the system.

So after consulting with our attorneys we had followed up our initial correspondence sent to KPMG a few months later with a letter again inquiring of their intentions, reminding them of the impact of the delays.

It was clear from before then that they had no intention of proceeding with their application for release nor did they intend to breach their professional standards possibly for fear of being exposed and sued by us. KPMG was in a win/win position. If they did nothing the system would not hold them accountable as is normal in Jamaica; and if they were pressured by the court to do an unfair valuation, a law suit from us could take 10, 20 years or never. So they have done nothing.

I realized that together with a Justice Sykes' ruling they could see to it that Justice is not done for a period of up to . . . "forever".

So while I agree that KPMG could not as professionals arrive at a fair valuation using corrupted data, I also thought that KPMG might have felt that they were being pressured or influenced by the court system to act outside of their professional standards. Although their stated ethics conflicted with the decision handed down by Justice Sykes, if they proceeded, it could appear to be a challenge by KPMG on the decision of a judge. I understand this hesitancy, but they nevertheless had an obligation to carry out their application and pursue the matter in court. Doing nothing caused a stalemate that handed us more irreparable financial and emotional damage, some of which they knew had been done already.

Whether or not proceeding with the release application would be sending a message to Justice Sykes that he was 'naughty' is not the point here. KPMG had a duty to do what is right. They were the ones that set the 90 day period and prepared the letter of engagement for both parties to follow. We took them at their written word and we endorsed it.

I have said before and I need to reinforce it here, this kind of conduct by professionals is not unusual in Jamaica. It is the type of behavior that international professional companies dare not try in developed countries or in some 'cleaner' developing countries, without seeing great risk. In Jamaica it is "*no big ting*." The volume of work made available to international professional companies in Jamaica is somewhat proportional to the level of cooperation they give to the establishment. It is not unusual for an international firm to breach standards or ethics and easily escape consequence by going to the courts, using one delaying tactic or another, or forcing their victims into securing bonds that are out of the reach of the average complainant. In addition, the abuse of power wielded by such companies is often protected by 'untouchables' in the judicial and political arenas.

Time, money and fear are powerful tools that determine what happens in Jamaica. Who is it then that is most likely to have easy and undisturbed access to these tools?

The realities I must face.

As I met with friends and sympathizers to ponder the issues at hand, I heard comments of "*impossible*", "*sick country*", "*everybody a tief now*". Such reactions strengthen my resolve to lash out against this scourge of unaccountability.

I continue to ponder why KPMG would act the way they did. In fact, through their actions (or lack thereof), KPMG have essentially ensured that any valuation will be done unfairly or never done at all. If done unfairly the minority shareholders are big losers. If not done at all the company will never be wound up, and the minority shareholders may never reap the fair value or any value for their shares.

Yes, I agree that KPMG could not have done a 2001 valuation in 2003. They definitely should not have done a 2001 valuation in 2005, and they have even more reason not to do one in 2015. Additionally, to do any valuation at any time using financials proven by the Public Accountancy Board and the Appeal Court to be tainted or flawed through gross negligence on the part of the company's auditor, and in the favour of the partners, would be unforgiveable.

KPMG ought not to have played any part in depriving any party of justice for over 11 years. So far their actions seem to suggest they have joined with the partners in playing the same game: delay forever and deny us justice for as long as it takes us to surrender. What they do finally will indicate their true level of integrity and will.

Continued strident pursuit of elusive justice . . .

Despite the disappointment in the actions of professionals generally, it should never be said that I didn't exhaust all avenues for justice.

The Prime Minister of the day, Bruce Golding was embroiled in the embarrassing 'Dudus" imbroglio, but which Prime Minister in Jamaica has escaped some embarrassment?

On June 9, 2011, I wrote to Prime Minister Bruce Golding including the following:

> "We bring to your attention a case of extreme corporate abuse that Government and the justice system have failed to adequately address for 10 years.....
>
> I was Managing Director for 23 years and my wife and I own 33.33% of EML group of companies. The business by then was financially strong and owned vast real estate holdings as a result of profits from its core business being prudently invested.
>
> Since then ... 2002 ... my wife and I have been unable to get any Financial Statements, un-audited or audited for any of the three companies in the group....

We signed a consent order in 2002 relating to the valuation and sale of our shares to the brothers, estimated by KPMG to be completed in 90 days. That order has been deliberately frustrated resulting in us going to court more than 60 times over the last 9 years. Legal fees alone exceed J$20 million....

The legal system has been used and abused in order to deprive us of justice and of the value we worked more than 20 years to accumulate.....

The group's Auditor was taken before the "Public Accountancy Board" and found guilty of gross negligence relating to the company accounts. For this and more the Auditor was suspended from practicing for six months and fined $1,000,000.00....

The Court appointed KPMG to carry out a valuation of our shares. Nine years later they applied to the court to terminate their appointment on the grounds of frustration and on the findings of the Public Accountancy Board. They have stated categorically that they will not attempt a valuation. To do the valuation based on corrupted data would breech their professional standards...

None of this has brought us any closer to resolution. More than JA$82 million dollars ordered held in an escrow account by the court has been used without our permission or input. Less than JA$ ½ million dollars remains. This breech is confirmed by The Privy Council....

The group of companies has operated for 10 years without reporting their activities to minority shareholders, or the Government. We are concerned that even as our assets are being dissipated we may be accumulating massive indebtedness to Government....

How can a group of companies operate in Jamaica without accountability to anyone? How can they do this for 10 years and continue to do so today?

> The question now is . . . . . WILL GOVERNMENT MAKE THEM ACCOUNTABLE?
>
> We believe local & foreign direct investments are suffering because of shortcomings in our Justice system, the relevant Government Ministries and the time it takes to settle corporate disputes. This is [these are] some of the first areas looked into when prospective investors begin the process of due diligence......
>
> It's easy to say this is a legal matter and must be settled in the courts ...... but where is justice if it is not in the Court?"

Thc Prime Minister responded with copies to various departments including the Attorney General, and the Revenue Department. I had been though the AG's Department and it was not a confidence builder but we had nothing to lose by revisiting.

Our letters to KPMG continued to be ignored. It was time to again try to get the attention of the Chief Justice. On August 18, 2011, I wrote to the Chief Justice reminding her that I had written to her on three separate occasions in 2007 and that "another 4 years had passed bringing delays to 9 years longer than expectations." I complained about a judge having been overruled by Appeal Court and Privy Council yet was back on the case. I thought that he should not sit on any subsequent matter involving us. Also, that from as far back as July 2010 the KPMG matter was referred for hearing in front of that same judge.

The Chief Justice responded to me on August 26, 2011, followed by a letter from her Registrar on September 2, 2011, instructing that attorneys for the parties should meet with her to set a date. This was an instruction that should get all the parties going. There should be no need for our attorneys to be timid especially when the instruction was coming from the top of the Judiciary - or, so one would think.

I kept getting the nagging impression that it was possible for KPMG to feel intimidated by connections in the court. Indeed as time passed it appeared to be a real challenge on KPMG after the decision by a judge to not set aside the Consent Order. But I held onto feeble consolation that in the field of professionals doing what is right and what was in the interest of justice had to be the priority.

Our attorneys immediately wrote to KPMG's attorneys and copied all the parties quoting the Registrar's letter stated:

> "A review of the file shows that the matter came before the Honourable Mr. Justice Rattray on July 30, 2011 (sic) and was adjourned to be fixed before the Honourable Mr. Justice Sykes for further consideration."

Additionally, the parties were to consult with the Registrar. The Registrar's letter had a 'typo' and should have read "July 30, 2010", but that should have had no effect on the order given. Despite these instructions to meet with the Registrar to arrange a date for a hearing of their application to be relieved from doing the valuation, I know of no effort by KPMG to get a court date to this point.

The 'top' continues to command no respect

It seems that not even the Chief Justice dares to buck the system. Why? Who is it that is so powerful?

It is not about an injustice to us only; it is about an injustice to the nation.

Some things happen out of incompetence or coincidence but when they are unjust and happen this way repeatedly, there has to be motive. There has to be some special influence applied.

All this was in 2011. It is no surprise that now, more than five years after the Chief Justice intervened, there has been no obvious attempt by KPMG to act. While still awaiting a response to the Chief Justices instructions my next effort was to seek audience with Attorney General Braham. He already had the Prime Minister's letter in hand. This was on the eve of General Elections, and I waited to see what would happen.

The 2011 General Election

Andrew Holness called the General Election in December 2011 and ran a campaign that openly revealed he would have to apply some "bitter medicine" to arrest the sliding economy if he won. The PNP, in their typical campaign mode, promised an agreement with the IMF and candies like "JEEP: Jamaica Emergency Employment Programme", which was just another name for 'handouts'. This strategy has never failed to get the attention of voters. The PNP won.

From the conduct and promises of the PNP it appeared at that time that the PNP were unaware of the gravity of the collapsing economy, although they had played a huge part in creating that collapse. For decades the JLP had been seen as lacking the ability to convince voters of why they needed to carry out their painful promises in the interest of country. They were usually given the task to govern an economically depleted country. On the other hand the PNP were seen as spenders and were able to tell the people practically anything and never fulfill their promises, yet still appear to be 'caring' for supporters to retain their votes. The JLP tended to be always in repair mode, fixing the problems created by the opposing party. The PNP consistently did what was necessary to stay in power even at the risk of putting the country into bankruptcy. Both parties were seen as corrupt, though, with the JLP being perceived as sharing the spoils among a few and the PNP allowing more of a trickle down to the masses. The situation in both was definitely unsustainable.

This is the predicament that Jamaica faces even today. Corruption in any leadership they choose; more fiscal responsibility from one party and more debt and trickle down from the other.

My efforts continue

My attorneys wrote to the new Attorney General Patrick Atkinson on January 24, 2012 for an appointment. Nothing happened, and after more than a year I had no response. In July 2012, I noted from a newspaper that Basil Cunningham, who had manipulated the books in favor of Michael, had passed on. After eleven years, Basil Cunningham had died and the true state of the EML group accounts had not yet been fully exposed. The truth about the accounts and what was done with the missing funds remains a mystery.

We had exhausted all the normal channels of justice that one can imagine and we remained in the same place as we were at the start twelve years before, only more 'aged' and financially weakened. I often thought of how perplexing it was that the people exhaust their funds seeking justice while their country exhausts funds in ways to deny its people justice.

Not having heard from the Attorney General since my letter in January 2012, I found it necessary to put the matter before the Hon. Mark Golding, Minister of Justice. My letter to Golding was dated August 15, 2012. I am being very frank here: I did not expect a morsel of good from any information I had placed in my letter before Minister Mark Golding. I was not even afforded the courtesy of a response, which is not unusual treatment in Jamaica these days. To get one, people usually take placards to the street, and even then the promises are rarely fulfilled. Were the Ministers of Government responding to the type of complaints as I had made, the problems assailing our country would not have been critical as they are now. Going further was only for the records.

Despite my being aware of the pressures under which the group Jamaicans for Justice has operated—chief of which are the large number of cases of murder and other excesses—I thought it necessary to at least put on record the events over eleven years of typical manipulations, corruption, incompetence, fraud and depravity carried out by the same leadership seen as role models that have presided over Jamaica for more than 50 years, the same leadership that has presided over the very depravity that Jamaicans for Justice fight so hard to remove. Like none other, they have continued to be strident and resolute in exposing the abuses carried out on people. Sending a copy of this letter to Jamaicans for Justice was only a formality. They already had their hands full and I wasn't sure if any of the attorneys who assisted them in their fight for justice was in any way part of the reasons for the state of affairs in the country. That is how complicated things can get in Jamaica.

Benevolent groups need attorneys to handle matters in the court—the very courts which are already corrupted and where many attorneys either suffer in silence with the problems or form part of the problems. It is hardly impossible for benevolent persons and groups to avoid accepting help from such sources, whether or not they are genuine. Help is always welcome especially when it is free or nearly so. But one should never assume that help always comes from only good people. The best place for bad people to shelter is among good people.

The stand continues

Isn't it so very obvious that the court system in our matter was being used to frustrate natural justice? Is it not clear that it is being used to create a situation where one party can win by stalemate while the powers that be are indifferent? Is it not clear that through the justice system the most heinous crimes can be sanitized? Despite all this to throw in the towel would be a great injustice to Jamaica.

Next was my visit to my Attorneys' office on September 28, 2012 to provide copies of titles owned by Basil Cunningham, the auditor who had spent more than three years fighting the PAB and the Supreme Court to escape the charges of gross negligence. He had failed to pay any of the costs awarded by the Courts, and we had to try to collect from his estate. At that meeting Lynne and I were presented with a bill of costs for our opponents' legal fees, as Justice Sykes had ruled. That bill of cost was in excess of a shocking J$22 million. This was amazing and typically brazen! Many who saw it referred to this as an act of fraud. I had been before the Courts for more than 10 years on more than 70 other occasions and totaling more than 100 days, with judgments in our favour, and we did not receive anything near that kind of cost. Additionally, more than three years fighting Basil Cunningham did not cause us to be refunded as much as 10% of true costs.

Many complainants abandoned their cases when slapped with this type of injustice. I suppose I'm a sucker for punishment.

Yes, this cost will stand if and when a judge sanctions Justice Sykes's ruling, but I already know what is likely to happen. It seems the ploy here by our opponents' legal team is to force us into voluntarily accepting what is unfair. This case history shows that they can achieve any end they wish, even as judgments are made against them.

This type of strategy is not unusual in Jamaica. In fact it is quite typical of large organizations or 'connected' persons and companies who use the court costs - padded if required - sometimes by way of requesting a bond, to deprive others of justice. It is typical of the ruthless administration of injustice in Jamaica.

How many persons can match their access to funds with the worth of large companies, especially international ones?

On October 26, 2012 I received an email from my attorney stating that the matter of costs would be before the court on October 30, 2012. Up to 2015, I have heard nothing further. This is even more indication that the 'strategy' has to be a less than honest act on which I will have to wait even as KPMG is playing the delay game. It's simple: Apply pressure by way of ridiculous costs which the history of this matter shows can be made to stick, even through the court.

A sudden and overly late response.

On November 8, 2013, I received a copy of a letter from the partners' newest attorneys, requesting of the Registrar a hearing date for the release of KPMG as court appointed valuators before Justice Sykes in the EML case. This hearing date—which five years earlier was requested through the Chief Justice and by us—was being requested this time by the partners. I viewed it as pretense—only appearing to care … or did they know something I did not know? But after all "*a nuh di Chief Justice run tings*" and "*when di tings ready it ready*". Other than a façade, what else could it really be?

In 2015 the request means nothing more than that if there is ever a sitting it will be before the same judge as before who had no good ethical reason to hear the matter.

It is in spite of all this that I have continued to pursue a path to justice by documenting my experiences in the court system and in various Ministries of Government. It is in spite of a court system that has the power to organize for the delay of Justice forever, that I must expose and hope that it will open some eyes one day. I see no great hope in the near future because this type of carnage is not unique to Lynne and me. It is routinely levied on the people of Jamaica. But hopefully, some benefit can come from this; hopefully some help can be found both locally and overseas to save this nation.

The transformation of this beautiful island of Jamaica took perplexing, but educating routes that could create a template for other countries to avoid. The route I personally have travelled might help to explain how we got where we are and possibly why.

It is pointless criticizing or even pressing for change in a nation that has gone bad, without looking into the past, the culture as it was, the steps taken that led us there and the steps we are taking now.

PART II:

Jamaica Today

CHAPTER 11

JAMAICA 2010s

While my own experience is instructive of the kinds of problems facing Jamaica today, it is inadequate to describe the biggest and deepest issues. Therefore, in this next section, I quote liberally and often from articles in the Jamaican print media because they are usually the most consistent and trusted sources of information available. External sources understand very little of the Jamaican culture. They see glimpses from our gifted musicians and from our athletes but have had limited exposure to our history.

I take good and well intentioned journalists very seriously, especially when I know they have been around for a long time and write for longstanding reputable newspapers. Unlike our typical leadership over decades, I need not take their word with a grain of salt. I have the same respect for credible and outspoken columnists and contributors who are not necessarily journalists in the purest sense of the word. Their perspective allows me to explore what I believe will be the most pressing issues facing Jamaica over the coming decades if we are to turn the nation around from its present course.

On December 29, 2011, Portia Simpson Miller of the PNP defeated Andrew Holness and became Prime Minister on January 05, 2012. This election carried a clear indication from voter interest that the people of Jamaica were tired of politicians. They had lost the little faith that they had left and had lost interest in the leadership of both the JLP and PNP. A popular cartoon from December 2011 put it accurately:

JEEP

More than 30 years after the handouts of the CRASH program, Portia Simpson introduced a new program to help the poor called JEEP (Jamaica Emergency Employment Program) In fact, this was nothing new, but it was wrapped in a new name that fooled only the uneducated and those who were ignorant of our political history. JEEP was a political gimmick that essentially referred to the same doling out policies from the terrible 70s. These programs had been used for decades to trick the people into believing that there was a special effort to care for them. It had more meaning before an election than after, because without handout money the 'JEEP' would 'bruk dung' [1].

Simpson-Miller's predecessor Andrew Holness did what was considered to be the one ridiculously unforgivable thing that killed his campaign: In his explanation of the hard times that were ahead, he told the electorate that there was "bitter medicine" to come. What he said was the truth but the metaphor cost him. People did not want to hear the truth, as the truth meant honesty, integrity, and fiscal responsibility.

The truth meant an overturn of the handout and 'eat a food'[2] culture. The truth meant that professionals would have to be transparent and failing that would be brought to book. The JEEP, curried goat, oxtail, [3] and other promises resonated with the people who, in all fairness, knew little about collective commitment to work diligently.

Despite the huge numbers of students coming out of university, we were still bereft of the entrepreneurial skills and the spirit of enterprise that would cause us to provide viable and sustainable solutions for employment.

As corruption remained the most conspicuous of Jamaica's problems. Greg Christie, from the Office of the Contractor General (OCG) wasted no time in writing to newly appointed Prime Minister on her first day in office with extensive recommendations. The local *Observer* Newspaper recounted: [4]

> As explained by the OCG, the recommendations "have been specifically crafted (a) to significantly enhance transparency, competition, accountability and probity in public contracting and licensing in Jamaica; (b) to ensure compliance with the Government's Procurement Procedures and Guidelines; (c) to eliminate waste and inefficiency in the award and implementation of Government contracts; (d) to prevent fraud and corruption in Government contracting; (e) to strengthen the independence of the OCG, and; (f) to generally win the battle against corruption in Jamaica."

Christie's letter to Prime Minister Simpson-Miller, copied to many other high ranking officials, was extremely clear and telling. Its expression of urgency and scope of measures indicate the level of corruption in Jamaica that should cause anyone to register that high level of concern.

Endemic CRIME

Clearly, from Greg Christie's plea, many should wonder what previous governments have done to curb corruption. Why has the culture of corruption remained so prominently and persistently on display? Kickbacks, extortion and bribery are followed by tame government responses. They pretend to do a 'little something' to fool the people into thinking they are dealing with the problem, then little gets to court and, whatever does, seems to go nowhere. We see desperation galore as they seek outlets and escape routes. Ponzi schemes become attractive. Lotto scams are prevalent. Debacle after debacle— police corruption and brutality, sanctioned killings, rape, murder, child abuse, extortion—most all are hidden away, lumped and trivialized under a single topic: Crime happens everywhere in the world.

Ponzi Schemes

Extortion schemes started in small Jamaica where 'everybody knows everybody'. 'Wolves' donning lawyers' clothing and introducing them to overseas bankers, as their close connections take tens of millions of US dollars, from trusting Jamaicans. As veranda talk puts it, who better to protect criminals without implicating themselves than lawyers who act in the interest of self, of Party, or of affluent connections? Extra protection disguised as 'lawyer client privilege' always comes in handy.

In many high profile cases, Ponzi operators were accused in Jamaica by a governing party of not being legally registered to do business in Jamaica but were allowed to settle elsewhere, appear legitimate, and avoid prosecution, even as the accusers themselves invested with them. This gave credence to the legitimacy and safety of investors' money placed in those schemes while the Financial Services Commission (FSC) – the regulating body that should bring them to account - gave the impression that they were taking action.

I was not acquainted with David Smith who was the main operator of the infamous Olint Ponzi scheme. However, he had the trust of so many persons of the highest reputation and so investing in his club seemed safe. When the Government of the day gave the impression that they were going to shut him down, many thought that this was unfair. It was seen as an effort to deprive investors of good returns and to protect the banks from losing deposits to Olint. In addition, it was common knowledge that prominent professionals and members of Parliament invested in Olint. What better message of credibility could one want?

The element of trust played a most important part in bamboozling Jamaican investors, both from the point of view of trust in David Smith and misplaced trust in Government officials. Distrust for the bodies that govern us is high, but we were to learn that too many of those who were respected for their reputation of integrity had been either masquerading as such or had given in to the culture of corruption.

One of the ploys used by David Smith to deceive investors was that, unlike the banks that were self-serving and often rapacious, the Olint organization was a club and did not need regulation. This became even more acceptable as heavy inputs from the top echelon gave support to him.

David Smith's Olint Ponzi scheme left Jamaica—some say it was "escorted" by prominent persons including Jamaican attorneys —to operate from the Turks and Caicos Islands after being introduced to bank connections there. Help from so-called 'persons of integrity' played a huge role. Smith was not alone.

Smith only got indicted because of US intervention. Had the USA not intervened, David Smith might still be ripping off the people of Jamaica even as he settled amicably with both Jamaican political parties. He is now in prison in the United States, but his protectors and partners remain free after stealing and sharing millions from investors.

No sooner had Smith settled down in prison when speeches from the peers of the same tainted politicians sounded off for solutions like enforcement of regulations. A presentation by prominent spokesperson in the PNP, Delano Franklyn [5] to the Public Seminar on Corporate Governance hosted by the Financial Services Commission at the Jamaica Pegasus Hotel in New Kingston on March 15, 2012 spoke of the need for "standards of conduct and a consistent, persistent, and relentless national assault against the erosion of social and ethical values in the society." In the same speech the admission was made that Jamaica already had a flood of regulations to ensure public sector oversight but that we needed to "become far more proactive in the application of these laws and regulations . . . [including] . . . a strong regulatory framework to strengthen corporate and public governance operating in a society underpinned by good values and attitude."

So very true. This same values and attitudes rhetoric had been flashed around by Mr. Franklyn's party since the 1990s, but apparently it was not intended then to also apply to our leaders. What hypocrisy! And somehow we just don't get it. Why do we, the educated, continue to entertain this insincere and repetitive political spatter? Mr. Franklyn makes great points in his 'sermon', but where was the Justice system in all that? What of the leadership from which the people take their cue?...to achieve the 'strong regulatory framework to strengthen corporate and public governance operating in a society underpinned by good values and attitudes.'

In 2015, other Ponzi scheme bosses and participating organizers were still enjoying the fruits of their evil. Many benefitted from the delays in the justice system—like those I had endured— that might eventually set them free. More importantly, some were spared the need to have to expose the various skeletons they have in their closets, such as the names of political figures on the dole. How much more brazen can it get when it is exposed that a senior politician - a Permanent Secretary in the Ministry of Justice - provided bail for an indicted Ponzi scheme boss awaiting trial? What are the consequences expected for such action? Frankly none, but who really cares anymore?

Lotto Scams

Only a Jamaican could, without formal education, operate a system that fleeced educated people in first world countries of millions of dollars and continue do so for more than five years uninterrupted. Their abilities to change, manipulate, and deceive are well adapted to the social, economic and political climate that has existed for most of the 50 years post independence. Their leaders have created the conditions that have given them little choice but to eke out survival, and have also taught them well by example.

One of the ways in which the Jamaican scammers ply their trade is to gather the detailed personal and private information of

Americans from tourist accommodations and from local call centers. If asking for it by gentle means was not rewarding, threats were carried out. When threats did not work, we all knew what happened next. Death is a very persuasive tool, and its message works well with those who won't hand over information. It works well with the retired elderly Americans too. Unaccustomed as they were to being terrorized in their own country, it didn't take long to force them into yielding. Again the victims of the scam experience the same gentle introduction, but death threats to them and their family follow if cooperation is not forthcoming. There is no mercy shown for the elderly regardless of the medical conditions that they might have been suffering. The threats of violence, rape of grandchildren, murder, or arson is alien to the retired American. I listened to some of these recorded threats and I can understand why these threats extract thousands of dollars from older persons who are used to a peaceful retirement. In addition, Americans have grown accustomed to a culture that includes a reasonable amount of trust. It is not unusual for a shopper to get a call from a store like Wal-Mart giving appreciation for a recent purchase by drawing lots and offering a free cruise trip. Innocent Americans soon learned that Jamaican scammers would capitalize on that strategy to con them out of their life savings.

The involvement of Jamaican political figures and police officers as partners in the scam has often been speculated. Frankly, this is not surprising either. The scammers do better with this kind of protection as the loot is said to feed the handout culture. O to see the mansions owned by young men who have neither formal skill nor profession! To see the barefaced scammers cruising in multi-million dollar cars! To see the 'bling'[6] at exclusive parties where thousands of dollars are incinerated for show!

Internet blogs by many Jamaicans who defend the scamming suggest that the money stolen by scams are 'entitlements', an indication of the levels of values and attitudes prevailing in the society. But scamming is not limited to the poor and underprivileged. On the contrary, it is an imitation of examples set at the top of society.

After billions had been stolen, the USA finally got fed-up of waiting on the Jamaican justice system to do something. Fearing American intervention, our leaders scrambled to deal with scamming. Yes, only when the USA jumps all over Jamaican authorities do we see a rushed effort to deal with problems.

Senator Susan Collins of Maine, at a March 2013 US Senate Committee hearing in Washington blasted Jamaica for not doing more to end the problem particularly in recent years. She is quoted as saying:

> "I think they are finally taking it seriously, but it has taken a number of years for them to do so and I would like to see them put the effort in this, in stopping this scam, as they put into enticing Americans to come vacation in Jamaica. A lot of money is spent on that."

She was clearly angered. And who wouldn't be. More than 30,000 calls are made into the United States daily to defraud elderly people. Senator Collins was very aware of the level of corruption and protection from within the government of Jamaica. She once called the government "arrogant" and insisted that "they clearly know they can continue to operate without consequence". In the same hearing Senator Bill Nelson is quoted as saying, "We want to see them extradited to the US. That will have a chilling effect on a number of these people who think they are bulletproof."

Senator Collins and Senator Nelson seemed to be aware that people who are protected by our 'untouchables' don't go to prison or hardly to Court in Jamaica.

In a single scamming scandal, we told the world that our leaders lacked will and caring. Honest hardworking people cannot find protection for themselves in Jamaica, much less expecting protection of some tourist visitors' data. We were effectively wiping out thousands of investment and employment opportunities, not just because of the immorality, but because of our refusal to do something about it.

Just as troubling was the high number of ordinary Jamaicans who look at scamming as a victimless crime. Some saw it as revenge for alleged crimes done to Jamaicans by others in the past, referring even as far back as during slavery. Some felt that anyone stupid enough to send thousands of dollars to scammers did it out of greed and deserved to lose it. This is the type of thinking that has become increasingly ingrained over years and is indicative of the values we can expect in future Jamaica. It is astonishing that these 'scammer sympathizers', many of whom have themselves been conned out of investments by failed Ponzi schemes, actually entertain these beliefs. It can't be a matter of revenge for reparation, since Olint and many other Ponzi schemes that stole their money were operated by Jamaicans. They were content to keep quiet about the bad that was inflicted on their own people, even as they condoned the bad that their own inflicted on others. This is values and attitudes the Jamaican way.

How can these criminals be put away when the Police are involved and on the take, the politicians seem part of the scamming operations and too many benefit from it? It's power over values here.

A contributor to the daily Jamaica Observer on March 17, 2013 [7] put it succinctly:

> "The criminals benefit directly; the private sector benefits from monies the scammers spend to buy cars, fancy clothes, construction and building materials, etc; some members of the police are said to benefit from extortion and shaking down scammers; politicians benefit because the flow of easy money into poor, political garrisons is putting less pressure on them to address community needs like roads, water, jobs, and security…"

As the saying goes, when America sneezes, Jamaica catches cold. The politicians only rushed to put into law the Reform of Fraudulent Transactions Special Provisions Act because Uncle Sam sneezed real hard. Government misread the loss to Jamaica as a gain that would help the terrible GDP-to–debt situation as well as satisfy the "eat a food" mentality. It has always been easy for politicians to get together and make laws overnight if it will save their necks or keep them in power, as it is never about country. Apart from the famous "law is not a shackle" instance when the Prime Minister illegally declared a national holiday and then rushed to Parliament to legitimize it, or the recent instance when the government announced their intention to raid the National Housing Trust funds and rushed to Parliament to make it legal, this anti-lottery scam bill is the fastest I recall any law has ever been rushed through the House - and it only happened when Uncle Sam cracked a whip.

It is so fortunate for Cayman and the Turks & Caicos that they are still British Colonies. There the British are not afraid to tackle corruption from the very top of the ladder. Chief Minister, Prime Minister or Judge — here in Jamaica we protect them at all costs.

We handed over our sovereignty to the United States and British governments to indict the criminals we protect. We are now handing it over to the International Monetary Fund as well. From as early as 2011 Jamaica has been taking instructions from the IMF. We are in a relationship with the IMF that forces us to meet quarterly tests which puts us in an economic straight jacket similar to Greece. We scam and steal from Uncle Sam and then we beg them for loans.

Meanwhile, very few heads turn at the news that between 300 and 400 murders in Jamaica were related to the 'lotto scamming'. Over 70% of murders in St James during the scamming between 2011 and 2013 were also reported to be related. Yet there is no real outrage from society. Rape, murder, immorality, injustice continues, and it is just our way of life.

Under an insightful article entitled – "Lotto scamming, bling and morality" [8] Published: Sunday Gleaner - March 10, 2013

Journalist Ian Boyne said:

> "*Dr Ana Perkins, trained at Boston College and Cambridge University, now at the University of the West Indies. Her lecture, published as a 66-page booklet, was titled* ***Moral Disease Making Jamaica Ill?: Re-engaging the Conversation***.[9]
>
> Perkins says Jamaica is suffering from moral degenerative syndrome (MDS). The causative agents for this disease are *"poor socialisation, inappropriate values and attitudes, lack of personal responsibility, reduced moral sensitivity,*

> *imagination and reasoning"*. The symptoms are all around us - *"widespread disrespect for each other, murder, rape, larceny and robbery, petty and white-collar theft and dishonesty, among others"*. . . . .
>
> "But, remember, that is the model set by the middle and upper classes. Granted, you might say they work for theirs, though ghetto people know that not all of them do. Some get their wealth through corruption and political connections. Our middle and upper classes don't provide an overwhelmingly inspiring moral model. The people featured on our social pages flaunting their wealth and uptown bling are also saying that these are the things which matter most. Ghetto people know that among them are some of the biggest tax dodgers, and 'bly' and contract recipients. Dem cyaah tell ghetto people nutten!"

A response made to this article states. . . . *"It must be noted that the level of corruption in high places is a testament to the measure of our moral and ethical standing."*

Former Minister of Justice Delroy Chuck admitted that in 2008 the lotto scam was well established and that Jamaica was already meeting with USA officials on the matter. The law to correct it was not put before the House until 2013. This is a simple indication that neither government was in a hurry to do anything about it, they were not concerned enough for the senior citizens in the USA that were being ravaged. Mr. Chuck commented that former Commissioner of Police Hartley Lewin had complained to him that the Scam was having a corrupting influence on his police officers. The Commissioner was actually implying that they get up off their asses and do something about it in Parliament. He was implying that he needed to be given the teeth to act before his police officers were further corrupted. Here we had a Commissioner of Police who wanted to accelerate reduction of crime while Parliamentarians had their feet firmly on the brake pedal.

What are we reduced to when people are happy because the money fleeced from old people in America stimulates business in Montego

Bay? Does the resulting relaxation of social pressure on the people serve to paint the government in good light?

Meanwhile politicians and their activists are arrested for show, and then quickly released; political persons involved make some money to hang onto votes while the Commissioner of Police takes blame for not doing what he can't.

I can't say it any better than cartoons in a daily newspaper . . . .

Ticket Extortion by Government.

Late in 2012, in support of an amnesty to persons with outstanding traffic tickets, the government displayed on its website a list of persons reputed to have outstanding unpaid traffic tickets. My name was included for a speeding ticket some 9 years back. Also on that listing was a fine of J$10,000 from a ticket served on my wife for driving an unlicensed vehicle some years before. My wife's ticket/fine was proven to be unjustified. It had been reversed by the Traffic Court and therefore had no right being displayed on the database of the government site as unpaid.

Almost all persons who were prompted to visit the site were shocked to see their names listed as having unpaid tickets. Some even denied receiving tickets that were listed. Many had not bothered to log on to the site because they were sure that they had no outstanding tickets and a huge majority of the driving population did not have access to the internet to check. To add to the chaos, most drivers in Jamaica don't file away paid ticket receipts. Many of those were nevertheless prepared to fight the issue. I was upset with some of my friends who had decided to again pay amounts erroneously listed on the site as outstanding. They did so for simple reasons I could certainly sympathize with. Why risk the hassle of being pulled from your home on a specious warrant? That is a clear indication of the level of extortion and injustice that is expected of law enforcers.

It turned out that the government's listing was bogus, resulting from contaminated data in the traffic department and probably even in the courts. There is so much corruption that many speculated that the contamination was deliberate to hide the fraudulent removal of funds from the government's kitty.

The huge public outcry that followed in the media led to the withdrawing of the site by government with a promise that the data would be corrected and the conditions of the amnesty revisited. Not long afterwards, the site was again posted to the web as 'corrected,' and callous threats from the police hierarchy attempted to scare people into paying what they did not owe. My ticket was removed from the list, but my wife's and most of my friends were still there in error. Drivers for some companies discovered that they were listed, only because employers implored them to log onto the site. Some discovered that they were listed for vehicles which they had never seen nor driven. Yet many who were innocent continued to pay for tickets that they had already paid, having not filed away the receipts. Fear of imminent injustice was the reason.

To whom does one complain? What of the traffic matters that were contested in court, discharged, and still on the list? Is it that the records of the court were mislaid or were they not passed on to the relevant department that stored this kind of data? Is it that data in the courts was also contaminated? Was this data accessible without having to visit the court and spend days searching?

Never before had the records of the tax department been treated with the distrust that was displayed by the public in this matter, but the Jamaican saying *"Every day bucket go a well one day di bottom muss fall out"* is fitting here. Injustice has been on this path for a long time and from the pulse of the public many were not going to take it lying down.

The messages here were clear. Government could not be trusted to keep the very records that are part of the paper trail for accountability. Whatever government wanted they would try to take. Is there any wonder it is common to hear ..."*Government too tief*" ... *"dem want money so dem decide fi tek it"* ... *"If dem so brazen an tief, den why mi cyan tief too?"* What kind of system messes up people's data, and then penalizes its citizens for the mess up?

Then suddenly, the matter seemed to be left alone. The exercise was a shakedown attempt by the government desperate for revenue. I believe that the government knew they needed desperately to invade the pockets of the people soon or the political implications would not be to their suit. This does not mean that it has been abandoned completely, though. Quite typically they might be waiting for memories to fade before springing the "amnesty" on another rainy day. Or maybe some police will eventually use the corrupted data to extort money or 'lock up' innocent civilians when it is to their suit?

What is the difference between the lotto scammers and government again?

Police corruption, brutality, sanctioned killings

The media, despite some amount of intimidation from the political activists and from partisan activists within their ranks, continue to play a vital role in Jamaica. I sometimes think that they are too soft on the leaders in civic and political society, but I more often feel that way out of frustration, as leadership becomes more callous, uncaring and unstoppable.

Since early 2000s, the media have turned up the pressure somewhat, exposing the crimes, mismanagement, corruption and more.

In the 90s when the world was booming economically, Jamaica was hell bent on its own destruction. The year 2013, imminently poised for terrible times in the economy, saw a media less inclined to be lenient. They have been professionals for the most part and have at times worked without fear or favor. Specific journalists stand out in this regard and most exposures of terrible incidents have been delivered by way of some brave journalists in the media. Only brave ones dare lash out against police corruption, brutality, and sanctioned killings.

I have learned to appreciate the skills of those reporters and columnists, and I have gained increasing respect for them as they risk exposing ills in a country so violent and corrupt. But some political interference places pressure on them. In addition, libel laws that suit corrupt officials are still in place. Lawsuits are therefore quite effective at silencing anyone in Jamaica including the media. This is good reason for government to keep certain laws in place.

I am always impressed by journalists' varying styles and clarity, probably because I struggle with it. But I am most impressed when the truth is laid out impartially. Journalists who become my favorite reads are typically due first to their frankness in telling the truth, next by their political impartiality, and finally because of how they say it.

A truthful and frank commentary in the *Jamaica Gleaner* of March 27, 2013 titled,[10] **"Only in this country!"** said:

> "Justice has fled this country. Good, strong policing, underpinned by the respect for citizens' rights and status as human beings, has also fled this country. Only you, me and the long-sufferers of police abuse, victims of miscarriage of justice, along with the recipients of token sympathy and empathy from politicians, remain in this country....
>
> ...
>
> In this country, seemingly anything and everything goes. Kill a helpless man on video, then walk free. In this country, you can dress up in police garb and grab your gun, then go to a yard and crack the skulls of a few law-abiding citizens. Only in this country could the penalty for that be to simply remove said policeman from front-line duty until the controversy dies down in the media..."

Truer words have never been spoken.

My experiences with the Attorney General's Department smacked of the same corruption that is to be expected anywhere in the entire system. Compared with most horrific injustices, my matter differs only in that I was spared the blood. But I felt the terrible pain that the majority feel.

After the police shooting of a man as viewed by video replay on television media in Jamaica and shown all over the world on YouTube, the justice system proceeded to mishandle the case just as badly as they'd done to mine. Ballistic samples disappeared. Also, what happened in the case involving the reputed Don Tesha Miller, where evidence was deemed to have been planted by the Police, and gross fabrications were presented to the court as fact? All of these were very typical. The fact that no one was held accountable for any of this is also typical. I am convinced that cases are often presented, even at Supreme Court level, with a deliberate intention for them to be so weak that they are allowed an escape route at trial or at appeal. That type of corruption is difficult to prove and escapes consequence. But when there are missing ballistics and exhibits, doctored statements and missing witnesses there are persons who are accountable and they ought to be pursued.

Police brutality

Taking a closer look at some of the recent instances of police brutality, such as the Buckfield murder, the Tesha Miller case, the Bungles case, or the brutal killing of a pregnant woman, who are those involved in seeing to accountability? ODPP, Police, Post mortem department, Balistics department, Supreme Court. Those areas are where most of the trouble resides, not among common civilians. That is also why civilians have no trust or respect for any of those departments.

It is not unusual in Jamaica for witnesses to be killed; in fact it is kind of expected. The very persons designated to protect them cannot be trusted. Their superiors— the politicians and their cronies— are no better. Two or more witnesses have disappeared or been killed on a single case after their statements which include their addresses were leaked while in the possession of the police, the same persons appointed as protectors. It is hard to recall even one police officer brought to account for any of this type of crime. Stories of witness statements slipping out of the possession of the Police and found in possession of persons wanted for questioning about murder; bullet exhibits missing; defendants framed. Yes, this kind of thing happens anywhere, but today in Jamaica it happens and no one is held accountable for any of it. We don't hear of anyone serving time for this type of obstruction of justice. Yet we wonder why there is silence from the public.

Groups like Jamaicans for Justice fight tooth and nail, sacrificing family and self to follow up on matters of injustice. But the deeds are too many and too protected for them to tackle effectively. They know the obstacles, and the fight to remove them is difficult when the powers that be rely heavily on having these obstacles in place. No act of murder, for example, results in conviction if the powers that be want it that way. It also works the other way if a conviction is needed we know what will happen. We know for instance, that the dons will go to prison only if they are deemed by politicians to be "uncooperative." Frankly, whatever the political leadership wants, they will get.

In July 2010, the world watched on YouTube as uniformed Policemen beat and shot an unarmed man while he was lying on the ground. Citizens egged them on to shoot him in the grisly scene.

I watched the video on the television news, and were it not for the cellular phone technology available today a murder might have been made to appear as an act of self-defense. The fact that citizens could encourage a police officer to kill in an extrajudicial manner might sound surprising when on other occasions they shout and block the streets in protest over police killings. What does this say? It says that trust in the system is nearly nonexistent, and the people want justice however they can get it. If that means killing a man in the streets, so be it. The citizens know that the policeman is licensed to kill. What greater indictment is there of the people in our system?

FORGIVE ME FATHER, FOR I AM CORRUPT!
ARE YOU A COP, SON?

WISH I COULD HELP!
HOW ABOUT A BIGGER AXE?
GOVT
JCF CORRUPTION

On Friday March 22, 2013, I read an article published in the *Jamaica Gleaner* under the heading "The appearance of injustice" [11]

> "In 1999, a mentally retarded youth named Michael Gayle riding his bicycle did not give the right answer to the verbal challenge of the security forces, and received the beating of his life from agents of the Jamaican Government. He who posed no physical threat was beaten mercilessly by cowardly men well-armed with high-powered weapons, schooled in the law regarding the arrest of citizens, trained in the science of restraining persons who resist arrest, and drilled in the art of self-defence.
>
> At the coroner's inquest, the police blamed the army, and the army blamed the police; and the stories from those sworn to protect us were so convincing that the coroner's

verdict was manslaughter, not murder. And not one name was called. And 14 years later, no one has been held responsible.

And this is the fundamental problem: The State gives privileges to its own - a fundamental and profound conflict of interest. I am not a supporter of the death penalty under any circumstances; but if a policeman (an agent of the State) or a party political activist (an agent of the party) is found guilty of murder in the course of doing his work, the law of the State enacted by political activists exempts them from the death penalty. Ordinary citizens could, of course, be put to death. . ."

Foreign help with investigations

Foreign help,—by way of experienced high-ranking overseas police officers—has been deployed within the police force in an effort to stem crime and corruption, without great success. They might have done a great job helping with investigations and supervision of stages of serious crimes committed, but they have been rendered powerless to protect the exhibits, the statements, Post Mortem reports, and the witnesses all at the same time in every case. For them to be effective under the existing conditions, they would have to do and secure everything themselves. As soon as critical files leave their hands, they are back in the same old corrupted system. It is with shame to suggest that the persons holding critical evidence should be foreigners. In fact it would be necessary under the present persons and system to remove every Jamaican that has a hint of political polarization from access to critical information—a near impossible task. So we are right back at accountability, the failure of the corrupt politically polluted system to hold persons to account. The answer must therefore include apprehending those in senior positions who fail to bring offenders to account.

Former Assistant Commissioner of Police Les Green (formerly of Scotland Yard) was one of three British Officers recruited in 2004 to serve in the Jamaica Constabulary Force for a few months. Those months turned into eight years. He must have gotten a boxing lesson or two during his tenure. Les Green was seen as a man of integrity, a man who stood up for justice. He was expected to be experienced in the techniques used in carrying out investigations, but I am quite sure that he was clueless about the level, the extent, and the dreadful impact of a culture of corruption on his job in Jamaica. I bet that his experience investigating shootings in London's Jamaican community was a walk in the park compared with what he saw here in Jamaica.

His interview with the British newspaper *The Mirror* in 2013 drew mixed reaction from Jamaicans. There was the usual division in Jamaica as indicated by the blogs. The majority who commented, agreed with him, but Jamaican pride often overtakes the truth. Leaning too far on the side of pride has not helped us much. I saw nothing wrong with his statements to the British press. In fact he was very kind by understating and restricting much of his criticism.

He was reported describing Jamaica as a place "where life is cheap, guns rule and drugs are rife." A place where "unlike the UK, the answer to conflict is very quickly violence and extreme violence," and where "there were occasions when there were several murders in one attack." A country that "once we had 13 different firearms used in one attack on a house," where "you have to have a very methodical mind to manage that process especially dealing with 1,600 murders a year," as was seen in 2009. His statements were not news in Jamaica, only hurt pride. It was true when he got to Jamaica in 2004 and remained so in 2013 after he had left.

His description of the country as "a wonderful place with wonderful people . . . wherever I have gone I have enjoyed it" is also true. I have heard this said from my eyes were at my knees but it serves as little value now except as a camouflage and distraction to tourists and foreign investors who might feel comfort from it.

Les Green brought a much-needed level of professionalism to Jamaica, and the Jamaica Constabulary Force must have seen benefit from it. Yes, his time here was of great value to Jamaica and is not lost, but he must have realized by the time he was leaving that he could not change what he saw without big changes at the leadership level of the country, where he had no say. He must have realized that the absence of proper crime-solving technology was not only a resource problem but a combination of problems too coincidental to have been there without design. He must have realized that his success was dependent on his ability to manoeuvre within a corrupt justice system.

Jamaica has been blessed to have many bright police commissioners of integrity with the will to clean up the force. Why then have they had so little impact?

On March 21, 2013, The Observer Newspaper carried an article by a seasoned and respected veteran journalist *"Between a rock (the police) and a hard place (the gunman)"* [12]

> "I was first assaulted by a policeman when I was 15 years of age (1965). It happened again when I was 39 (1989). In the first instance, I was told, 'Yu full a moth eh bwoy', then wham! Right across the face. One eye swollen for a few days.
>
> In 1989, I was attempting to make a social intervention (ask questions) as I observed a policeman physically manhandling a young teen-aged girl in Spanish Town while a gleeful crowd gathered, seemingly eager to smell blood.
>
> While speaking to one policeman, I am grabbed from the side by another and hurled into the upright of a chain-link fence at a place called Marcus Garvey Park in Spanish Town. Spectacles broken and twisted, bruised on the cheeks and bleeding from along my eyebrows. Policemen with their guns trained on me.
>
> …
>
> The irony is, if at four in the morning you find that a prowler is attempting to gain forced entry to your house, you will be calling the police, that is, if you do not reside

> in an inner-city enclave. There you can always call up the 'local authority' and have matters dealt with…"

I am not for one minute suggesting that the police put away their first aid kits. But I am suggesting that they can only gain the respect and the trust of the population when the system can guarantee justice.

One of my favorite public persons, Reverend Roy Notice, in a letter to the Editor of a local newspaper, wrote on June 5, 2013. Pastor Notice, known for his integrity and fearless sermons of truth in the "LETTER OF THE DAY" wrote under the heading – ***"Rogue cops killing faith in police force"*** [13]

"THE EDITOR, Sir:

> Rampant injustice in a nation gives rise to anger, frustration and can lead to revenge. These emotions can become fertilisers for violence, crime and brutality.
>
> There is a link between injustice and crime in Jamaica. Many Jamaicans are of the view that too many of the members of our security forces operate as a law unto themselves. The accusations of extrajudicial killings, police rape and disrespect for the citizenry cannot be ignored. These factors, coupled with economic hardship, other social injustices and a deterioration of traditional family values, make Jamaica a ticking time bomb."

The enormous respect that I have for Rev. Notice – and I am not alone here – will always cause me to pay attention to his sermons and writings.

Well intentioned print media attracts credible and outspoken people who are not all journalists, some say this is so for selling the shock content, but I find this less so within a Jamaican setting.

The outspoken Rev. Dr. Notice who carried a message in 2007, to the discomfort of some politicians present at a Prayer Breakfast sitting, was again in a letter to a local Newspaper, speaking out. The failure of other sources from the Churches to demand what is required for justice begs the question, why were they so strong when they rightfully demanded an apology or resignation of Prime Minister Bruce Golding, yet so weak when the people are most in need of justice? Where are their voices for the rights of the people?

CHAPTER 12

EXTORTION, KICKBACKS, BRIBERY, AND MORE

Corruption is sometimes quite subtle and well hidden. A typical example is applying for permission to do a project (like a subdivision, a housing scheme), or even an application for a simple building permit. One provides all the necessary information required for approval but then gets the run around for years, until one takes thc hint and employs 'special professional help' at great cost. That problem is transferred to the professional, who provides the same information which was given originally only rearranged in different format as a cover. Approval is granted after money has changed hands. One does not have to be "in the know" to figure out how the professional gets approval.

This is the route often taken by those who are not willing to pay the bribes, but when faced with rejection and losses from delays, will commit to the act through someone else. This happens more often these days, particularly among those who have held out against bribing but have found survival impossible without it. Staying in business often requires this conduct. One becomes an unwilling partner in the corruption process by proxy.

It works the other way too, where bribes are paid outright by applicants thus sparing the professionals any indignity to do it.

These kinds of corruption are not new, just bigger. Once, a bribe had to be paid to a handful of departments; now, paying bribes to more than ten departments is difficult to avoid. Once, a bribe started with what was considered a reasonable sum and a similar amount was paid at each step. Today the great fears are that as an application moves from department to department and the 'kickback' fee increases, there is a point where the applicant is in limbo and may not be able to afford all the bribes necessary to complete the approval. Interestingly, bribes are often necessary for projects funded by international lending agencies that seem to display little care for accountability. I have seen this through poor supervision on their part.

In January 2013, when I last inquired, to have a housing scheme approved one had to run the gauntlet of some 16 separate departments (water, NRCA, Fire Brigade, etc.). The continuous increase in departments required for approval helps only to satisfy an increase in demand for funds to feed this culture.

It is so difficult to adequately give a complete picture of a nation that has been fooled, pillaged, plundered, raped and practically left for dead, all by its own people. One is confused by the enormity, variety and frequency of the wrongs. But, there is no one else to blame but ourselves, though the very poor and uneducated among us are by and large blameless.

The British—often derided as 'our colonial masters,' 'our slave masters,' 'rapacious imperialists,' and more—handed Jamaica over to us back in 1962, leaving us totally in charge. Haven't we made a mess of it? The more we search for solutions, the more new obstacles appear, old obstacles that have become such an enshrined part of our culture over the past 50 years that new ones are merely offshoots that seem so normal. Reversal is so hugely dependent on political will that it may require many generations to adequately bring about a reversal.

As a businessman I see the intolerable problems; I know some of the answers but I can't see where people with the guts and the conviction to do something about our problems can be easily found. So implicated are most that those without skeletons who can command the trust necessary are very few, many of whom prefer to remain silent and alive. But we can't give up. We must at very least start to address the problems, even if we have to do so with help from abroad. International help would remove the type of corruption that is aided and facilitated by agents from other countries. And it is corruption that is the basis for all the tribulations in Jamaica today.

After some 40 years of corrupting influence, the population has adjusted their values to blur the difference between right and wrong, fair and unfair. Once personal gain can be had, beneficiaries don't mind calling most acts 'fair'. It is important here to stress that I speak not just of what happens in every country, but what it is commonplace throughout Jamaica. Stealing electricity is the norm. Finding 400 illegal electricity connections in a small community is normal; finding only five legally connected in the same community is also normal. Handouts are our way of life. Any act, even if seen as difficult to achieve but deemed necessary is made legal in the minds of most.

In 2012, a local television news station conducted an informal poll by way of interviews with anonymous persons on the street. 100% stated that a popular DJ who bribed an official in the US Embassy in order to get a visa had done nothing wrong. In fact they thought he should be allowed to keep the ill-gotten visa.

A typical racket among contractors in the construction field is often engineered with the word "overrun". It is not unusual to see a contract start out at say $10 million and at the end of the contract turns out to be $45 million, an over 300% overrun allowing ample room for kickbacks.

Government projects have been known to overrun 1000%. What causes a 1000% overrun? Such errors are not likely to come from engineering or architectural miscalculations. It is outright corruption; kickbacks also funded by excuses like 'impractical or unworkable specs', unsupervised 'variation orders', or 'extras' deliberately left out of original contracts or deliberately added to justify overruns.

The Contractor General's Office is replete with evidence of these, but he is blocked from applying the consequences that would deter future incidents. Professionals form part of this kickback behavior by endorsing payments like overruns that are obviously padded. In fact most overruns are fabricated costs billed to the taxpayers in addition to what is known to be fair contract prices. These crooked charges by professionals give credence to the legitimacy of the funds paid out to contractors and is one of the 'smart' ways of camouflaging kickbacks to look like honest work. I cannot recall a single instance where a professional has served time for this type of practice; not that an indictment would get past "connections" in the courts in reasonable time or at all. Such is the state of professionalism there.

The fact is that the taxpayers who foot the bill for kickbacks from construction contracts and supplies are of no importance to the powers that be.

Any deliberate strategy that would deprive anyone, in any way, of their right to justice has to be seen as dishonest. Obstacles placed to guarantee this are not only from within the civil service and the courts. Professional companies and private individuals form a large part of this. The power of politicians and their connections is most evident even among so called professionals who seem to have fitted well into the corruption culture to earn their quota of business. I am particularly disappointed when international professionals use their perceived integrity to be part of dishonesty, degrading themselves by conforming to the systems, aiding and abetting to get their share of the spoils.

I refer to my personal experiences here. What is it about KPMG's conduct in the matter in the EML case that points to international integrity? It is KPMG that recommended a time required to complete a valuation. It is KPMG that has contributed in large part and continues to do so in stalling a matter which in their professional field must be seen as unfair and disastrous for one of the parties. Arranging to stall a matter in the courts in their own interest or that of others is not unusual on the part of professionals, and it is as dishonest in Jamaica as it would be in the USA and Europe. They ought to be acting in the interest of justice everywhere. For the justice system to work, professionals must be exposed and removed from their trusted positions when they cannot be relied on to carry out their work without curry favoring and maneuvering between the raindrops.

If auditing companies like KPMG, Price Waterhouse, and Deloitte are not here to contribute in values and attitudes, professionalism with integrity, and to keep the standards high in business, then we don't need companies of their sort in Jamaica. We already have a lot of those here. This is further reason why international professionals should be subjected to investigation, the same type of investigation that I personally called for previously from various government departments and from which I got no response. Exposure of these professionals makes it a win/win for the rest of the world. They are certainly not here to extract funds from the nation in exchange for staging and passing on examples that lack integrity.

Begging again for an IMF Bail out

Over the period of some 40 years we have borrowed and squandered repeatedly, and now we can't pay our debts. We always seek a short-term bailout, which will inevitably be squandered like those before it. We have learned well from the 70s that votes are up for grabs, particularly those of the uneducated and the poor, as long as handouts are made available. The votes and funding from many of the middle class are up for grabs if 'favors' can be made available.

It does not matter if there is no work and no production, as long as funds can flow to the people. Whether those funds come through drugs, kickbacks, extortion, or robbery is of little importance to the powers that be. What matters is that politicians '*free up di money*' so people can '*eat a food*'. The more that is generated through illegal and

immoral means is the less that is required for government to find by taxation. We all know that this type of funding is not sustainable in any society much less in a just one. In fact, even in an unjust society sustainability comes at a high price. High crime leads to little investment, and higher crime leads to even less investment. The time eventually comes when too much borrowing is used to make up for the shortfall in handouts and the country heads for the cliff.

One problem is that all the lenders know that we are about to go over the cliff. Some feel we are already over the cliff, and the result is that nobody wants to lend to Jamaica. Only the IMF is available, and only after the IMF sets the conditions is any other lender likely to step in to help. The IMF is actually playing the role of facilitator that should give others some confidence to lend to Jamaica. They are doing what should have been done over 40 years ago.

We have been to the IMF several times, begging. They know what we did with the funds each time we got it, and if they are smart and caring enough they ought not to be in a hurry to encourage more squandering.

But it is much too late for just a plain old bailout. We all saw the devastation over the past 40 years, and we know that to cutoff the squandering is a deathblow to many politicians, particularly those who are in power at this low point. Politicians will therefore look for any possible bailout so that they can squander all over again. A great bailout is forgiveness of debt, but it is great only for the politician. It is a deathblow to Jamaica.

I hear the talk from politicians that we need “forgiveness”. Having used the funds we borrowed to buy votes so that the powerful can stay in power at the expense of the people of Jamaica, we seek to start over the same game at the expense of other countries and investors. The forgiveness of debt would no doubt allow a repeat of the same cycle—“borrow and squander”, buy more favor (or votes), hold onto power and hopefully get another ‘debt forgiveness’ down the road.

A forgiveness of debt by any creditor would be a huge disservice to Jamaica if the cause of the creation of the debt is not addressed. Any write off can only be helpful if the cause of that debt creation is removed and guaranteed never to happen again. Debt created in a corrupt society is guaranteed to proliferate in the absence of justice. The solution is the same as is required for every area of failure in Jamaica: Do what is necessary to guarantee justice in the long term.

An easing up of the conditions by the IMF would send the same bad old message. After over 40 years of living like a sponge, it is time to pry ourselves from the teat and fend for ourselves.

Meanwhile, I see that the political manipulation of facts is in progress. Somebody has to take blame, and it won't be the political leaders. There is always a way to fool the people over and over again. Already I hear of blame being placed firmly on the 'harsh' IMF. Amazing! We go begging and then want to blame the only volunteer for helping us.

A most apt and interesting article in the Daily Gleaner published May 31, 2013 [1] puts it so clearly:

> "While some argue and say what they will about what a depreciating currency will do, others know the IMF's position is empirically correct and are taking steps to protect their valuables and their savings.
>
> The Bank of Jamaica responded with deferring silence. They know the IMF is right and they could not pick a fight with our main financial supporter."

A blogger responded to the article:

> "We are in a downward economic spiral of low or no growth, declining or stagnant productivity, declining jobs and consumer demand, declining value of our dollar, declining tax base, increasing gap in our balance of payments, increases in borrowing ,increase in poverty, increase in public ignorance, increasing imports and increased debt to GDP. Now we beg "the wicked IMF to save us" as we continue to live an unsustainable life style. We are a country unwilling to face reality led by governments which have become masters of distraction."

It is so clear that if we keep running to the IMF, as we have done for the past 40 years, we are either extremely unlucky or we have been consistently incompetent, corrupt and incapable managers.

The destruction wreaked on the nation by successive political leaders has again put us in huge trouble. The chickens have now come home to roost.

The world from time to time experiences economic crisis. That is normal. I need not explain what has happened to our economy because it seems that we have always had self created problems in our economy from back some time about 1974, with the only exception being the 1980's – early 1990's.

From my experience in business I have watched and learned from the failures of other businesses. The longer and deeper a company stays in debt without producing, the harder it is to get out of debt. There is a point where meeting interest payments and repaying the debt become impossible. That point is 'past the tipping' point. You bleed to death or you crash and die. Jamaica is at or past the tipping point. The ball is in our court.

An article in the UK Guardian explains our predicament simply:

> "Jamaica is sitting on the curb slowly bleeding to death," says a hedge fund manager. "They can remain there and gradually wither away or they can walk into traffic and get run over by a truck. It will be brutal and they may spend a year or two in intensive care, but that may be what they need in order to walk out on their own two feet."

This is hard to swallow. Cold hard facts face us . . . crash and die, or grow ourselves out.

The IMF set out requirements that include huge adjustments. So where is the growth plan? The IMF requirements seem onerous only because we have flittered away our chances in the interest of political one-upmanship. There is not enough slack to continue with handouts for the purpose of funding votes. It seems the only way to fund votes now is to create jobs; which brings us back to employment through investment. That takes us to the urgent and desperate need for an investment friendly climate. It reminds one of the song "There is a hole in the bucket dear Liza. . ."

One would think that this was an eye opener, but weeks after the signing of an IMF agreement I saw no effort to do anything differently.

I am not the only person complaining about this. I am stunned by the failure of the leadership to act and to do so with great urgency. It is as if they don't understand the consequences, or are waiting on a miracle bailout that will never come.

I read an article printed on June 13, 2013 referring to a presentation to the *Gleaner* Editors' Forum by Dr Gene Leon, the outgoing senior resident representative in Jamaica for the International Monetary Fund's (IMF). He clearly and simply explained that "wishing away" the debt was not an option, the problem still remains; without Key Policy changes, nothing else would change. He further simplified it with an analogy:

> "Supposing tomorrow God would give us a wish and that one wish was to get rid of the entire Jamaica debt, [so] you wake up tomorrow morning and you have zero debt," he said, as he sought to illustrate his point. "What guarantee would you have that in five years' time, in 10 years' time, the debt is not exactly back where it was? Ultimately, it is the policies that you are going to put in place."

In supporting Leon's point, Dr Damien King Head of the Department of Economics at the University of the West Indies added: [2]

> "The issue is not so much the elements of the $70-billion adjustment programme. The real issue [lies with] the mechanisms of fiscal governance that got us into this position and have kept us in this position. And if you want to understand many parts of this programme, you have to recognize that… so, if we are going to sit here and try to think up some easy get-out of this deep hole, … it doesn't exist,"

Seeking to put the IMF deal into perspective, Mr. Leon, explained that:

> "Jamaica is now faced with a 150 per cent debt-to-GDP ratio, as well as accumulated net indebtedness to other nations of about 125 per cent, or one and a quarter times what is produced annually . . . this is compounded by 40 years of less than one per cent economic growth, caused by low productivity, lack of competitiveness, rising energy costs, and inhibiting bureaucracy."

As much as I dislike the subject of economics and as difficult as I find the expressions used by economists, I find his explanation very clear. Everything he said about GDP and growth I instinctually understand from my time in business, especially during the 70s.

Growth is necessary to get out of Jamaica's huge debt. Belt tightening without growth does not solve the debt problem. More and more borrowing is not the solution either. To achieve growth, investment is needed. To attract investment, trust and confidence is needed. To inspire confidence, the government has to provide a climate where investors have access to accountability for their investments—less frustrating bureaucracy, a working justice system, a trained or trainable work force, reduced crime rates, and leadership that would enforce transparency and accountability. What we need most of all is a political leadership that will stand by their word and not make unpredictable and rash changes in policy that would create and exacerbate mistrust; a leadership with the resolve to put country before votes.

But we have heard these promises many times before. The leaders have a lot of convincing to do. In this regard, I personally have not seen a move to urgency since 1990, and I get the feeling that many really believe that a 'forgiveness' is on the way. Somehow I get the gut feeling that political gimmickry will be used to make the fall appear to be softening.

As I write, I hear and feel the government's enthusiasm. A Chinese company wants a piece of Jamaica. A piece of prime real estate it seems. But it's Goat Island, a natural fish sanctuary that provides a source of livelihood for thousands on the south coast of Jamaica. The future survival of local indigenous marine life and land species are now threatened with extinction.

In hard times politicians make sacrificing the environment seem like a proper thing to do. Governments in Jamaica engineer destruction of the economy and then destroy the environment under the pretense of saving the livelihood of the people. Yes, they drive the country into poverty and then they can sell anything to justify getting cash to survive in an unchanged lifestyle, no one dares to successfully challenge any sale or anything to bring quick cash when the people are suffering because of the policies they themselves created.

Who can argue against that? Why should we permit the people to starve for the sake of a "few fish and some lizards" on Goat Island?

Never mind the fact that they plundered and created the problems; never mind the historical trend that indicates the likelihood of them also plundering the proceeds of any sale of Goat Island or any other fixed assets.

Jamaica keeps on selling assets as GDP climbs. That is sure confirmation of an economy in trouble. We sold the Air Jamaica lot at Heathrow, other 'diplomatic' overseas holdings, the cement company, the Bernard Lodge Sugar Estate, the Munymusk Sugar Estate, Frome Sugar Estate, as well as major insurance companies, banks, utilities, and transportation infrastructure all by way of protection for the poll collectors. We've sold even more than that, too. Next we are talking about selling Goat Island and huge parcels of land—possibly over 5,000 acres for a start—to take advantage of an opportunity to gather some more cash.

But what will happen to this cash? What is it that dissipated the gains of the distant past that would cause us to need more in hand to dissipate? Soon we will have no assets left to sell, and then what will be left of us?

It is worthwhile here to reinforce the analogy as presented by Dr Gene Leon, the outgoing senior resident representative in Jamaica for the International Monetary Fund's (IMF):

> "Supposing tomorrow God would give us a wish and that one wish was to get rid of the entire Jamaica debt, [so] you wake up tomorrow morning and you have zero debt . . . What guarantee would you have that in five years' time, in 10 years' time, the debt is not exactly back where it was? Ultimately, it is the policies that you are going to put in place,"

To proceed with any large investment without a guaranteed change in the justice system ensures that it will be business as usual. Proof of change must not be by way of words from political leadership. It has to be by action that would give independent, non-political persons prosecutorial powers with the capability to remove the "untouchable" status of all those that exist today. The proceeds of any sale of the country's assets should be handled as if it were a loan and ought not to be exposed to the plundering, theft and corruption as we have seen over the last 50 years.

We don't need more promises; we cannot trust more promises, and we don't need more time to act. Now is the time.

Raid on the National Housing Trust (NHT).

Desperate times show up the true qualities of leaders and the level of trust we should place in them.

The National Housing Trust (NHT), a great idea put in place in 1976 by former Prime Minister Michael Manley, is one of those institutions that has performed creditably since its incorporation. It was as set up as a trust should be. It directed that: employees were to contribute 2% and employers, 3% of gross salaries. The funds held in the Trust are to incur interest which will be treated as loans, and which can be repaid after 25 years in the case of employers or after seven years in the case of employees.

These funds held in trust by government are used specifically to provide housing for the people who need that start.

With the exception of some amount of political favoritism from both political parties and probably some collateral impact from the Operation Pride scandal, the scheme had been of benefit to a tremendous portion of the population. The working classes in particular have benefitted well from this trust.

The very nature of a trust gave some confidence that provided a feeling of security – even to me who never had to use it for my personal housing. It was one of the few government organizations that were considered reasonably well-run. A large portion of these gains were passed on to those seeking mortgages at lower interest rates. Applicants who might not have been able to buy earlier could rely on the trust for their opportunity to buy a home later.

After the hard work and sacrifice by donors and potential applicants, the government raided the coffers of the NHT to relieve it of some $45 billion in order to settle debts, while ignoring the cries from society to leave the trust alone. Assuming godlike powers, they used their majority in the House to change the law that would restrict them or even delay them. Like rapists, they do it with contempt and without remorse. What is to prevent them acting this way with investors—or with anybody in any other matter? They have in the past broken the laws and then changed them to take effect retroactively. So this type of action isn't shocking, but what does it say about the promises made by the government? Who would want to invest in a nation that pilfers the people's money?

The money they took was not borrowed, it was taken for the purpose of paying unrelated debt. Yes, debt that should not have been created in the first place. Any surplus that could have been used to serve more applicants or better serve all participants by way of providing lower mortgage rates has vanished. Former Chairman Howard Mitchell, under whose watch some of these gains were created, should be seething at this. From passing this law, governments will take from this 'cash cow' as they wish without even having to inform the people that the availability of housing to contributors will be diminished accordingly, possibly one day entirely.

This kind of autocratic governance is typically carried out with defiance and impunity. It continues today after flagrant breaches on government property in 2013 by Member of Parliament Richard Azan, the *Gleaner* of April 21, 2013 in a commentary by political affairs reporter Gary Spaulding, [3] stated:

> "While the JLP has historically transformed divisiveness into an art form that keeps the party out of governance for long periods, the panache of the PNP has been no less than legendary in the manner the organisation handles stressful scandals - until now.
>
> "Richard Azan, the Portia Simpson Miller loyalist from North Western Clarendon, has catapulted his party into the throes of the first scandal of the 16-month-old Government. Even as the party continues to be battered in the press and by civil society, the embattled politician appears to be anchored in the Cabinet.
>
> ...
>
> Given Azan's strong support base, inside and outside the Cabinet, his political career hasn't yet been pronounced dead. There is still a pulse.
>
> Why should he resign, as he is in 'good company'? How dare members of the public call for him to quit when resignations have been demanded of some of his senior colleagues? . . . .
>
> What is troubling is that unlike her predecessors, the Simpson Miller administration appears to have abandoned the notion of ethics and anointed Azan an untouchable."

A response on this from Ontario Canada speaks for itself:

> "...Regardless of his motives, zeal must never trump judgement, rules and process. When this happens, and by a member of the Cabinet, sanction must be applied. But, what can

we really expect poor Richard to do if Portia and Cabinet, the ones who must crack the whip, have assured him? "Richard, my loyal servant, you have done well for the small businessman. We will not discipline you but, like Pontius Pilate, we will leave your fate to the OCG investigation. In the meantime, issue an apology and keep your mouth shut."

CHAPTER 13

THE BROKEN JUSTICE SYSTEM

The people who are supposed to provide and secure justice—politicians, judges, Justices of the Peace, lawyers, civil servants, DPP, the Attorney General—are all so intertwined that I would prefer not to address all of them together but rather approach each one as separately as possible. It seems fairer to start where the buck should stop. One might assume that means starting with the politician, and in a sense that is understandable. In reality, politicians in Jamaica (and possibly worldwide) cannot be relied on to hold each other to account. I believe the system can be seen as unbiased only if accountability is enforced by persons independent of politics. Unfortunately, in Jamaica there is no such 'independent top' in the justice system with powers to see to consequence. The civil service in which my father was employed has moved from a body independent of politics to one almost totally intertwined with it. The actions of the civil service are therefore too partisan to be relied on for change. The civil service, from recent history carries it out by instructions from the politician.

Who then is in place to press for change?

I feel that the only tool I have left as a civilian is to place blame by exposure. I must dwell here expansively on the officers in the courts, their corrupt conduct, and their professional incompetence. The interconnection between all in the system will not allow me to address each independent of the other. They are all connected in some way, and as I speak of each I am aware of implications caused by one on another.

Judges

The Supreme Court is invariably where the first buck stops. Challenges in the Resident Magistrate Court and even in departments governed by professional bodies (like Public Accountancy Board) go to the Supreme Court and usually stop there. Why do they stop there? Because few can afford to reach the Appeal Court, litigants quite often are forced to accept terrible decisions after exhausting their assets and in many cases getting into debt seeking justice.

A businessman in financial difficulty knows when things are hopeless for him, and might go into survival mode by taking from the business at the expense of his partners. His partners might have the ability to plunder the company at the expense of the other shareholders. A judge needs to pick up on this behavior quickly. A good knowledge of commercial transactions along with the effects of inflation and devaluations is a huge plus for justice. Recognition of, and appreciation for, the impact of delays on business is absolutely essential for justice to be administered in the face of conflict. 'Commercial case' judges worth their salt must be familiar with the devastating impact of delays in Jamaica when the Jamaican dollar devalues and real estate prices fluctuate extensively, as has been the trend over the past 35 years or so. They would know the devastating hurt that extensive delay in the courts could cause to one party. They would know when to protect minority shareholders when one party is in control of a company's assets. They would be able to recognize the dangers, pitfalls, and tricks used against the minority, as these are done mainly by way of delays.

Unfortunately, one cannot assume that this is to be so in Jamaica because the line separating incompetence and corruption is presently too blurred. For that reason there is little room for honest investors in Jamaica.

It should not be difficult for any Judge in Jamaica to understand the difference between 2008 and 2001 values. He damn well would not sell his house in 2008 for 2001 values because he would incur losses of more than 150%. A judge cannot plead ignorance of this if he has lived in Jamaica for an extended period. I say all this to highlight the point that the main problems in Jamaican courts must involve corruption at all levels.

The damage that time does to assets and the opportunity that time gives to those covering for evil is so very critical in a just society. In countries like Canada, England, and the USA, if such blatant malfeasance takes place the offender is exposed to prison or seizure of his assets, and time is fairly compensated. This acts as a necessary deterrent for bad behavior and an incentive for investors to get into business without fear of injustice in the event of conflict.

Judges in the system hearing matters, particularly commercial cases, ought not to tolerate the enrichment of one party at the expense of the other and under no circumstances should one party be allowed to out wait the other party by depleting that party's ability to fund his way to justice. This is so common in Jamaican courts, and it speaks to the quality of judges.

There is no doubt that the majority of Judges in Jamaica are of absolute integrity; but why should we accept those that are not. Without corrupt judges, corrupt persons cannot manipulate colossal delays, nor can they consistently arrange for unfair results in the courts. This is plain common sense. In order to successfully manipulate the system inside the courts, one has to know who can be manipulated and one has to have access to the persons who can arrange for which judges sit on which cases and when. One has to also know which judges will play ball. This is where the 'connections' to and from the Registry, the offending parties, the attorneys for offending parties and specific Judges become complicit. It is impossible for Supreme Court documents to be continually mislaid by the Registry in the same case without the collusion or knowledge of court employees, lawyers, clients that benefit, and some judges. Judges who are part of this conduct are being unfair to other judges whose reputations are unquestioned. It is therefore ironic that this actually amounts to an injustice being administered to other judges by their own. I don't believe that correcting this is totally the responsibility of the voting public; they have already, to a large extent, been coerced into joining the politicians as part of the problem. Judges ought to clean their houses or be cleaned by independent bodies. We all know that the political leadership should see to the provision of systems that ought to make sure that everything is in place to guarantee that offenders who choose to go wrong do so at high risk. But from what I see, I won't hold my breath any time soon.

Judges are a reflection of the culture of the country; a culture that they help to form whether by high standards of integrity and honesty or by actions of incompetence, dishonesty, or even by looking the other way. In Jamaica, when the man in the street looks the other way, he is acting innocently within the prevailing culture out of concern for the safety of his family. Survival is the most valued attribute within his culture. He is also acting with total distrust for his protectors in the system. When a judge looks the other way, he is the ultimate reason the man in the street loses trust.

To further stress an earlier point, it is obvious that the 'repeated' selection of certain judges to sit on specific cases could only be dishonest manipulation for the benefit of one individual or party capitalizing on the known or perceived incompetence of some judges.

Likewise the presence of fair and honest judges is a comfort to honest parties but unfortunately, among other tricks, they are easily bypassed by simply arranging for important documents to disappear when those judges are slated to sit. I saw this happen too often.

Who are those with full knowledge of which judges are to sit, and when? From my personal experiences I have noticed, for example, that when opposing clients don't turn up for Supreme Court the case is always adjourned and delayed for other reasons. This happens too often to be coincidental and would seem to indicate that they knew beforehand what was going to happen. The blatant absence of one party when this happens shows the level of impunity with which 'connections' flaunt their wrongs. From personal experience in a single case, these types of delays occurred at least seven different times at other critical points, resulting in delays of more than 10 years at great expense to us. It begs the question, who in the Registry is responsible, and who else could have influenced these strange and well-timed occurrences. In my case, it was definitely not us, since delays seriously hurt our cause and our wallets. It also begs the question, why is it most judges do nothing about the perpetual 'missing documents' scam? They just look the other way. Why is this typical 'no accountability' situation tolerated by any judge?

Similarly, it is difficult at the best of times to separate culprits in the police force from any or all the other enforcers inside the justice system. Police are blamed for not preparing and handling cases professionally, while judges are accused of handing easy bail to individuals charged with deadly crimes. The truth is that the inefficiencies and corruption inside the system make this likely from both sides, or frankly from anywhere inside the system. No doubt, many of the escape routes criminals use are arranged through the courts with some influence from politicians— the very persons placed there by the people to provide security and justice.

The trend set in the courts is that there is no decision that can be seen as being nearly predictable because there is no obvious perception of the difference between right and wrong, even among some judges. The systematic abuse of the courts has escalated and been traditionalized over the past 40 years. Even judges seem to adjust to changes in culture that allow them to think unfairly and without consideration for the oppressed. Some decisions are taken with such surprise that many bewildered observers often assume some judges are eccentric, inept, or 'on the take'. People who can hardly afford to go to the Supreme Court and definitely cannot bear the costs of going to the Appeal Court, much less the Privy Council, are unable to fight an injustice and often surrender early, leaving in place horrific precedents for future cases.

Some argue that the Privy Council ought to give way to the Caribbean Court of Appeal because the British Privy Council does not have an understanding of Jamaican culture and therefore should not handle Jamaican cases. Hogwash! They need not to 'understand' our culture; murder is murder. Corruption is corruption. We have created new distorted perceptions of justice and seen more delays and more unpredictable decisions handed down in Jamaican courts than honest leadership should tolerate.

One saving grace is that up to January 2008 there were still some honest, intelligent competent judges in the Supreme Court of the highest integrity who continue to operate as consummate professionals. Honest people have difficulty getting before them. I however hope that these are the only ones slated for the Appeal Court. I dare say that as far as I have witnessed the justice system fall in a single generation, the Appeal Court seems doomed to the same fate as the Supreme Court by the next decade or so.

Fortunately, the caliber of Appeal Court professionals in knowledge, experience, honesty, and understanding of all matters has managed to remain high. As a result, Appeal Court decisions tend to be seen as more just. The real problem here is that this is an asset only to those who can afford the costs of appealing. Getting to and past the Supreme Court is so costly, mainly because of delays– deliberate or not —that one can hardly afford the Appeal Court after exhausting funds in the Supreme Court. The honest person will most often throw in the towel before appeal stage and possibly even consider leaving the country. In effect, this rewards the 'bad guys' (the same ones who manipulate people within the system). It adds to the message that manipulating here is risk-free. What is also unfortunate is that many of those who have been dealt injustice in the Supreme Court, apart from going into shock, assume that the same corruption exists at the Appeal Court level and avoid the risk of even trying. They would rather not risk another unjust blow at great costs in the Appeal Court.

The matter of awarding costs is also puzzling. The court routinely awards costs to parties that are not only unrealistic and unfair, but often so ridiculous that it is seen as outright dishonest. On the flip side, some costs are cranked up ridiculously high as a means to scare one side to the point of submission. Sometimes the costs awarded are acts of outright robbery. Judges ought to know better, and to approve these outlandish costs is an act of complicity.

Another unfortunate problem is that the Supreme Court Registry has to be the most corrupted office in the land. The words "delay" and "mislaid" has to have caused more damage in Jamaica than any other. The Registry is part and parcel of the tricks used to discharge selected cases, everything from petty crimes to murder. From the educated we often hear excuses of "incompetence," and undoubtedly that this is a small part of the problem. But the man in the street knows the problems run deeper: *"Dem tief, dem get buy out"* [1].

The man in the street is disadvantaged by way of education, an affliction deliberately applied by his 'masters'. He understands corruption and he is aware of the "*runnins*" [2] inside and outside of the courts, but alas he is powerless to execute reform. The "big man" uses the 'incompetence' excuse and the 'limited resources' excuse; the "little man" sees it as *"dem too tief."*

Out of adversity often comes some good. Before and during the earliest parts of my experiences in the system, I would describe myself as an unyielding proponent of capital punishment. So strong an advocate was I that I often told friends that I would pull the hangman's lever at the gallows for free. It is my stunning experiences with injustice in the Jamaican courts, supported by the lessons from fellow Jamaicans who have whispered to me in confidence about their experiences that changed my mind. Today I abhor capital punishment in Jamaica. So naïve was I of the extent and serial nature of corruption in the Jamaican justice system that, in hindsight, to have offered to pull the hangman's lever is now a shameful admission on my part. Now it is more obvious to me that had more persons been willing to overcome the fear of speaking out, I would have been wiser sooner and able to take a stand earlier. There can be no greater injustice than passing a death sentence on anyone, using a system known to be corrupt.

What have judges been doing about the problem? As part of the justice system, can they be distanced in any way from the level of corruption we see? Can they be absolved in any way? Are they that unpatriotic that they can see the frailty, indiscretions, and failures of their peers inside the system and continue to accommodate them? They are so hugely powerful that the very Prime Minister of the country can be held accountable by them and sent to prison. Yet Ministers of Government, politicians, police, and lackeys of all of the above remain untouchable.

From my experiences, I have come to the conclusion that Supreme Court judges operate in cliques. Cases are directed to particular judges in a clique by way of adjournments or through the Registry. The cliques do not exist by themselves but are 'connected' to departments like the DPP, the Attorney General's Department, Lawyers, Police, and others.

The system might require some upgrading no doubt, but that will be absolutely useless if non-compliance by those within the system continues. The courts should be forcing compliance by their actions and by their example. As long as interference by connections continues at the present brazen and uncaring rate, we can only expect worse. 'Untouchables' will continue to *'run tings'* through their contacts inside the courts and outside. Irrespective of the great efforts by Commissioners of Police, absolutely no progress can be made if there is no trust in the courts.

Despite my terrible experiences in the Supreme Court that surely qualify me to detect corruption anywhere, I feel that there is some hope, but only if change is made aggressively and now. A simple but huge step would be to have bodies comprised of fearless educated persons of unquestioned integrity, people with no skeletons in their closets reporting to an Anti-corruption Agency. There is great need for this as a matter of urgency; these should enjoy the benefits of the wide prosecutorial powers of the Anti-corruption Agency that would ensure them being spared any interference by politicians. They would obviously be recommended and sanctioned by the Anti-corruption Agency.

Attorneys and judges among themselves can understand that one can argue a point, communicate afterwards as if nothing happened, and still remain impartial. Typically this is not the belief of the average man, so it is incumbent on the judiciary to behave in a manner that the average man can understand. Indeed this might very well be why judges in America are appointed by input from the average man. They have to comport themselves in a manner that is in accordance with principles understood by the average man. In Jamaica the average man thinks *"di whole a unu understand mung unu self but di whole a we tink unu is tief."* [3] Taking the conduct of Justice Sykes as an example, he chose to sit on the same matter after his ruling was rejected by both the Appeal Court and the Privy Council. I believe that he would have lost his place on the bench in the USA, and he must know it too.

Court Resources

Lack of resources is one of the most feeble and cowardly of excuses used by those who preside over the system. What does transparency and accountability in terms of resources cost? So, yes the courts may need some resources, much of which is missing because of the very corruption we are trying so desperately to stamp out. Ample resources were in place 50 years ago, and the funding required to sustain it was stolen by politicians. So as the argument often goes, this suggests the absolute necessity for more resources as priority in order to get justice. But this is merely an excuse, a distraction, which can only be valid if accountability is in place to prevent a repeat of the plundering of funds needed for these resources. The system needs people with the honesty, integrity, and dedication to their country that will help to discharge their duties with the will and resolve necessary to ensure justice to all, but the system will only sustain it if all can be held to account.

Over the past twenty years, as creeping corruption infected the courts, the system became increasingly clogged by delays. As new delaying ploys were developed and permitted by people in high places, the clogging naturally increased. As the corruption process grew, so did delaying ploys. The increased clogging, in addition to manipulations within, caused newer cases to be subjected to even longer delays. Had an effort been made even after years of delays to hold offenders to account by way of exposure and swift penalties, doesn't it stand to reason that there would be a significant reduction in new cases, which would in turn reduce the clutter? And when I say 'swift penalties', I mean doing so while at the same time ensuring that any interference from 'string-pullers' is also exposed and the guilty parties punished.

Case in point, a friend outlined to me in 2012 that he was scaling down his business after an employee stole more than $4 million in hardware. The offender was identified and the police called in. The employee admitted to the offence and begged for leniency. As soon as he was out on bail, the feedback was *"Him nah go no weh"* . . . *"Police seh him wi tek $2 million*" [4]. The case sat in the court for years, and eventually the matter escaped the court system without as much as the complainant's knowledge. My friend scaled down, not because of that single incident, but because of similar occurrences with intolerable frequency. He said *"The fact that an employee near the bottom of the ladder at work can in a few years own 5 houses free of mortgage and brazenly drive a new Benz, not having won the Lottery or inherited anything, explains why many businesses fail.* Simply put, stealing is risk-free unless you are very poor and unconnected, mainly because of the courts failure to provide justice.

Another friend told me about a professional, a chartered accountant, who when caught after stealing millions of dollars admitted to it and explained how it was done. Years later, the case is still delayed. The culprit is 'connected' well enough to get employment at another company and in the same capacity. That type of person will always find a job in Jamaica, especially if his skills can earn his employer a lot through other than fair means. He becomes a good contact for a price.

The gravity of the failing economy compounded by the corruption throughout Jamaica has given the media much fodder. In January 2013, I noticed a headline in the newspaper reading: [5] *"Fear fuels not-guilty verdicts"* A judge, Justice Paulette Williams, was quoted complaining that there were growing fears in St James that guilty men were being allowed to walk free because jurors were too afraid to deliver the correct verdicts. An overwhelming number of not-guilty verdicts were returned by juries over a two week period. She is quoted as saying "Even in cases where the quality of the evidence is good, they still find the defendants not guilty.....So far, everybody put before them has been found not- guilty because they are afraid to serve justice."

Here, jurors don't trust the system to protect them. I can't understand why Justice Williams should seem surprised at the fear shown by jurors. There is nothing unusual there, and she has sat on the bench long enough to know that the system which she represents has failed those jurors. Justice Williams cannot escape scrutiny even after such an expression of concern; she happens to be the same judge from whom I requested verbatim notes and a detailed ruling over 3 years before. As of January 2015, I have failed to receive them. That by itself has certainly diminished my trust and respect for the officers of the courts, particularly since her ruling was one that in my opinion showed a lack of respect for the Jamaican Appeal Court and Privy Council rulings. I suppose the same would apply had the Caribbean Court of Appeal been involved.

In March 2013, on a matter involving a Ponzi scheme, a letter to the editor of a Jamaican newspaper. [6]

> "The taxpayers of this country must hold the persons appointed to serve in our judicial system accountable and efficient. No lawyer, judge, police, clerk of courts, or stenographer will appear out of goodwill. Someone pays them, and I think we have paid far too much for nothing."

Resident Magistrates Court

My experience in the Resident Magistrate Courts is limited mainly to hearsay; I would imagine that the Resident Magistrate's Court is more hectic than the other courts, though. Apart from handling smaller cases, it leaves the perception of being the poor man's place to seek resolution or be punished for the more minor offences.

As is expected, the standard of Resident Magistrate Judges and prosecutors (rightly or wrongly) are perceived to be below those in the Supreme Court. In some cases Justices of the Peace preside as "Lay Magistrates" and pass sentence from the same bench. I know of a Justice of the Peace who has lied repeatedly in affidavits, has deliberately obstructed justice, and who still sits on the bench in court handing down judgments. But sadly, there is no one to whom one can complain. This should never be, but are we to expect different? Are Justices of the Peace expected to act with any more integrity than Resident Magistrates? Logic says that I should think not. Unfortunately, I already know what standard exists in the Supreme Court. Need there be any further comment therefore on the Resident Magistrate's Court?

Since I prefer to back up my opinions with personal experience, I will go no further on Resident Magistrate's Court except to say, if only by comparison, common sense should be a good guide of what to expect.

Lawyers

A link of huge importance between society and the justice system is the lawyer. Law firms and lawyers in Jamaica cannot be absolved of responsibility for the state of the nation today. On the contrary, as officers of the court they have a duty to take a stand against corruption in the very system that provides their livelihood, even if doing so is financially less profitable. They have tremendous advantages that protect them, as they often invoke attorney-client privileges. This exposes them to opportunities that can provide for them financial gains that are sometimes less than honest.

Lawyers—not to mention judges, prosecutors, and other officers of the court—more than any other profession have not challenged the newest Jamaica. They too often behave as if all parties in any matter are people of integrity. Loopholes that could be avoided in a first drafting, when treated casually, will go back to court. Their handling of contractual agreements, not surprisingly, often ends up under challenge that will drag out cases for 10, 15, or even 20 years. They know the true state of corruption in the system; they know that often judges will treat it as casually as some lawyers wish. They know of the high level of incompetence in the system, and they are aware that they will be the biggest winners in a case that is haunted with delays.

Most law firms in Jamaica carry a big stick (some much bigger than others) and the reasons are obvious. In most countries crime in any form is the lawyers' mint, but where there is corruption the lawyers shouldn't plead ignorance. It begs questions relative to Jamaica, such as who protected David Smith of Olint as he fleeced trusting investors of millions? What law firm (or firms) was involved? Who introduced David Smith to the bankers in TCI, and what position of responsibility does that person hold in a firm? Did David Smith partner with people who earned millions of US dollars from the Olint Ponzi scheme? What is the connection or relationship between them and the law firm (or firms) in question? What are the connections between any political party and these lawyers or law firms? What prevents these persons from being placed in the cell beside Smith? And a most curious question here is, if indeed the head of any law firm was involved in any way, what levels of integrity and ethics should we expect of the lawyers and staff in that firm?

These are questions not likely to be asked by the big guys in Jamaica. But Smith is in prison in the USA because of the damage he did to American citizens. Somebody ought to answer for Jamaicans. The laundering in these Ponzi schemes was damaging to Jamaica and Jamaicans local and overseas and lawyers can't be assumed innocent here.

OCG (Office of the Contractor General)

The area of Contracts is possibly the avenue through which the most corruption between government and the private sector travels.

It seems so odd that an Office in a Department of Justice—placed there for the purpose of seeing to accountability and transparency in the government, with particular responsibility for accountability in the costing, tendering, execution of contracts and selection of contractors— can be so different from every other justice division in its reputation for integrity. The Office of the Contractor General is the only office within the justice system and within the entire civil service that escapes the perception of serious corruption.

It is no accident that I heard little about the Office of the Contractor General despite its existence from as far back as 1983. The OCG, as it is called, was formed from recommendations by former Prime Minister Edward Seaga who had concerns about the "lack of probity in the award of Government contracts in Jamaica, and the need for a Commission of the Contractor General to deal with the problem." But the difference between corruption in 1983 and 2013 is the difference between chalk and cheese. So inconspicuous was the OCG that its existence slipped me until Greg Christie's arrival.

Since Greg Christie was appointed to the Office of the Contractor General in 2005, its reputation has been nothing short of exemplary. I had intended when writing not to dwell too much on the great achievements in areas like sports and music or on other positives that might continue to distract us from the terrible path my generation has taken, but I can't resist looking at an office of which we are so proud headed by a man with guts and a true patriot of Jamaica. Christie is a man who served his country above self despite the risks, a man who could not have handled his job with such fearless resolve without the support of his family. So often we see the man and neglect to see those who stand with him, face persecution, ridicule and risk along with him. My gratitude to them, and in Jamaican expression: *"nuff respect."*

A media news print in referring to the man "Dirk Harrison" who was to head the OCG on the departure of Greg Christie said candidly: [7]

> "His appointment comes in the wake of the departure of the controversial Mr. Greg Christie, whose seven-year tenure was characterized by an arrogant but well-meaning boldness in the face of withering criticism from administrations both green and orange JLP & PNP...Dirk Harrison ought not to be baited into trying to fill Mr. Christie's shoes but define his own legacy. We expect him to be unwaveringly courageous in the face of criticism from government ministers and other officials who would rather he turn a blind eye to stipulations. . ."

Another article written by a respected veteran Journalist states: [8]

> "People in positions of power and responsibility in the public service will bow to the politicians who ask them to bend the rules and to facilitate their whims and fancies because they would rather keep their cushy jobs rather than fight any corrupt encroachments.
>
> This is why this country does not begin to realise the value it has in Greg Christie. We will never begin to understand what a treasure Greg Christie is and we can never

> pay him enough for his uncommon courage, fearlessness, inflexible commitment to integrity and even his feisty temperament..."

Under the heading ***"Greg Christie hits bull's eye"*** [9]and published July 1 2012 in the Daily Gleaner, the same respected veteran Journalist contributor continued in what I consider an excellent read:

> Greg Christie departed from the usually myopic way in which the corruption discourse is conducted in Jamaica, which is to focus purely on the institutional and legal factors, while ignoring underlying moral and cultural issues. He gave a most nuanced, sophisticated and philosophically sound analysis of Jamaica's corruption challenge.

The Ministry of Justice

Mark Golding is well known to be a bright attorney who had made successful investments in the area of finance and can be described as an attorney who is strong in the drafting of agreements and contracts. He is also known as a supporter of the governing PNP. But before I give any further opinion on what to expect from him, we should look at what he was handed and who preceded him over the previous 20 or so years.

Mark Golding took over the role of Minister of Justice from Delroy Chuck, who is also an attorney and an opposition Member of Parliament for more than 20 years. Mr. Chuck held the post of Minister of Justice for a short period of about 6 months, and this reasonably short stint as Minister of Justice, to some extent, forgives him for the state of that office even as the level of corruption remained unabated during his watch. If change occurred it was not conspicuous enough to notice. He was therefore not allowed a fair opportunity to accomplish considerable transformation. His reputation for integrity is not in question here. However, as a longstanding attorney and Member of Parliament, his voice against the scourge of corruption within the political parties has had no impact. His is just another voice in the chorus. I quite understand how the politics works; good people, surrounded by wolves, are much safer feeding with the pack than trying to curb the pack's voracious appetites for power and enrichment. Those like Mr. Chuck are outnumbered, possibly because they waited too long to stand.

Prior to holding the position of Minister of Justice, Mr. Chuck spoke through his articles and at functions regarding the lack of will as our leaders saw the country run amok with murders, larceny, Police brutality, and extrajudicial killings.

Surely, Mr. Chuck in his profession as an attorney has been long aware of the level of unchecked corruption that has eaten away at the civil service. He has seen it become the norm in society while the government is unable or unwilling to hold to account those in the very position appointed to give us justice. Back in November 15, 2000 I read an article by Delroy Chuck that I thought then was somewhat overstated. At that time I 'brushed' it aside. I had not yet felt the brutal impact of injustice

But in 2008 I searched for it again. I found it through Google and was surprised by his accuracy. I was wrong back in 2000; Delroy Chuck was spot on. His foresight was obviously better than mine, and I figured that I owed him an apology. It is not often that I think in praise of post Independence politicians, but in 2000 I saw the bad and not the extent, possibly because I was not familiar with happenings in the courts and I had by then been accustomed to taking what politicians say with a grain of salt. I had to again peruse Chuck's article. He was obviously aware of and unhappy with the level corruption and in fairness to him I must give his full context.

His 2000 article titled '*The will to fight corruption*' [10] stated in part: "At last, I hope, the country is waking up to the frightening spectre of corruption. Indiscipline, criminality, corruption and crassness have become so embedded in our social fabric and political culture that only a national effort can successfully eschew them. We must summon the courage and the will, and find the mechanisms, to fight and curb these social cancers; otherwise, we would have failed in our duty to ourselves, to one another, to our country and future generations."

...."The political culture that breeds patronage, tribalism, corruption, indiscipline and divisiveness cannot take our country forward. It may help to win elections but in the long run it creates the environment for crookedness and criminality. The electoral process that facilitates irregularity, malpractice and corruption sets the stage for corrupt government" ...

"What moral authority do our political leaders have when they speak out against thuggery and indiscipline after the charade of the recent election? Why should the rest of society take our politicians seriously if and when they initiate and promote the fight against crime and indiscipline when their very political authority has its genesis and foundation in dishonesty, thuggery and corruption?"...

That was in year 2000.

Mr. Chuck's outburst in 2011 about his abhorrence for the state of corruption within the Supreme Court was again like water on a duck's back. At best, he had created only a 'perception' of having the will to speak about change.

An October 2011 article by *Gleaner* writers Arthur Hall and Nedburn Thaffe titled "Corruption Choking the Courts" [11] featured Minister Chuck during his brief tenure. Of particular interest also was the response from the comments, which speak for themselves. "It is for this reason that one of the priorities of my ministry under our Justice Reform Programme is to build trust and confidence in the justice system," said Chuck as he told the graduates that they are entering a system that is being threatened by corruption. "There is corruption within the court and the justice system, where the police have been paid to say they cannot find a witness, or persons have been paid to have documents destroyed - amongst many other things," said Chuck

...."Cases languish on the books for years with very little progress, clients become frustrated and cannot move on with their lives, sometimes they appease their grievances by taking justice into their own hands," added Chuck. He noted that developments in the system leave lawyers with a bad reputation as being of no help while the justice system gets a bad reputation of being of no use. "What I'm asking you, what I'm exhorting you, do not be tempted to contribute to the problems of the after Justice system." He told the graduates that if Jamaica cannot remove corruption from its justice system, it is unlikely that corruption will be removed from anywhere else.

It was uncanny there how Minister Chuck snuck on his political cap, avoiding the fact that widespread corruption was not likely if judges known to be of integrity and fair play were conspicuously in place. In typical Jamaican political style Mr. Chuck softened. He was being much too kind to the judges or at the very best, non-confrontational.

The comments posted below the article are particularly telling. Comments on blogs often show a kind of awareness, cynicism and distrust, mixed with intelligent deductions and keen solutions which are so often, discarded speedily by our leadership. One user wrote:

> *182 missing children - NOT ACCOUNTED FOR - last year alone!5 Billion in praedial larceny each year!$50,000 dollars in gold missing from the Half Way Tree Police Station. A whole beach missing! A whole convention center of missing chairs and rugs! Over 80 gangs in Jamaica doing more dirty deeds... murder and mayhem! Churches have to have burglar bars and alarms! Court cases can take as much as a decade long! Trafigura & light bulb schemes!*

Another sagely noted:

> *Not all instances of corruption have to do with the lack of opportunities or your " right environment." Many very wealthy and greedy Jamaicans in spite of their wealth continue to be very corrupt.*

Another summed it up best, perhaps:

> *Where in Jamaica, pray tell, is there no corruption?*

Previous to Mr. Chuck, Mr. A J Nicholson was the Minister of Justice. Heading up such a critical department in a country as corrupt as Jamaica requires more than integrity, it requires the will to stand up to political party influence, and it requires the will to stamp it out. Mr. Nicholson's political Party led Jamaica for some 18 consecutive years during which most of the decline took place. Was Mr. Nicholson therefore a contributor to the problem? As Minister of Justice he had a duty to act in the interest of Jamaica in a way that would see to justice and stamp out corruption from all departments, especially the courts. It didn't happen.

Mr. Chuck passed the baton to Mark Golding of the newly appointed PNP government and he wasn't long in his post when he spoke at a function among judges. The press reported on this on February 12, 2012 under the title - Integrity Of Justice System Intact.[12] He started by outlining a number of measures to improve Jamaica's justice system.

Responding to the United Nations Development Programme (UNDP's) Citizen Security Survey results on the justice system in the Caribbean, Minister of Justice Mark Golding, chose to look at the state of the justice system from an optimistic point of view; clearly a political view point.

The Minister preferred to say he saw the glass as "half full". With the exception of Minister Chuck, I don't think other Ministers of Justice have seen it any other way since independence. I call this '*fool di people politics*', a practice certainly not suited to someone in charge of justice but then, why disturb the status quo? Why remove power and control from the hands of the politicians'? What Minister Golding should have said was that for 36.3 per cent of judges to be corrupt, was absolutely unacceptable:

> "The minister went on to sound pleased since this was consistent with the 2007 Jamaica Justice System Reform Task Force Report that acknowledged the tradition of judicial probity among Jamaican judges, and which stated that "the greatest strength of the Jamaican justice system is the

> widespread confidence and belief in the integrity and commitment of the judiciary".

He seemed unhappy to accept the validity of the UNDP report which implied that some "57 per cent of Jamaicans believed that the justice system was corrupt". As politicians do so well, manipulating words, selectively, he implies that "After wide consultation, the Jamaica Justice System Reform Task Force Report (2007) did not make any suggestion of the 'Court System' being corrupt". In other words, the report was a reference to the justice system and not the judges. How consoling!

The Minister went on to state that:

> "In our 50 years since Independence, there has only been one incident in which corruption has been raised with regard to the judiciary - a magistrate who was convicted and sentenced to a term of imprisonment, over a decade ago. From my own perspective, having worked in the legal profession for well over 20 years, I have neither directly experienced nor heard of specific instances of judicial corruption."

What was the Minister saying there? Did he expect the untouchables to be sanctioned? Did he mean that all was well and acceptable with the judges? He had to know that one of the reasons for corruption in the courts was because not enough judges were being held to account for corruption?

> The Minister appeared to disagree that the system was "plagued by systemic corruption, but he conceded that the country's legal system was still faced with many challenges that cause delays, frustrations, and sometimes injustice.". . . .
>
> "It may be that the level of acquittals in the court, weaknesses in the collection of evidence, well-known cases of fabrication of evidence, difficulties in securing witnesses due to fear of reprisals and the like, and the inordinate delays

> in disposing of cases are factors impacting public perception and these statistics. The perceptions reflected in the survey statistics may have more to do with the existing weaknesses in the justice system rather than actual corruption".

I am stunned by the level of naivety here. I must ask: In what country does the Minister actually reside?

It is amazing that only the Minister and those who might comprise part of corruption enhancement fail to see that judges have presided over enforcing the laws, passing judgments for decades, in the most corrupt country in the English-speaking Caribbean. Despite their input, corruption has increased exponentially inside and outside the court houses during their times on the bench. It is just so damn clear!

Every country that has fought off the scourge of corruption has had to find the will to purge the judiciary of corruption, and the USA is no exception. In such countries, corruption had become so bad that the judges themselves had to possess the will and resolve to overcome fear of death. I know of no other country on earth with the level of corruption for as long as in Jamaica, yet we continue to pretend that there are angels on the court's benches. We must be special.

Surely *36.3* per cent corruption would place the Supreme Court conservatively where I think it is now. I am not the only victim still waiting on justice! Injustice is being served daily in the Supreme Court, under the very noses of over 30 judges, who despite their stated competence and integrity have been unable to slow its escalation even for a while. Who could ever believe that a society riddled with crime and corruption—one of the highest in the world, with politicians bypassing accountability in the Courts for decades and with no end in sight, with connected persons charged with gruesome murders, out on bail for years and not expecting to get to Court before witnesses lose their memories and documents disappear—would just happen to have a full complement of judges, all of high integrity?

Had the Minister stated that there were some on the bench who personally act with integrity but look the other way when their peers sin, I would quickly believe that. But while doing so, I wouldn't even hazard a guess at the percentage.

The minister did not take leave of his speech to the Judges just yet. He continued:

> "As for the view that powerful criminals go free, the justice minister said there was no doubt that the task of securing convictions of financially well-resourced, ruthless criminals is particularly difficult".
>
> "Nevertheless," he argued, "There have been high-profile cases where successful prosecutions have been mounted and the convicts are serving long sentences.

Minister Golding continued to disappoint me there. What '*high-profile cases*' was he talking about? A couple of dons who were known to have fallen out of grace with their politician bosses? He was certainly not referring to David Smith of the Olint Ponzi scheme or any of the other multiple of financial criminals who operated in Jamaica. He knows that the Jamaican justice system did nothing about them. The USA had to put David Smith away. The other Ponzi scheme operators have avoided conviction in the Jamaican system more than seven years after all the schemes crashed.

The don he was referring to, Dudus Coke, was so well protected by the Jamaican corruption that he never had an indictment in Jamaica. He was only convicted in the USA after pressure was applied to his Jamaican protectors here.

> The minister continued . . . "the negative perceptions may be altered by improving the capacity and efficiency of law enforcement and the legal system so that users of the courts have greater confidence in the services being provided." . . ."The justice minister also said that the Jamaican Government is working with its bilateral partners to increase the capacity within the police force in relation to intelligence, investigations, and case preparation. . . "The Evidence Act

is being amended to allow video-recorded evidence as a counter to the intimidation of witnesses. We will be reviewing Jamaica's criminal procedures to eliminate steps which produce unnecessary delays."

"Greater emphasis is being placed on the training of judges and other judicial officers employed in the court system."

I read the media outline of this presentation that was made to the Judges and only realized that I was not losing my mind when I read the following comments on the Ministers speech:

"*Sir, you can believe whatever you like. As my friend Motty Perkins once said, as long as politics can influense the choosing of judges and the acceptance or rejection our courts the justice system is corrupt.*"

"*i can distinctly recall when people were saying a couple of years ago that the police force was corrupt a lot of big people in society coming out and saying this was rubbish. they are singing a different tune today. how many instances of corruption does it take to establish corruption in the system, 1 or 1 million senator golding? because i havent heard the queen pass gas does not mean she does not do it. i have been before the court more than a few times and i wouldnt like to relate here what i have seen transpire. someone i know has personally told me that a lawyer said to him he can whisper in a judges ear and get the decision he desires. we must speak the truth my dear sir and i suggest to you that some of what you say in the article is not the whole truth.*

"*I certainly hope Mark Golding will improve the justice system because I certainly do not agree with the claim that the integrity of the justice system is intact.*"

"*This editorial, its content, and Mr. Golding's response don't sit well with me. It was difficult to read. Simply because*

I had to contain myself (in spite of my inclination to do otherwise) in order to get through it.

Mr. Golding, if this judical system looks good to you, it must be on paper only.

There most definitely exists a 'great divide' between the haves and the have nots. The uptowners and the average 'down trodden Jamaican'. Because the average/majority of Jamaicans are having a warm time with this so called justice system.

All these (many/vast and varied) things which you cite as weaknesses which need to be [strengthened] to improve the system is rather curious to me. Because they are not in fact extricated, removed or independent parts of 'the judicial system'. Are they? (do we need witnesses [preferably live unintimidated ones] to testify at trials in order for law and justice to be meted out? Do we need judges to not act in a corrupt or destructive manner? Including taking bribes, or themselves not to be intimidated, threatened, coerced, harmed or strong armed by dirty politicians/government? Do we need to look at the full picture, instead of regarding 'the justice system' as only one isolated little aspect of it? That which you deem to be intact?!)

Mr. Golding, the whole thing works hand in hand. All these parts need to work together in order for the whole machine to operate or function properly.

People arrested and thrown in jail/prison for 6, 12, 15 years without as much as a bail hearing or an eye turned to their case is injustice, and it's a part of the justice system. Not separate.

If ever there is a case of 'who feels it knows it' this is it.

The people in the street say the justice system is corrupt. Because the justice system is corrupt. They are the ones who are put through this system. They are the ones who are made to endure it.

No 'sensitization' write up or hand book from Paula Lewellyn can solve or even remotely alleviate the problem.

The DPP, the judges and the justice system are the ones who desperately need 'sensitivity training' not the other way around. As the people are already profoundly/intimately sensitized to the hell called 'the Jamaican justice system'.

He who feels it knows it Mr. Golding... So let's not try to re-invent the wheel here. Or try to call a spade a shoe lace, or try to explain away corruption and the hunger for sanity.

I really would like to indulge and even support your disposition Mr. Golding.

But when you say/think 'the glass is half full' what exactly is it half full of?

Is it half full of blood, sweat or tears Mr. Golding?"

"My Gosh!!

How could you even try to pull this garbage on the people Mr. Golding?

How could you even stand to utter such things out of your mouth. In this country, in this time, and in this situation and condition which the people live?

I only hope you realize that by saying this, that you yourself are shouting from the mountain top that YOU ARE COMPROMISED. YOU ARE NOT INTACT. And should not be trusted with this post of ministry which you now hold.

This inandof itself is a startling, disappointing and painful revelation Mr. Golding.

What scale are you using to judge "intact"?

THE SCALE OF OPPOSITES???"

"to whom it may concren[concern] yes there is corruption in the justice system.and also in the government the police

> *the lawyers .then how can the people out there can respect the law if those who should governer the people they are corrupt and with respect for the people of jamaica. jamaica will never come back as in the 50th and 60th and 70th because you have those gangster running the country..may god have mercy on the people of jamaica.to show corruption look what are happening with this government their pay and not evening start to do the people work. and a counrty without money.they should be ashame."*

Again, we must look at the internet commenters responding here. They tell a lot.

It is a fact that every Ministry and indeed every aspect of life in Jamaica is seriously affected negatively by the failure of the justice system. The female employee who is required to have sex with her boss in order for her to get a promotion may well be expecting fairness from inside the Ministry of Education, but the enforcers fall under the Ministry of Justice. And if you say that she is part of the cause of failure because she should have reported it, I ask you this: Where would she get justice? If she reports this, can she trust the police? Can the police put trust in the government or any of the courts? And even if so, at what cost does this come to the woman? What if the tables were turned and the woman had falsely accused her boss of harassment? Where would he get the justice required to clear his name?

Whatever is required to cause complainants to speak without fear has to be installed before we can get anywhere. It is worth repeating here that the single most impacting act that would positively affect the entire country is to clean up the justice system, starting at the top. What amounts to castration of the Contractor General and refusal to empower independent agencies with authority to clean up, guarantees, at the very least, business as usual.

Any person with the standard of education and intelligence qualified to hold a position of a Minister of Government is expected to speak intelligently and with honesty and do so with the facts at hand. It is impossible for me to believe that average people in Jamaican society know more about what is happening in the courts than the Minister of Justice, who has lived in Jamaica for decades, and who has been a practicing lawyer in Jamaica for much of his adult life.

Despite my disappointment in him, I still have to clutch to the belief that he is not dishonest. For that reason, I would rather see a naïve yet honest person in power than a smart and corrupt one. Sadly this has been a forty-year problem in Jamaica which we keep fixing with band aids.

The expectations from this is that Mark Golding's brilliance in law will continue to be seen in his ability to do things like preparing amendments and new laws, thereby leaving corruption in Jamaica to fall victim to his naivety. The message remains 'business as usual'.

It is easy to have a 'soft' person handle a smooth running operation and keep it on track. It is impossible to reverse the devastation from corruption that has become part of the culture over a period of 50 years, supervised by someone who is soft and out of touch with reality, while at the same time is expected to have the will to stand up, prosecute, indict, those among his peers who are already shamelessly supporting the very corrupt practices he is duty bound to eradicate

Director of Public Prosecutions (DPP).

The Director of Public Prosecutions (DPP) holds the position in the Jamaican Justice system matched only by God. No one else has the power to influence who he or she prosecutes and who not to prosecute.

The argument for this power is somewhat understandable; the DPP ought to be out of reach of all influence including political influence. That is what we all want to see, but I am bothered by the frequency by which people of 'importance' and 'connections' escape the arms of the law. There is no better example than the frequency with which this occurred after some 40 matters were investigated by the Contractor General and recommendations for prosecution made. I can't recall even two of those matters being prosecuted in that five-year period. The people of Jamaica are aware of the level of corruption in society; they resent the disparity in prosecutions and convictions between connected and unconnected; they have grown to settle for a level where they expect selective behavior like poor defenses followed by no convictions, but now they have to also accept a regular no-prosecution situation.

Yes, the tampering with evidence, the disappearing files, the unavailability of pathologists, disappearance and tampering of forensic exhibits, dying witnesses, witnesses overcome with amnesia, and delays by the courts are all obstacles to the DPP, and they obstruct justice. I am also bothered because I have difficulty recalling instances where persons have been convicted or even prosecuted for obstruction. This is most common in almost all cases in Jamaica. Personnel, who have exhibits in their care and lose them, never seem to be held to account. There are so many cases of murdered witnesses, and rarely do prosecutions or convictions result. So frequent are these occasions where the law is not applied that we have grown to expect nothing else. Cases are delayed causing pressure on witnesses who keep looking over their shoulders for hit-men, eventually giving in to the pressure to avoid giving evidence. In a multitude of cases documents disappear, memories fade, and no one is prosecuted.

The present DPP Paula Llewellyn has such a dismal record that I ought to give her a fair break at explaining a particular matter that had drawn the anger and shock of civil society. So, to be fair to the DPP and in the interest of clarity it is worth looking at an explanation by the DPP in its entirety, regarding the failure of the system in a blatant shooting seen on a video recorded and transmitted worldwide on the Internet.

Giving a detailed outline of "Why the Buckfield case fell flat" [13] her verbatim statement was published in the Daily Gleaner, March 20, 2013. The DPP explained:

> "The ethics of a prosecutor do not allow us to do anything other than to place the available evidence before the court. We are not telepathic or in control of what a witness is going to say in court. We are dealing with human beings who have minds of their own, and it was quite clear that Det Sgt Kelly was popular within the community of Buckfield and that Mr

> Lloyd, who the police were trying to capture, was alleged to have just murdered an elderly woman of the community.
>
> The prosecution's case will only be as good as the quality of the narrative outlined by eyewitnesses and the other evidentiary material available.
>
> […]
>
> Our inability to adduce the video evidence, which is 'clear as day', if we accept that it is unaltered, draws attention to the need for our citizenry to play an active role in the administration of justice beyond the mere expression of public outrage, that is, to make themselves known and available to give evidence when called upon so to do, in the public interest.
>
> It is unfortunate that this matter, as discussed in the public domain, has suffered from uninformed commentary. The prosecution of any case has to be within the context of the law, prosecutorial best practices, as well as ethics, and must transcend petty-mindedness as well as prejudice or sympathy for any party in this matter.
>
> In the final analysis, each case has to be assessed on its own particular merits and the relevant law. The prosecutorial authority which I head welcomes constructive criticism and will always strive to facilitate clarity in the public interest."

The full explanation by the DPP says a lot. It shows the fear on the part of witnesses to come forward or to cooperate in any way; it shows disappearance of evidence as in the ammunition lost in this case; it shows the problems as with post mortems; it shows typical delays among other things which obstruct justice. Fear and distrust is written all over this case. And it really begs the questions: Was the handing over of the bullets that were removed from the body during post mortem done in a way that is considered normal, and why has nobody been held accountable for the disappearance of evidence as in the ammunition exhibits?

The release of the policeman was not unexpected. Our history explains it and the public anticipated this. The clear message from the current generation in Jamaica is that murder is OK. It could not have been demonstrated any clearer than as in this video. Onlookers who witnessed this shooting were actually egging on the police officer to kill a man.

It is so symptomatic of the type of values to expect from the present generation, and it is not their fault. This is what they have been taught by their leaders over the past 40 years. This is how they see the administration of justice.

The Azan Affair

Let us look at another of the typical examples why there is reason to place distrust in the Office of the DPP regarding improper conduct on the part of political and private sector leadership.

Ten shops were constructed on government property in Clarendon without the required authority of the Clarendon Parish Council. State Minister Richard Azan, the Member Parliament for North West Clarendon admitted to instructing a private contractor, John Bryant, to construct them. Rent was collected from the occupants of the shops by the contractor, and all this occurred with the knowledge of the Parish Council.

Enter the Office of the Contractor General (OCG).

Then, with a full report presented, the OCG sought to have the DPP determine whether their actions gave rise to a Conspiracy to Defraud the Revenue of the Clarendon Parish Council. The OCG also referred the Mayor to the DPP for "allegedly knowingly misleading the office during the conduct of the investigation."

It was no surprise when the DPP ruled that no criminal charges were to be laid against former State Minister in the Ministry of Transport and Works, Richard Azan but that the Mayor had charges to answer.

To the best of my knowledge, no one has ever been held to account on this matter. It is clear that all Members of Parliament are free to build on government lands and collect rent for same through their political party office without following the legal guidelines or any procurement guidelines provided that there is no proof that the Member of Parliament put any of the proceeds in his own pocket. The fact that it is done for the benefit of one political party does not seem to be an ethics problem. Amazing!

I am not alone in my thoughts here. Peter Espeut, a respected journalist, in his article of September 27, 2013 "*Ethically challenged"* [14] *wrote:*

> "Who is responsible for the education and training of politicians - leaders and followers - in the ethics of their profession and pursuit? It seems to me that, whoever it is, is failing badly, because both major Jamaican political parties are ethically challenged."

...Former Minister Richard Azan says he has no regrets for breaking the law, because what is important to him is helping his constituents. And his constituents have no problem with him breaking the law to help them. The law must not be a shackle to progress! They are all ethically challenged. ...

ethics

The trouble is that all of the above is par for the Jamaican political course, and now seems so 'normal' that few in politics see that kind of behaviour as corrupt. People who go into politics for personal gain and advantage are not going, all of a sudden, to be concerned about ethics...

The Richard Azan affair is not over. Despite being labelled politically corrupt at best by the OCG, he remains a member of parliament, and a justice of the peace. Remember that Azan's stamp as JP - but not his signature - appears on rent receipts. Was the staffer in his constituency office authorised to use his JP stamp? The matter is not yet over."

I believe that the writer Mr. Espeut was mistaken when he said that "*the matter is not yet over"* and I think he knows it. . . It ended when it started - as the blog comments tend to confirm. He is either being facetious, or like many of us, he perseveres with a level of misplaced trust that is really a kind of hope - which probably gives some comfort. Although it is the norm for members of parliament to conduct themselves in this way, the folks seem too battered, too down trodden, too dependent on this leadership to risk taking a stand.

The Role of Social Clubs and Charitable Groups in Jamaica

Social Club activity has been on the rise since the late 1990s. Kiwanis Clubs, Rotary Clubs, and the sort all play a stabilizing part. I am thankful for the many efforts on the part of citizens who contribute to improving the state of the country by way of social welfare programs driven by these social clubs. God knows we need them. The great camaraderie in the spirit of giving back to society by way of funding social projects or by their free professional input is irreplaceable.

However, I must admit that I fear the impact of the increasingly endemic corruption around these clubs. They are comprised of some in civic society known to travel unsavory paths, even as I take consolation from their giving back some of what they have taken or earned. Giving back is creditable, but sheltering diminishes their usefulness.

While these clubs try to avoid politics – and to some extent understandably so – they have often utilized the opportunities to invite speakers who are known to be outspoken in their presentations. Clubs have avoided openly criticizing politics but have facilitated constructive attacks through these guest speakers. I can't blame them for this because we don't need any conflict or division within the clubs by what may be perceived as political interference.

Many of the old stalwarts in these organizations have remained faithful and selfless as the need to address the problems of crime, violence, poverty increases. The Salvation Army, The Red Cross, Food for the Poor, Brothers for the Poor, Jamaicans for Justice, Missionaries for the Poor, and Mustard Seed Communities – to name just a few— have done fantastic work. My concern has not been about these nonprofit organizations, but that the dependency on these organizations has been increasing exponentially as the economical and social conditions in Jamaica plummet. While they do good work for the people, they are inadvertently not helping to discourage political plundering as they substitute for what government should be providing from budgetary commitments. Obviously, they have little choice but to tactfully do so in silence.

I strongly believe that charities should work in combination with social justice programs to be gainful. I believe effective social programs must provide opportunity rather than rely on charity. Replacing opportunity with charity kills the spirit in entrepreneurship. Charity by itself will not bring about what is necessary for long-term change, and long-term change must include justice.

Does abuse of charity weaken the poor? It must. It does not provide a solution in the long run. It is a temporary fix, a stopgap measure while the hardcore problems worsen. Politicians like to speak of empowering the poor, but a handout does not empower; it creates dependence. It marries the poor to their situation. So effective social programs must provide opportunity rather than charity.

In Jamaica, compassion flowing from charities like 'Food For The Poor' will continue to be abused by successive governments who have catered to the dependency culture which they themselves created. The poor will thus continue to be less empowered as dependency grows. When this happens government guarantees absolute power for itself as they become the lifeline of the people who cannot fend for themselves. This situation is exacerbated with the rhetoric of "entitlement" which bamboozles the people into believing that they are entitled to handouts like 'reparations' and they don't have to work.

So, the social justice that requires folks to work in a cooperative way, to develop the ability of the poor to rise above their conditions, is withheld in the interest of political power and control. This is widespread and typical in Jamaica. When politicians fail to provide the people with real opportunities this should not be considered as coincidence, but rather, a deliberate strategy to keep the voting majority beholden to them.

What then has been the result? Jamaica has been driven into debt to maintain this culture. This puts a tremendous load on charitable institutions as they try to cope with new and enlarged dependent garrisons.

'Garrisonisation' [15] requires a lot more help than charities can give, and what the taxpayers can't make up has to come from somewhere else like kickbacks, overruns, extortion, scams, padded contracts, or from wherever possible – legally or illegally.

Even today, social justice is practically nonexistent in the garrison communities. It has not been about teaching a man how to fish, but about giving him the fish every single day. There must be a point where the charity donors realize that they are not healing but are simply 'patching' the problem. They can't catch up with the demand. They must realize that given time, as poverty climbs, they will be feeding almost an entire nation which would be an incentive for the poor to live as they are, and for the government to care for the people through charity organizations while they manipulate and control the people using funds that were marked for doing what the charity organizations have to be doing. What won't some do for power and control?

From this dependency lifestyle children grew up seeing their parents and grandparents living in absolute poverty, and they too have to bear the indignity, the contempt and the injustice as they too are slated to be fitted with the same shoes.

It is fair therefore to say that charities have inadvertently contributed to the dependency culture here. They must however, be commended for their humanitarian effort that has reduced suffering and saved lives. Sadly, it is no longer seen as a stopgap or alleviation outreach. It has evolved into a socioeconomic imperative.

It might seem heartless to say that charity organizations contribute in some ways to the further degradation of the poor through their irrepressible compassion, but the callousness and the parasitic history of Jamaican leadership over the last 40 years leaves no doubt that even charitable organizations are preyed upon.

CHAPTER 14

WHO IS REALLY TO BLAME . . . AND WHY?

"He who passively accepts evil is as much involved in it as he who helps to perpetrate it. He who accepts evil without protesting against it is really cooperating with it."

—Martin Luther King, Jr.

All of us who have let even minor wrongs pass without taking a stand have some blame to take. By our inaction, we have further empowered our leaders to bend more rules. Today we are weaker, more vulnerable. Our leaders are more powerful, more corrupt, more controlling, and many who have followed their conduct now have skeletons hidden in their closets.

The New Zealanders who sought to invest in Jamaica lost their shirts because they dared to trust Jamaicans and, more embarrassingly, the system. That is not the message we should send to investors.

Some argue that our politicians are really not leaders; they are manipulators. I agree. They manipulate the population through their pawns in the civil service with the cooperation of the private sector.

Meanwhile, we must always remember, the only thing equal to, or worse than the devastation that has taken place in Jamaica over the last 40 years is the silence and inaction of so many as it happened during those years.

"Those who cannot remember our past are doomed to repeat it," the philosopher George Santayana once warned. If we don't know our past, we can't successfully chart a clear course for the future, avoiding the pitfalls along the way.

Jamaicans know the scourge of political divisiveness and the greed that fuelled the post-independence times. We all know that the poor and uneducated remain exploited by many of the educated who monopolized on their ignorance and will likely continue to do so. The citizens of Jamaica have followed the cue of their leaders; who else should they follow?

Our leaders tore down principles of responsibility, transparency, and accountability to their own benefit. Why then should we blame a child for stealing an orange when that child's role models in government steal millions without consequence?

Yet, for how much longer are we going to be consoled by the fact that it is our leaders who have ruined us? When are we going to stand up and demand accountability? How long before we admit that by our own actions and inactions even the good folks have facilitated and promoted the appalling culture established by these leaders? Some of us may even be so self righteous that we will never admit that in one way or other we have slackened on our civic duties and responsibilities. When we get involved in an assortment of bribes, back-door deals, 'bandooluism' [1], 'links' [2] , 'hustling' [3], '*runnins,*' [4] and 'string pulling,' we are part of the corruption and we are failing our country. When we react supinely to dishonest non-violent acts that appear so simple and harmless, we are failing in our civic duties, and untold miseries must be bourne as a result. When we raise children who promise to make their own future a nasty one, we are tampering with the progress of our country. When we pay the Policeman for a 'bly' [5], grease the palm of a customs officer, 'drop a money' to the civil servant, pay the Court Registry employee to "mislay" some court papers, or get a favor from a Judge, we are perpetuating and further corrupting a 'sick' culture.

How many of us bother to obtain a driver's license? Is it because it is made difficult or impossible to pass the test unless we grease a palm? Or is it because we have lowered our standards to believing that it is OK? Both, I believe. How many of us in government service fail do our jobs unless we are "paid off"? How many files have you moved from the bottom of the pile to the top for a "*ting*"? [6] How many lie flippantly in court with the certain knowledge that there will be no consequence?

Our leaders set this standard, and as a general rule they never face consequences. Because our leaders are never held accountable regardless of how blatant or brazen the offence, it has created a pervading culture of *"anything goes"*. As the man on the street says, *"a no nuttn"* . . . *"anyting a anyting"*[5] . . . *"a di runnins."* [4]

It is indeed a great shame that to guarantee that one gets justice in Jamaica, one has very few choices. One can either take the law into one's own hands literally or through a don, or one can 'get into bed' with the necessary 'connections' and be on the side of the 'untouchables'. Many of us are urged to wait on poetic justice or retribution hoping that 'what goes around will come around' and "the sins of the father to affect generations later". These thoughts smack of injustice; why should the offenders escape consequence for their punishment to be handed to an innocent person? The 'what goes around comes around' theory is consolation that was likely planted in the minds of the oppressed by their oppressors. To not take a stand because redemption will come one day is a cruel joke.

In Jamaica, the poor man and the oppressed man, having waited all this time for reckoning, has wised up somewhat. He can only trust the don as his protector, his only help in trying times, his Robin Hood, his only source of justice. He has long ago discovered that what is for sure, going to the courts without having some connections and expecting fair results is at best like rolling dice. In fact, if an opponent is 'connected' or financially of substance in Jamaica, he is already the winner.

The very reckoning one awaits might only come about when there is total degeneration of government to the point where the people see no hope and can take no more. When they reject new promises; when death is not a worry and is perceived as better than the pain they feel; when life becomes cheap; at that moment, extremism like a Caribbean "Arab Spring" may begin to look attractive.

As Thomas Jefferson once said, "Every government degenerates when trusted to the rulers of the people alone. The people themselves are its only safe depositories."

Lending agencies

I cannot absolve lending agencies from responsibility for this mess. Banks, both local and overseas, have been part and parcel of the destruction of Jamaica. They have capitalized on Jamaica's failure to be fiscally responsible and have profited immensely. They have witnessed the plundering and it is within their place to recognize the folly. It begs many questions - why have loan conditions of international banks' been made so attractive and so easy for so long? Knowing the level of political corruption, why were non-political independent bodies with prosecutorial powers not made mandatory conditions for monitoring loans given for specific contracts? Agencies like the IDB and the World Bank, local Financial Institutions - all knew what was happening as financial institutions raked in huge gains.

They all must have recognized at some time before the point of collapse that the culture of corruption they had encouraged to develop could not change without completely removing corrupt political access to such funds.

Tolerance of the Powers that Be

It is a common occurrence in Jamaica to "shut up" objectors with libel suits that never seem to see a start or an end in court. It is therefore a frustrating waste of effort to complain of anything that will impact negatively on the power of the politicians. Any complaint or exposure by way of the media is usually silenced quickly with a letter from one's lawyer, and we all know what is likely to happen in court. The media are not just silenced for a while this way; they are rendered dumb until a hearing date can be arranged many years later. For this reason, such lawsuits in the courts are for the benefit of lawyers, the connected, the wealthy and the guilty. The court is a sure means of hiding the truth for prolonged periods, sometimes for a lifetime.

Talk show hosts are often vehicles used by society to register dissatisfaction in the most vehement of tones, after which there is only silence. This forms one of the huge impediments to cleaning up the country. Around 2009, some discussion in the press implied that the matter of libel laws was being addressed by Parliament. To take it for granted that there would be speedy or willing action in this regard was naïve.

We have grown accustomed to hearing promises, waiting for fulfillment, and suffering the pain and disappointment from the resulting "nine day wonders".[7] Without doubt, it deters the innocent from speaking up since to sue would likely cost a lot with a strong chance of unfair results.

When is the right time?

It seems that the nation is waiting to hit rock bottom. But one gets the feeling that the politicians are using their smarts to keep the people just above the bottom. As long as the folks have a little hope, their politicians can maintain control. The PNP government in particular is gifted this way. The people seem to believe that the JLP over-tightens the belt and that the trickle down would be better from the PNP. In 2013, as I witnessed the crumbling of the Jamaican economy I was convinced that had the JLP been in power, the population's intolerance for drastic fiscal adjustments by government would have driven the people to the streets.

International Professionals and Contractors

Practically every curious lead we follow implicates the involvement of professionals in nefarious activities. It seems professionals are the head cooks and bottle washers who are common to almost every act that leads to corruption. Yet these are the people most qualified to correct these ills.

From back in the late 1960s we have been concerned about the rising incidents of bribes and kickbacks on government projects undertaken by international companies. As a young and naïve teenager, I saw some of it back then but only grasped the severity of the impact years after. It convinced my boss then to get out of the business he was best at. I would be stupid to think that any such contracts in Jamaica since the 90s could be free of 'bandoolu' [8], bribes, and kickbacks. I am now quite aware that international professional companies play an active part in the corruption process in Jamaica, and no doubt, in other third world countries. Auditing firms internationally are expected to be of high standards for obvious reasons. More than any other professionals, auditors are relied on to see to accountability of investments of billions of dollars. Despite their reputation for being creative they are supposed to be squeaky clean and very familiar with the word equity. I can't speak to how they behave generally in developed countries, but for damn sure they are not seen as angels in Jamaica. Common sense says that professional companies, local or international, would starve for work in a country as corrupt as Jamaica if they didn't 'play ball.' But I had always thought better of international auditing firms since I thought they would have more to lose.

The conduct of KPMG in my court matter could indicate a Jamaican 'business as usual' attitude, and that in a Jamaican setting justice was not necessarily expected of KPMG in carrying out their professional duties. To me, they were no better than the very court to which they applied for relief. Their application to the court appeared to be a stalling tactic – certainly not with equity in mind. KPMG stated clearly – and I believe truthfully - that with their failure to receive requisite materials necessary to carry out a valuation in a timely manner as per a court order, along with their refusal to rely on tainted financials prepared by Basil Cunningham, they should be relieved of responsibility to carry out the valuation. Though I believe that KPMG said this much too late, I believe that KPMG correctly filed in the Supreme Court for relief from the agreement.

But why leave it there? Years after filing, KPMG has still managed to avoid delivering justice. They applied a typical Jamaican kind of justice by avoiding the courts and could do so forever in this matter if they wished. Every effort to have them act has failed.

The messages I get are that court costs affect their bottom line and that their bottom line is more important than what is fair; that they are part of the establishment that can do wrong and be spared consequences; that they do not necessarily form part of those international professionals who we should rely on to raise standards and integrity in Jamaica.

I also find it difficult to understand or accept why companies like Price Waterhouse, KPMG, **Deloitte & Touche, and** Ernst & Young should be allowed to operate in any country - especially in the third world - using their corporate names to enhance their credibility and boost their chances of acceptance, while the head offices in foreign countries remain unaccountable for any negligence on the part of their agents. It doesn't sound like justice to me. Surely these agents operate for a fee. Surely their head offices set and advise on their standards and ethics. Where then is the 'big name' advantage if smaller countries are denied access to their bosses for accountability. Why should any firm be allowed to legally hideaway in some first world country like Switzerland, out of reach of the arms of justice while their surrogates/agents represent them with very limited assets exposed? What could these organizations have that so need hiding? What is to deter the unprofessional temptations that these agents are expected to reject in corrupted countries that relentlessly bury the very things we rely on these professionals to unearth?

The Caribbean region has been seeing an increased spate of corruption in recent years, and no doubt international companies have been having a field day in this regard.

The Cayman Islands and the Turks and Caicos Islands (TCI) have seen many persons trying their luck at corruption. However, they are colonies of Britain and offenders have not found shelter from British justice. These colonies have been prosperous models that have brought their delinquents to book. Their successes in this regard have exposed and highlighted Jamaica's absolute failure to discourage corruption.

Government Boards

Government boards are an avenue by which private sector selections and volunteers sit as directors on boards to serve the people of Jamaica. These selections are done through the Ministers of Government for respective ministries. Directors are therefore selected by the political party in power to serve all the people. Although some non-political persons are selected, the very selection of the directors by a corrupt political party tells us what is likely happen.

These boards are supposed to monitor, advise, regulate, and approve the behavior of various departments and government-owned companies that are responsible for receipts and expenditure of taxpayers' money. The directors are, by law, supposed to be accountable, but they never seem to be brought to account for the wrongs over which they preside. The law permits imprisonment and fines to be applied to directors who become part of dishonesty or gross negligence, but I can't recall a single such penalty being applied. There has therefore been no disincentive to sit on boards which continue to act without integrity.

On August 31, 2010, [9] an influential businessman and former executive of a large successful company, James Moss Solomon, resigned from all government boards with immediate effect. He is quoted as saying that he had lost faith in the credibility of the persons elected to serve the nation:

> "You know we come to a point in time where sometimes you have to stand for something…My resignation is due to my inability to accept the numerous incidents that impune the credibility and honesty of those elected to serve the nation from both sides of parliament," Mr. Moss-Solomon said.
>
> "They need to have more respect for people," he declared. "There are many things going and the nation is getting poorer and poorer by the minute."
>
> Moss-Solomon contended that the situation continues to deteriorate in the face of the obvious failure of the leaders to do what is right."
>
> "He was critical of the People's National Party (PNP) for the retention of former state minister in the energy ministry, Kern Spencer, in Parliament, even as he challenges criminal charges relating to the Cuban light bulb scandal in which millions of dollars were allegedly misappropriated.
>
> Moss-Solomon also frowned on former PNP General Secretary Colin Campbell's plan to return to representational politics after his involvement in the Trafigura scandal."
>
> In commenting on the governing Jamaica Labour Party (JLP), he chastised the party for keeping Joseph Hibbert,

> former state minister for transport and works, ….. after serious criminal allegations were made against [him]."
>
> "It is not the first time that I have had the cause to resign from various positions, even as a schoolboy. If you believe in something you need to stand up for it, if you don't stand up for something you will fall for anything,". . . "There are a lot of people who have called me to say congrats on the stance that I have taken. I can only hope that those who have called would take a similar stance themselves," he said.

What followed when James Moss Solomon resigned? He resigned from several boards all at the same time, yet absolutely nothing happened. He probably expected as I did, that others experiencing similar problems would follow suit. Not a 'single Jack man' followed. How disappointing! It sent a message that people on boards playing leadership roles were not yet committed or ready enough to throw caution to the wind, and risk taking a stand; nor did they care much for the general public who had to pay the price as a result. Here those in positions to impact on leadership were communicating to the public that they were not compassionate enough, not concerned or fearless enough to stand up. They agreed with what was happening or had not yet overcome their fear of persecution. At the same time, politicians were being given the message that the country was not yet near their tolerance limit, so they could carry on with business as usual.

The news media were replete with high praise for Mr. Moss Solomon, a brave man indeed. A few persons responded with 'hogwash' comments that inferred that he should remain on the inside in order to influence change. That never happens in Jamaica! The majority on a board will carry the vote which the powers that be want, and no government department is in a hurry to investigate any complaint that might act negatively against 'connections' within the establishment.

Personally, I am no longer prepared to give any kind of personal time to any department of government or affiliates. I have sat on boards to serve and have seen it all. On these boards the only option I had when unhappy with the level of accountability and transparency was resignation. Speaking up didn't work. When a vote was called for a decision, the majority invariably went with the flow. After all, the flow was with a body that was selected mainly from partisan loyalists by the government in power. The minority that would be honest and act in the interest of country were only there to give some credence to the board and to give the impression of integrity.

Onlookers are unaware that the Jamaican democratic process of 'majority vote' kills the usefulness of honest board directors. In effect, the public is fooled into believing that their presence there means that the board follows the 'up and up' path.

From my personal experiences and the cowardly response of some to Moss-Solomon's strong message, I finally concluded that remaining on the inside of any board within a system that is devoid of transparency, accountability, and integrity was useless. It is hogwash to suggest that in Jamaica good people appointed to these boards must remain in place in order to deter corruption.

People often say that you can't change a problem from the outside. I agree in principle, but this is Jamaica. You damn well can't change it from the inside either. The level of fear and apathy is so high and so politically controlled that when anything is put to a vote, the majority of directors follow the dictates of the political directorate, leaving a minority to ineffectively oppose. This is one sure way for the powers that be to get whatever they want – whenever they want - while at the same time give the impression to the public that people of integrity preside over their affairs.

In Jamaica, sitting on the inside only gives credence to the wrongs. The few who vehemently oppose the wrongs are made to be toothless bulldogs, marked as obstacles to be bypassed. They have no one from whom their objections can get honest responses.

The only option therefore is resignation. While some are fearful or unwilling to follow suit, a message can be sent by going it alone.

Private Sector Corruption

The path travelled by private sector businesses between 1974 and today is best described as a roller coaster ride like no other ever seen in Jamaica.

The climate and messages provided by the political leadership over this period have had little to do with country and a lot to do with how the politicians can retain power. Money in hand, by whatever means, has been a key requirement for holding this power. Where does the money come from? From the taxpayer directly, from loans which come from the taxpayers indirectly, from gifts or grants, from the improper removal and manipulation of funds from contract kickbacks, which eventually becomes debt to the taxpayer. So with the exception of "giveaways" from friendly countries, the taxpayers are stuck footing the bill.

Private sector businesses are the majority of the taxpayers, but they do what is necessary to guarantee that their bottom line looks good. They will adjust their charges for goods and services to make sure of this. Kickbacks are hidden away and obviously escape the tax net, while the taxed employees from the middle and poorer classes bear much of the burden of running the country, including the debts incurred from squandering and kickbacks. Those kickbacks go to various pockets: politicians' pockets for personal enrichment, politicians' 'bags' for "eat a food," and to other "handouts" necessary for retaining personal power.

The involvement of the private sector played a huge part by amassing funds from contracts from which these kickbacks were provided. The extreme level of corruption in successive governments was not possible without local and international Private sector complicity.

The saying that "one hand can't clap" surely applies here. Government needed willing partners to unscrupulously arrange kickbacks. The Office of the Contractor General is in place to deal with these problems, but agencies which are untarnished and independent of politics are known to be huge obstacles to this corruption. Again, the problem here is huge corruption between government and the private sector, both protected by politicians. Government reform must include accountability and consequence, which can only happen in Jamaica when the politicians are bypassed. Private sector persons enjoy the full protection of politicians and will continue to avoid prison as long as these politicians continue to be untouchable. Stronger oversight and support from private sector organizations is imperative for change, but how much can this help when powerful private sector companies and individuals are so wrapped up with government? A simple example here is financial institutions which have over-invested in government paper to make massive profits often find themselves heading for trouble and seek government bailouts. Government paper problems tend to happen when the government needs money. Those holding this paper dare not refuse a request from government for loan favours. Why? Because the word "haircut" from government would send too many scurrying to bathrooms. There are situations when a 5% haircut would put some institutions in bankruptcy instantly.

To make matters worse, the need for accountability has made the Office of the Contractor General become a target in Jamaica to be shot at with regularity. I am not at all surprised that even greater effort is constantly being made by politicians in power and private sector individuals to weaken the powers of that office. As great pressure from various connections continues to be applied to remove transparency from large contracts, the OCG struggles to have offenders held to account. When removal of transparency succeeds it will practically guarantee a ballooning of the same plundering that put us where we are today.

Politicians in Jamaica, particularly since the 1990s, don't want transparency for better governance; their interest is to achieve better control while they hide their wrongs. Even as the Jamaican economy is in steep decline, kickbacks for use in handouts continue to go a far way towards securing votes.

A typical way government uses to hide kickback money in Jamaica has been to sell assets, the proceeds of which are squandered. This way the pain is not felt immediately as the cash flows unproductively from the sale, and blame is avoided.

I was not surprised by the sense of relief within the private and public sectors when Contractor General Greg Christie departed. The investigations over a 7 year period (2005-2012) under his watch exposed a host of irregularities in private and public sectors, sending shady individuals running for cover from exposure. Although his efforts were typically hijacked by the justice system, an important message was sent. There was no hiding place from exposure of corruption and incompetence. The public had the option of deciding which.

I heard a story once of a director's meeting being held where a vote was sought to approve a matter that was obviously procedurally improper, lacking transparency and fairness. The majority of directors sitting were from the private sector. When it appeared that from the opinions of the majority the board was about to hurriedly endorse this questionable matter, a concerned director said calmly suggested that they seek the opinion of the Office of the Contractor General.

The resulting silence was deafening. There was no need any longer to pursue the matter. If it was a good thing, all directors would have been proud to show it off to the Contractor General. If not, there was need to hide it away.

I saw this as a show of respect for the integrity of the Office of the Contractor General. I believe that the sickness in the justice system became very clear to Greg Christie and he eventually saw where he could do nothing about the untouchables. He only achieved some amount of compliance because offenders so feared exposure.

The Church

Among the most powerful organizations in Jamaica, the church carries a responsibility for transparency and accountability which can impact the political leadership enormously, but with this at hand it is so disappointing that they have not used their influence for more good. In a country where talk is seen as cheap, they used it effectively to call for an apology or resignation from Prime Minister Bruce Golding. Where were they before that? Where have they been since? Their silence is part of the reason our political leaders rape, pillage, and plunder the assets of the country and abuse the rights of the people. They too have grown comfortable in a position of "looking the other way."

Despite this, I can't knock their caring for the poor, but they ought to realize that the more they see corruption and look the other way, the more mouths of the poor they will need to feed. There are some inside the Church for whom I have great respect, but too few are busy dealing with 'breakdown maintenance' instead of standing up against the causes of breakdown.

Jamaica is said to have more churches per square mile or per capita than any other country. At some point these churches need to be more concerned about the influence they have in the space that they occupy. They have a responsibility to turn over the tables in the 'synagogues,' in our Parliament, in the courts - everywhere in Jamaica that governs over peoples' lives. Is it that the church is so heavenly bound that it has no earthly use?

While the church may be fixed on that mansion in the sky, it should also remember, 'the least you do for my children that you do unto me'. Do not sit by and watch injustice and corruption tear the innocent, the oppressed, and the 'disconnected' apart. Or is it that perpetrators are paying tithes and offering, so hefty that the church dares not speak against them? Is it that many of the judges and other professionals of the land are themselves the ministers and high profile officers of the church?

As Martin Luther King, Jr. once said, "If we are to go forward, we must go back and rediscover those precious values - that all reality hinges on moral foundations and that all reality has spiritual control."

The Media

Jamaica owes its survival a great deal to the media. Battles fought from the 1970s were covered by brave men and women in the media. Much of their survival required government patronage by way of advertising, and there is no doubt that as they stuck their necks out they risked persecution.

The Jamaican print media is replete with complaints, exposures, and to a lesser extent investigative work. Hearing from trusted reliable and responsible sources replaces thorough investigative journalism . . . simply because 'the establishment' is quite adept at withholding information; and in that arena, although less than in the non-media arena, things are still under some controlling interests within which media contributors have to operate. Unlike in developed countries, libel laws are antiquated and silencing the media is easy, effectively delaying any attempts to get pass injunctions and lawsuits.

Today, just as in the 70s, the media takes a leading role. Even the journalists who were branded as sympathetic to certain political sides seemed to have grasped the gravity of the situation. In recent years, the print media became increasingly outspoken about the multitude of wrongs in the country, to the extent that I was often surprised at how regularly they ventured close to being sued.

But despite the vigilance, sometimes lambasting from journalists and other concerned citizens, governments have haughtily ignored them. I won't pretend that the media is comprised of mere angels because it is known that they go oddly silent at times to the benefit of their political favourites. I continue to ponder why so many readers have treated such strong exposure of incompetence and corruption in Jamaica by the media with such anger in response but with such limited action.

I have seen every possible style of journalism on display in Jamaica: outspoken, tongue in cheek, suggestive, rehabilitative, funny, assertive, arrogant, sarcastic, and more. All these styles are intended to send a message, but they have increasingly been ignored. It's almost as if the taunt is *"you can always stay deh chat, di whole a unoo lucky"* [10]. But most journalists are bound in this hostile socio-political climate where they may face persecution, serious injury and even death.

Having heaped some praise here on the media I must warn that the danger of unfair control over journalists and writers remains in the hands of media moguls who can unleash terrible persecution on unco-operative contributors by removing them as contributors, muzzling them or by shackling some their opinions, especially in the existing climate where the unavailability of justice is standard. This is more damaging in a small country where media sources are few.

CHAPTER 15

CORRUPTION HARMS INVESTMENT

It is dishonest to woo investors to Jamaica by misleading them into believing that all is good and then allowing their investment to be used as a private cash cow for untouchables. Such behavior is no different from a Ponzi scheme from which government and their cronies earn millions to fund their lavish lifestyle. Most worrying here is the fact that this is not the odd case, it is the norm. Should we be surprised?

The business climate as set by government determines how much investment business is done, when it is done, how it is done, who will do it and how it will progress. A government accepts or rejects suggestions from civil society, the opposition, the private sector, or even the police force. When they preside over a climate with its base steeped in corruption, they will attract entrepreneurs who are willing to fit into that type of climate. If the climate favors paying bribes and kickbacks, then that is the kind of investor they will attract.

The 'look the other way' and 'take a bribe' attitudes have created unfair competition in a large way. Honest investors have been forced to compete with businesses which use their connections to avoid GCT charges of 16.5%. Many businesses that rely on the incompetence of civil servants to take advantage of these tax breaks. One of the surest ways to keep legitimate businesses out of profitability is when unfair competition rules.

Investors who are prepared to 'jump in' are usually aware that preferential treatment makes business unsustainable. They know that at that rate their companies will go under eventually, but if they can "clean up" and extract as much as possible before the crash, and get out, then they will still clear a profit. This rules out long-term investments which are ideal for growth in any country, and any such investor worth his salt is likely to take the risk only if he is investing with borrowed Jamaican taxpayers funds. If he has the connections to arrange to be bailed out with taxpayers' money, as we have seen in the recent past, why not go all in?

Honest investors with the best of intentions who seek good advice from credible sources will stay away. They certainly would not be expecting the luxury of anything like resolution in the event of a business dispute with anyone.

Seeking help from professional firms can only be another gamble. Those with international names that are already adjusted to business in Jamaica and have therefore learned to survive inside a sick business environment will continue to operate contrary to the standards their names imply. They will watch their bottom lines flourish until the time when they are no longer able to rely on or afford 'connections'. Presently they differ from local professionals only by name and overseas status. They are part of the same leadership of the private sector and have learned to alter their ethics for survival under corrupting conditions. In fact many seem to have fit in very well.

Investors' losses are bound to include the loss of any time and principal invested; any losses or gains accrued over time before and after any dissipation; huge losses from devaluations that have made delays worthwhile for culprits; and interest lost as a result of dissipation and fraud. After all these, any attempt to recover would likely result only in further losses in legal fees and frustration and anger. All this is bad for investors' health and wastes decades that would have been better spent investing elsewhere.

As a final guarantee of disincentive to legitimate investors, in the event of any problem whatsoever, going to the courts is a no-no. Although getting to the Appeal Court might see your chances improved, getting there takes years. Eventually, options vanish when there is nothing left of assets to recover, and suing for disappearance of these assets will put the investor back where it all started years later. In addition to the risk of dissipation, suing for outstanding uncollected receivables yields no different results for an investor as delays are in place to protect and encourage those who don't mind owing. I speak as *"he who feels it knows it"*.

I don't know of any country in the world that can attract any sort of investment, short term or long term, while operating in such a crime-ridden environment presided over by brazenly corrupt political parties. Our civil service has become near totally political; our departments of justice are openly politically aligned – holding a clear reflection of each governing party; and corruption in the general populace has been taught, tried, and spread in endemic proportions. No investor is guaranteed the necessary unobstructed access to determine the integrity of operations where he would be in a position to detect "chicanery" and manipulations of accounts of the companies in which they may invest. The inner workings of such companies in which they invest can be hidden for years while the assets of the company are depleted without any accountability whatsoever or any consequence to offenders. Here there is no fair access to anywhere in Government to complain or seek redress even as the dissipation is in progress—not to the Attorney General, not to the Ministry of Commerce, not in the courts, not to anyone!

I remain puzzled at why anyone should expect investors to be attracted to a country where information on the status of their investment is blocked even while their investment is being traded and while deals preferential to selected directors are in place. Why should investors place their money where the plundering of investments cannot be prevented unless the offended investor is "connected" well enough? Why should they endure the hassle of requesting access to financial statements that can be withheld for years at a time with the support of government, all while assets are being sold out from under them? Why place their money where there is no way to recoup improperly removed company funds from interest bearing accounts for years? Why subject themselves to a justice system that ignores rulings from the highest possible courts—the Jamaican Court of Appeal and the British based Privy Council—and instead relies on the integrity of compromised judges?

Why would we expect anyone to put their hard earned money in a country where being "connected" is a prerequisite to getting anything done; where survival depends heavily on the fickle decisions that the Government makes, changeable at the snap of a finger; where the same officers of justice who saw to my demise are the ones who will deal with others, and likely will continue to hand the same type of injustice to investors, civil society and the poor?

What is it that would cause investors to ignore the culture in a country that sanctions murder, Ponzi schemes, scams, and other forms of extortion as a normal course of business? What upside is there in a system that ignores and perpetuates the numerous steps of bureaucracy created in government that extorts from the pockets of businesses at every step?

Investors are led to believe that they have refuge in our court system. That is a fallacy. I am not saying that upstanding institutions like the Appeal Court and the Privy Council make no difference. I am saying that there is only a slender thread on which to swing. My experience and that of others is that the Appeal Court and the Privy Council are given no respect at times, a clear indication of what to expect if Jamaica chooses to go to the Caribbean Court of Appeal in preference to using the reputable British Privy Council. The very persons showing this lack of respect today include some of the same persons destined to preside over the Appeal Court and the Caribbean Court of Appeal of tomorrow.

Without the Privy Council, Jamaicans will be able to bypass fairness without fear of successful legal challenge from any independent source. It will then strengthen and embolden the continuation of "survival through connections". Which investor is willing to navigate through all those preconditions?

Yet these only form the tip of the iceberg. Much of the other obstacles, as in that of crime, are a direct result of a failure of the very same system.

Questions from investors

Common veranda conversations in Jamaica— whispered often out of fear of persecution—are about the same obstacles that affect all existing and potential investors both local and overseas. I have sat on too many of these verandas to not speak out.

From these conversations, which are supported by my experiences, I believe that investors would like to have answers to serious questions before making any meaningful and long term commitments to Jamaica. Imagine a typical overseas investor looking for opportunities in Jamaica. Wouldn't he reasonably want answers to questions like these before committing to a deal?

- Where are the departments with responsibility for seeing to the prompt and fair investigation of companies and individuals that move funds around without any transparency or care for the assets of investors?
- Where are the departments with responsibility for seeing to the prompt and fair investigation of companies and individuals that sell the assets of companies without any transparency, accountability or the knowledge of the investors?
- Where are the government departments that should be seeing to the fair and equitable collection of the various taxes that would spare investors exposure to the risk of hijacking and dissipation of their investments, whether by deliberate manipulation or by gross negligence?
- Where are the government departments that would promptly pick up on the evasion of taxes?
- Where are the departments that should be seeing the balance sheets of companies, and in so doing respond to complaints by shareholders who need protection from fraud, dissipation of assets, and even the withholding of balance sheets from investors for years?
- Where are the departments with responsibilities that should respond by acting on the rulings of bodies like the Public Accountancy Board, and bring all the offending persons to book?
- Where are the mechanisms with responsibilities for preventing the unfair and false assessment of taxes from being applied by the tax department on minority shareholders even as information

relative to the assessment is withheld by the individuals controlling the companies holding those shareholders' investments?

- Where are the mechanisms that should uncover information on employee returns, financial statements, company returns and all that is relative to protecting the trust placed by minority shareholders, and which would protect investors from being ravaged by the justice system as funds are extracted unfairly by the Tax department?
- Other than inexcusable incompetence, what could cause a matter designed for execution in 90 days, take more than a decade, result in countless trips to court, cost millions of dollars to one party, and remain no further advanced than it was at day one?
- How does a person who is not willing to kowtow to the culture of 'connections', survive in a system operated in a way that causes any of the above challenges?
- How can due diligence be done to avoid injustices if there is no access to the books of accounts, and to individuals who are involved or implicated?
- Where is the protection for those investors? What is there to prevent rampant abuse or inaction by various government departments, particularly inside the justice system at all levels, the very persons with responsibility for protecting the rights of everyone?
- Where is the Jamaican Diaspora that continues to be quiet, even as they prop up the conditions of their relatives with their hard earned foreign currency remittances, allowing for the escalating slide in Jamaica to remain unchallenged causing an unsustainable increasing demand for more of their monetary support?
- And what are the messages that could flow from the likes of recent and other common occurrences?
- The snail's speed with which we arrest and deal with 'Financial Traders' who ripped off the people (like Cash Plus and OLINT) . . . even as we know that without the US and England, OLINT

and others would be free and still ripping off Jamaican people . . . what then of "Cash Plus ponzi scheme " et al?

- What of the "Trafigura" matter that has typically been rewarded with time and seems headed for nowhere?
- What of the Cuban light bulb matter? And what message can it offer?
- What of the many murder cases that have been postponed seemingly for an eternity as witnesses fret and scamper for many years . . . often disappearing.

Had Jamaica not been Independent, actions likely would have been very different . . . They would likely be similar to that of the British in TCI, Cayman, St Vincent et al?

Total Collapse

> *"When you see that in order to produce, you need to obtain permission from men who produce nothing — when you see that money is flowing to those who deal, not in goods, but in favours — when you see that men get richer by graft and by pull than by work, and your laws don't protect you against them, but protect them against you — when you see corruption being rewarded and honesty becoming a self- sacrifice — you may know that your society is doomed."*
>
> — Ayn Rand

My kindest and simplest description of the plight of Jamaica today is … a country in the hands of corruption, the corrupt, and the corruptible… a country with absolutely no governance, and with no sight of good governance in the future . . . a country with two major parties, neither of which is nearly prepared to offer good honest caring governance any time soon. The people have formed their own methods of governance because they have had no choice. The root cause of all this has been corruption which has become widespread throughout every nook and cranny . . . specifically installed and intended to enrich self, family, friends, party and protectors at the expense of the country and its people.

I am not alone here…

A beautifully written letter *"Didn't we almost have it all?"* [1] was "Letter of the Day" in the *Gleaner* of October 7, 2012. It said so much and so well that it attracted some 22 comments from both appreciative and unappreciative readers. It is worth reading if only to illustrate the differing, if not confusing views, that see us where we are as 50 year Independent country today.

"During our 50th anniversary celebrations, I was struck by how many of our leaders seemed to blame the British for Jamaica's failings. Jamaica had a strong foundation in 1962 on which to build a prosperous nation, unlike many countries which have left us pointing fingers from the dust.

Every one of Jamaica's top-tier high schools was built pre-Independence, and none equivalent has been built since. Maybe the Government was well intentioned when it took over these prominent establishments, which were mostly run by the churches, but instead of building on the strengths of these world-class institutions, 50 years later, not one is at the academic level it was in 1962!

Our business, government, art and culture communities are filled with pre-Independence graduates of these schools. I would dare say the two generations since 1962 have not produced great Jamaicans like Norman Manley (Jamaica College, 1910), Professor Louis Grant (Jamaica College, 1925), Wilmot Perkins (Calabar 1944), Herb McKenley (Calabar,1937) Professor Rex Nettleford (Cornwall College 1953), Louise Bennett-Coverley, (St Simon's College, 1932), Noel Nethersole (Jamaica College, 1920), Sir Hector Wynter (Wolmer's, 1945), Sir Florizel Glasspole (Wolmer's 1922), and Gerald Lalor (Kingston College, 1942).

Triumphant success

There are thousands of men and women, too many to mention here, who excelled despite colonisation and whose contributions made early independent Jamaica a triumphant success.

P.J. Patterson (Calabar, 1947) speaks about black people unable to get bank jobs before Independence, but he, who did a good deal better, does not share his impressive story. Born poor and black, educated at one of Jamaica's most reputable high schools, graduated with honours from University of the West Indies, then attended the London School of Economics, all during colonial rule.

His story is almost identical to others who made up his, and Jamaica's, longest-serving government. Men and women from humble beginnings, who studied hard and attended top-tier Jamaican schools, then studied abroad at the most highly selective universities in United States and Britain, finally returning home with prestigious degrees, all before Jamaica's Independence in 1962.

How different the child born poor today? What chance does he or she have of attending The London School of Economics, Harvard, or Oxford? For that matter, what chance does he or she have of attending Immaculate, Campion or Ardenne? There is a better chance of becoming a drug dealer.

The history of hard-working Jamaicans is long and inspiring, but during Jamaica 50, we heard mostly of those who were poorly treated and underachieved under colonial rule. Are our successive governments, who reap the benefits of an uneducated electorate, trying to deflect the blame that should fall squarely at their feet?

In 1970, after a decade of economic growth averaging 5.2 per cent per annum, the United Nations Development Programme estimated that based on its Human

> *Development Indicators (combining per capita income, life expectancy and educational attainment) calculated for 79 industrial and developing countries, Jamaica ranked first among developing countries.*
>
> *Take pride*
>
> *Mr Patterson said that Jamaica in 2012 should "take pride that more people have running water than before Independence", while more than 200 of our schools use pit toilets and are debating whether to use Patois because our children no longer understand the English language.*
>
> *Imagine the hopes and dreams of the proud Jamaican people on Independence Day 1962, who witnessed the first raising of the black, green and gold? Imagine the pride of Sir Alexander Bustamante and Norman Washington Manley who worked together to see this day they dreamed of as youths finally arrive. Both men died peacefully knowing they had left their beloved Jamaica far better than how they found it.*
>
> *They cry from their graves when you call their names from your pulpits; they had nothing to do with what you have become. You have squandered their accomplishments and undermined their struggles. You have put self before party, and party before country. Our national heroes brokenheartedly would never recognise the shattered remains of this, Jamaica, land we love."*

An improving debt to GDP ratio is a friendly climate for growth. A dependency culture is dead weight on this growth. Our politicians love to hold onto power by creating this reliance scourge, but dependency needs money and too much dependency spreads money thinner. If the balance of dependency and production wavers, so does growth.

More dependency often brings about more taxes. Too much tax is a severe drain on the resources of entrepreneurs, effectively reducing investment and the gains the country gets from the taxation. When taken to the extreme, wealthy investors move to more lucrative territory. In a perfect situation we need a balance with the right amount of social benefit to not kill the work incentive and to not scare off entrepreneurs, while at the same time providing enough welfare for food, health care and comfort for less fortunate among us.

The Jamaican government has constantly searched for money to borrow to make good on the outsize promises it makes to the people. These loans have ritually been squandered leaving Jamaica in serious indebtedness. The larger the indebtedness in relation to GDP the more difficult it has been, and must be, to get the trust of more creditors from whom more loans can come. Losing access to such loan funds has been a deathblow to the Jamaican politicians who needed this to distribute handouts among voters and their 'connections' alike.

So when loan sources dried up, there was no money to fund projects from which kickbacks could continue to flow. Where then could they best find a replacement for these loans? From sale of some of the country's assets? From raiding the coffers of the National Housing Trust? Or by selling even more of the county's assets? Yes to all of these, and no one dares to oppose these acts of government when the people are reduced to the need to *'eat a food'*, or worse. As is typically affirmed in communist takeovers, the powerful assume that no one will dare to oppose them when the people are starving.

And what role do charity organizations play here? Charities are usually run by people of compassion and conscience and are not likely to look the other way when people are in need. They have and will continue to take up the slack left by the lack of jobs in the private sector and from any sudden disappearance of 'handouts'. Under these conditions, their role as surrogates stretches them past their expectations. In fact, I would not be surprised if funds budgeted by government for social welfare get transferred elsewhere knowing that charity organizations will always fill in and not allow the people to starve. From this chain reaction, an overloading of charity organizations eventually results.

Few lending organizations are willing to risk lending to Jamaica these days, so the IMF has become the last resort. No one else wants to risk lending because Jamaica's leadership doesn't seem to have the intention to become fiscally responsible. Only the IMF is available and that is at a price. As is their reputation, the IMF lends under strict conditions. Their tight monitoring and quarterly "tests" allows other lenders the opportunity to ride on their back to extend further loans with less risk of being hurt from fiscal irresponsibility. When the IMF puts a foot down there is little or no idle money to lend for squandering or for funding projects from which kickbacks can flow. But rest assured that Jamaican politicians will find it anyway. This is the situation in Jamaica.

By 2013, the financial situation had thrown politicians into a tizzy due to the IMF's increasingly firm stance. The chickens returned home to roost. Where could replacements for these loans be found? Well, the charity organizations were already giving some help, but it wasn't enough. This kind of austerity situation is not ideal for securing votes. An additional source of more funds had to be found.

The time for fiscal responsibility had finally arrived after politicians over the years, under the guise of caring for the poor, had enriched themselves and their friends. Their slogans of *"power to the people", "better must come",* "*Deliverance, "run wid it",* all did their part to get the votes. They fooled the people as they sapped the country of its growth. But now they had much less cash left to continue fooling them. Much of the assets were already sold to countries like Trinidad since the debacle of the FINSAC 90s, and the alternatives were to sell more assets or to finally become fiscally responsible. You can guess what has been chosen.

At 2015, with the IMF at the reigns, Jamaica is somewhat restrained on the bit, but the assets are still being sold; bailouts still abound; the funds of the NHT and other government agencies are still exposed and abused; and corruption still on the loose. It is a cautious more restrained business as usual situation.

I can't see it possible for fiscal responsibility to be sustained in a culture of unbridled corruption. The indispensability of fiscal responsibility is not my thought here. It is how to remove the corruption that will allow for fiscal responsibility to start, an impossible task unless the political connections from which it feeds are removed. Frankly, I have no good reason to hold my breath for that in the short term either.

There had to be a way to get a free ride to tide us over until the next General Election; and don't misunderstand, this is exactly the mindset of both political parties in Jamaica.

Ah, some new and good news. Large Chinese companies have shown great interest in Jamaica as a great location for investment. This has been so for some years. The geographic location of Jamaica is touted as the major reason these companies in China are interested. A seemingly perfect hub location that would fit in nicely to take advantage of the projected expansions in the Panama Canal and South America in general would make sense.

The Chinese are not supposed to be sitting around waiting on Jamaica to make investments. Business is also about taking advantage of investment opportunities. That is what the cash rich Chinese are doing. When we crash our businesses there will be buyers, except that the buyers will be in a position to call the shots and state the conditions for bailing out that business. China is not taking advantage of us here. They happen to be running their businesses better than us and have the cash to help Jamaica on their terms while making a profit for themselves. The bottom line here is that we have destroyed our economy to the extent that few will finance us, and we therefore cannot afford to be choosers.

Had Jamaica been kept on track after 1972, we would be in a strong position to negotiate —or even better, we could go it alone. The persistent failures over the last 40 years have placed Jamaica in a poor bargaining position. The country has borrowed and squandered, borrowed more and squandered more, sold assets and squandered, sold many more assets and squandered more, borrowed again and squandered more again. I can't put it milder! With no one willing to lend, we are at the mercy of anyone who takes the risk to invest. In this case the cash strong Chinese can call all the shots. We will likely have to give in to investor's prices and terms irrespective of how rapacious they may appear.

No surprise we seem to be liked by China. The Chinese are showering us with gifts— stadiums, highways, infrastructure, and more. But we must acknowledge that nothing is free, and no one should expect the Chinese to be throwing money away on our account.

Unfortunately, I have not seen any sign of the intension nor the will to change the status quo. I see the same old politics, the same old Justice system, and sadly, the same old governing PNP party with the same old opposition JLP party, both parties saying the same old stuff.

The continued sale of Jamaican assets to countries outside of Jamaica is a matter for real concern, particularly since it seems there is little or no effort being made to become fiscally responsible. The gains made from sold assets are no longer expected to remain in Jamaica and why should they? More worrying, is the propensity for corruption on the part of governments, particularly, the governing PNP, which relentlessly puts great effort into bypassing the Office of the Contractor General. This has continued to guarantee an absence of transparency and accountability. A sale of more assets is likely to perpetuate the same reckless type of governance in the interest of power and at the expense of the people. In addition, the disregard for areas under conservation restrictions are likely to be trampled and their protection thrown out the window to the irreversible detriment of the Jamaicans of many generations to come. No one seems able to stop it.

Here again the old communist political adage is instructive: Who dares to oppose what we do when the people are starving? The history of government in Jamaica confirms this. They will continue to do it, and they will change the laws if they have to.

CHAPTER 16

SOLUTIONS

I have sat at the tip of the iceberg throughout my condemnations of our current state. I have been overly conservative, giving limited examples that ought to prove emphatically that Jamaica remains in the hands of corruption, the corrupt, and the corruptible.

From the start of the handout policy in the 70s, we catered to the creation of a non-productive society, which can only be reversed when the population is motivated to work. They will need to be motivated to have to really want to work. I have listened to veranda debates, the consensus of which would imply that this is nearly impossible over the short-term. This reasoning I can understand. Reversing a culture is not an overnight thing. However, corruption at the top has to be minimized before an attempt at changing the pervading attitudes can happen.

Our leaders, civic and political, must be brought to account, not just for what is happening today, but for all that has happened in the post-independence past. Only that can prevent such injustices from happening again. Only that will send the message to future leaders that there will be no hiding place. This is a critical component of securing the trust of investors and the people of Jamaica on a long-term basis. The trust that I acquired in the 80s diminished in the 90s and vanished by 2005. Only strong commitments and actions on the part of a new type of leadership can help it return.

Of the many excuses for our current state, a most insidious is the blame put on our former "colonial masters" from Britain. Certainly terrible wrongs were perpetrated on us—why else would we have sought independence?—but do you recall ever hearing, reading, or even dreaming of a time when an Englishman called on the Romans for reparations? Northern Europeans had been enslaved by them in the past, but they did not let it affect their future. Why? Because corruption, and plundering from the people in Northern Europe was not standard conduct. But in Jamaica, besides concerns about the political leadership teaching their citizens that they ought not to be working because their former imperialist masters owe them, we know what will happen to reparations distributed in a country being plundered by leadership corruption...a country devoid of the very justice required to harness and distribute any reparations due to the people, whether through education, housing, roads and all that is necessary for rebuilding the nation?

'Dem must give you what dem owe yu,' our children are told. That is political trickery that is so often used to excuse leadership corruption and failure. It works well on uneducated people. It places the minds of people who have read of the horrors of injustices of the past, conning them into being distracted from the injustices of the present. Children grow up seeing their parents with this attitude, and they too adopt that culture. The 'handout' lure meanwhile maintains a level of contentment even as the blame is placed elsewhere. The call for reparations helps to justify handouts in the minds of the people, keeping them tolerant of their political leaders. This only benefits the politicians who are nurturing support for the next election. It is to the benefit of the power seekers only. Drugs, extortion, robberies then make up for any shortfall. That becomes the way of life that replaces the older way of life and the newer "entitlement" culture eventually becomes a full time culture.

In any event, based on past conduct, if any funds were paid over as reparations, they would be immediately squandered. The money would rapidly and corruptly disappear into the usual pockets, further strengthening the culture of handouts. Reparations can have no useful impact on growth in the absence of justice.

How can one generation reverse all this? Short of a catastrophe that would force an entire country to either go to work, or die, I can't picture a reversal of this culture in a short time. We can only overcome this if we encourage work. The people can only work if jobs are available. Jobs will only be available when investors put trust in the country, and that trust will never come about if justice continues to elude us.

We have witnessed in Jamaica, the removal of our sovereignty that is tantamount to enslavement. A mockery has been made of our National Anthem: "… Justice, Truth be ours forever …. " The Jamaican people have been deprived of basic rights which progressive countries take for granted. They have been deprived to the extent that they have lost their dignity. Criminals no longer go to jail if they are 'connected', as most of the infamous ones are. They go to jail only if a developed country such as the USA or England insists. If there is an arrest, it is mainly for show and will be short-lived. Whatever is necessary for one to walk free will happen; lost forensic evidence, witnesses dying, or convenient amnesia are all expected and tolerated.

Funds removed corruptly from the government's purse is taken from taxpayers again and again. It deprives communities of doctors, child care, general health care, education, and employment, but worst of all, their rights. The same injustice that I experienced is the same kind of injustice that is used to shelter murderers and deprive the unconnected of their rights.

The level of trust in Jamaica is somewhere near zero. Corruption is completely risk-free. Any reversal of corruption has to include a belief that corruption has been attacked successfully; only then can the leadership of the country can be trusted. Without it, the corrected problems are likely to return. No investor worth his salt puts money in a long-term investment without trust in the leadership who sets the climate. I can't think of many businesses that might benefit the country better than those that employ people for longer periods. To get hold of those kinds of jobs, trust is indispensible.

A common escape route used to justify the lack of action by government is the word "amnesty". Amnesty forgives those who don't meet conditions while punishing those who play by the rules. Why should those who play by the rules compete against those who use their tax funds as interest-free loans? Such amnesty allows the government to collect from delinquent persons without consequence, offering even more incentive for their friends to cheat. This is a terrible message when seeking to regain trust. I believe that it should be always clear that you can run but you can't hide; that no one is untouchable. That message by itself is a tremendous deterrent.

History includes both the good and the bad, and the truth of these events should be recorded in the history books of Jamaica. Leaders should own their legacy, hopefully one of which they can be proud. At the root of all of Jamaica's massive problems are politicians, police, judges, lawyers, civil servants, private sector investors—all better classified as professionals. Putting them all together, one can just imagine the tricks that they get up to. They all need hear a very strong message that how they conduct themselves is guaranteed to be placed in the history books for all to see.

Jamaican politics tires and frustrates. It destroys and then welcomes those who do nothing about change. The uneducated I excuse. The educated who become part of doing nothing are no better than clones of their leadership. Returning justice to the people of Jamaica cannot be completed until every stone is unturned. The lawyers who take advantage of the attorney-client privilege should feel the menace of exposure. The laundering of money into bank accounts in countries like Turks & Caicos can hardly be accomplished without these lawyers who conjure up schemes with names like "Estate Planning" to sap countries of funds stolen from corrupted contracts and tax evasion schemes. "Estate Planning" is a neat cloak used to disguise the laundering and movement of money. All these activities must be unearthed, exposed and brought to account if Jamaicans are to again experience peace.

The major solutions: Narrow our focus; we can't solve them all at once.

The trillions we owe as a country is simply an indication of the level of corruption that has to be removed. The solution cannot be single-fold. It cannot be that we must abandon a lot of what is in place and adopt new ways. While I agree with the former Contractor General who suggested in a statement [1] "a holistic, surgical, sophisticated and intellectually rigorous approach to corruption," I realize that this takes time. A culture has been created and cannot be reversed quickly, but it has to be reversed if we are to see change. The reversal is in the hands of the powerful people … the politicians, the judges, the police, and their connections. We must urgently hold these to account. I depart from his opinion only for a while in order to focus on critical areas that require immediate change and on which all solutions depend.

We are all aware of the Teflon nature of politicians; they will fight to avoid what impacts negatively on their power. So why place a long list of necessary items before them when we know that their order of priority will vary? They will likely first institute the items that suit them, leaving behind the most critical items.

It is therefore pointless focusing on the accumulated sea of solutions when we know that many of the problems are mere symptoms of corruption. A call for more police patrols, more talk shows, more amnesties, a call for crime stop initiative, Caribbean Court of Appeal . . . all these calls create distractions and give the perception that we are doing something about our problems. There is so much talk about need for better education, police vigilance, better health care, and more. We cannot accomplish all that in a corrupt unjust society. Let us not forget the recurring and seemingly well intentioned calls for "values and attitudes" during a period of increasing corruption.

Also, the distracting politics of looking for more money to solve various problems is standard, and by itself allows for more corruption. Every problem area is directly affected by this scourge of the corruption. Removing the corruption automatically starts correcting injustices and solving problems. All solutions sought for problems in Jamaica are only band aids if they are installed without removing the real reason for corruption.

I believe that it is better to aggressively tackle the leadership—the political top and the judicial top—before applying additional pressure to improve the ethical standards, behavioral and attitudinal patterns of society in general. With a message sent to the top through indictments and trials free of perversion of the course of justice, much of the rest will start to fall in place. The business sector, civil society, the small trader, all cannot perpetuate corruption without the complicity of the top. The police force is an excellent example here. Commissioners of Police made efforts to lift the behavioral, attitudinal and ethical standards in the force with very limited success. Commissioners of Police have been given baskets to carry water. They have been dressing the sores while the top keeps creating them.

I therefore endorse Mr. Christie's sentiments, but prefer to confine immediate aggressive action to the 'untouchables' first as a priority. I find it difficult and unfair to pressure subordinates into "cleaning up" their acts while their superiors to whom they report, are busy pillaging and plundering at the expense of the very subordinates. Were it not for unrelenting opposition from the "top", the process of change could be made quite simple.

Impeachment – Seaga's Call?

I reflect on Seaga's call for impeachment, and wonder what he was seeing. Why did Mr. Seaga find it necessary in 1991 to seek support in Parliament for his proposal to enact impeachment penalties on high officials? What was he seeing then that he did not see in 1989 when he was leaving office as Prime Minister?

In 1989, he had the power to enact whatever proposals he deemed necessary. He had 100% of the House, but correctly did not seek to abuse that power since he had appointed watchdogs to prevent this. Knowing the type of person Mr. Seaga is, he was not known to make proposals for idle reasons. Despite having 100% power in his hands, he did not put forward his impeachment proposal at that time. He is known as a no nonsense man who did not hesitate to remove persons from his cabinet or from high office if he thought they acted against the interest of the country. Clearly he would not have hesitated if he thought such policy was needed.

So, was Mr. Seaga seeing a change in 1991 that bothered him? I believe he did. In the early part of the 2000s, he again tried to have those proposals visited but it went nowhere. Mr. Seaga's first request in 1991 might have been timely in 1991, but for sure, his 2003 revisit was too little too late. Such is the speed at which deterioration through corruption had taken place. Opposition to his proposal by then was expected, and it will be so in the future at every attempt to clean up the country.

Today, a combination of Impeachment proposals, Greg Christie's proposals, and independent anticorruption agencies with prosecutorial powers seem minimum immediate requirements to regain trust. We have waited so long that the impeachment proposals of Mr. Seaga by themselves are far too late. The most impacting start for correcting our problems, short of a benevolent dictatorship, is the urgent and immediate installation of an independent anticorruption body with prosecutorial powers and the widening of the powers of the Contractor General to include prosecutorial authority. "Independent" is the operative word there. The bottleneck lies in our ability to find the right persons who will remain non–political and impartial. This will have its early problems as the country is fast running out of people of integrity who are without skeletons in their closets and who would be best suited to participate in an anti-corruption body. The existing severe political pollution might cause a need to source from overseas because we can't draw only from a pool so saturated with corruption to find someone who will be required to pass any kind of judgment on anyone.

Thankfully there are still some people of integrity left in Jamaica who will likely only step forward when they are sure of the installation of a concrete agency that will be unyielding when faced with political interference. The introduction of a truly independent anti-corruption agency with prosecutorial powers will have to demonstrate reasonable success before the confidence of investors can be restored.

This must not be the 'end all' to solutions, but we must accept that nothing positive can be permanently achieved with corruption in place. It must be displaced. Action by such an agency will eventually lead to reducing bureaucratic red tape, which will in turn minimize the corruption influence and will make exposure much easier for those who are now afraid.

From all this, the effect of removing highly positioned corrupted persons will "domino" all the way to the bottom. The very leaders who put us where we are today will either have their turn seeing what inside prison looks like or become straight. The judges who have tolerated the conduct of these leaders, facilitating their tyranny, will themselves straighten up or have a look inside those quarters too; the Attorney General's Department will want to embrace cleaned up Judges; the DPP's department will do likewise; the police know what jail looks like and they too will become better persons, as they avoid it; The civil service will work more honestly, efficiently and avoid political influence; professionals will revisit good standards and values, and civil society will take their cue from all of the above.

The result of all this means more money in the government coffers to provide more jobs; better health care, better education, better roads, more and better housing, better justice, less crime; more investors with even more jobs. In short, a happier nation.

Yes, it will not all come overnight but over time, trust and respect will return.

The people will continue to feel some pain during recovery, but less in the long run than if they continued on the well-worn present path. They will see change and appreciate it because justice will be readily available. They will see fewer problems and find an honest ear to complain about fewer problems. They will find accountability resulting from their complaints, and be rid of those complicit in dishonesty.

With independent anti-corruption bodies formed and their prosecutorial powers securely in place, delays in the entire system will diminish as the system holds persons to account; the culprits who prey on others using the systems delays will find it not to their suit. There will be fewer matters before the courts as the advantage gained from manipulation of the system by crooked persons become too risky. The Police Commissioner will be happier doing what he does now, as his results would be more rewarding and less stressful. Judges, lawyers and the like would command more respect.

Meanwhile, all the short term fixes and 'maintenance' will continue but be more efficient and rewarding. While all these must be kept in place, we must believe that nothing will come together and work until justice is in place. Remember, it doesn't take money to achieve justice. Justice actually saves money but requires will.

Let us remove the power from the hands of those who have held it and used it to enslave us over the past 50 years. Let us put it in the hands of the good judges, the good JPs, the good police. Let us make it painful and unprofitable to be bad.

Avoiding the Caribbean Court of Appeal

What a great day it will be when we can confidently draw from a pool of judges of integrity to wean us off the Privy Council and to sit on a clean workable Caribbean Court of Appeal.

But, during the cleaning process, staying away from the Caribbean Court of Appeal has to be a necessity. I don't know how anyone could think of agreeing with a Caribbean Court of Appeal drawn from a pool which includes judges from a country that has nurtured so many of questionable repute. Many are beholden to one another—either by family, school, or political connections—are only a phone call away and bear the expectations of a "squadie" mentality, particularly after the reputation of leadership that we have in the Caribbean.

In contrast, the Privy Council judges know no one to call for a favor. They have no axe to grind. Why, during a time of escalating corruption in some Caribbean Islands, with Jamaica leading the way, do we chose to depart from that level of impartiality and integrity, to play around with trying something else using persons who can't command the trust of their own people? Because we are a sovereign nation? Rubbish! We have desecrated that sovereignty; we have shown the world that we ought to be supervised. We have been presided over by a bunch of scammer sympathizers who have over the past 40 years led us down a path of murder, slaughter, extortion, and every imaginable crime. Corruption has risen to a level that has placed us in debt up to our gills. We continue to be unmatched in the Caribbean, and we are possibly one of the worst in the world. All this has been masked by the distractions of our rich culture, tourism, exports, and all that fancy talk. What a great job of obfuscation where a facade can mislead tourists to visit Jamaica as we conveniently hide them away in all-inclusive resorts.

Making Professionals Accountable.

I have already trumpeted the critical role that professionals are required to play in every country, but most importantly they will have to play an important role in Jamaica's return to growth. They will have to reset the standards from which we all make decisions. It is however, common knowledge that in Jamaica, seeking redress when professionals stray from standards and integrity has been a waste of time and money. Here, smart people don't sue professionals; they are a known part of the establishment. It would be just as futile as suing their friends. That is how wide the net spreads.

That situation has to change during any cleaning process. We must bring professionals to within the reach of the law. Remove their 'untouchable' status. Professionals must again be forced to become clean. They must again be trusted. The courts rely heavily on the input of these professionals. Corrupt professionals make for corrupted verdicts. Corruptible judges are influenced by corrupt professionals, and the 'powers that be' have continued to protect both by their action and their inaction. Politicians' easy access to them must also be removed. We must ensure that political interference is not tolerated even as we need more fearless impartial bodies to investigate complaints or perceived behavior unbecoming their professions – we must see and expose what parts they have played in the demise of Jamaica.

While all of the atrocities of the past must be recorded in the history books and must never be forgotten, we must continue to accept that little will change until justice is readily accessible. The vanishing schools, Iran sugar deal, detention camps, Green Bay massacre, and numerous other scandals are embedded in our minds; the nine day wonders [1a] that followed should be lessons that strengthen our resolve to put an end to that culture and to remove the reasons they occurred.

What better example of the hypocrisy and of failures in the system is there than that of the tragic Armadale fire of May 2009? The ink had barely dried on the 2010 findings when commission members called on the government to release the official report only days after its contents were leaked to the media. RJR News was told that "What we have heard is that urgent action is going to be required by the relevant authorities and perhaps disciplinary, administrative proceedings will start but we don't think it's appropriate for there to be any further delay for the official document to be released to Parliamentarians and the public particularly since it has been leaked to the media and is in the public domain." The Bruce Golding–led government had tabled the findings before the House [2]. Public officers were expected to be held to account for their part and the government for "the inadequate facilities provided to care for children who are placed in juvenile correctional or remand facilities".

Of course this is what we expected to see our opposition members doing. But more than 4 years after the tragic Armadale fire the alleged "breaches of duty and administrative errors by the Department of Correctional Services, that public officials acted negligently and that a police officer acted unlawfully, resulting in the tragic circumstances at the Armadale Juvenile Correctional Centre in May 2009" appears to have been left where it was in 2010. The very "recommendations from the report and commitments made by Bruce Golding in his statement on March 2, 2010" which was so aggressively extracted by the ruling PNP remained hidden despite their being in power more than 2 years after Armadale's tragedy. So when the PNP party had called for "swift and decisive action" by government, that call was not about caring. It was an act for political mileage. Now that the JLP party is in opposition, they too show little about caring. Whatever mileage that was gained by one and lost by the other is tucked away in the past. It seems either protection by way of corruption or by way of incompetence. Why has the persons responsible for bringing the offenders to account not themselves been brought to account? As in the past, the memories of the people faded and other critical matters formed new distractions.

The need for an IMF

The heaviest criticism of the IMF comes from the beneficiaries of corruption. No surprise however, the masses are fooled into believing that the pain of austerity which has to be borne is the IMF's fault. Those who abhor the plundering of the country see the IMF as savior, not as doom. They are not to be seen merely as an institution to bail out countries by giving more loans. Their actions can only help if we live in ways that satisfy conditions intended to achieve fiscal responsibility.

The IMF conditions are only as strict as successive governments have caused it to be, having plundered and wasted the assets of the country and poisoned its people over an extended period of some 40 years or so. As strict as the conditions appear, the longer we wait to make adjustments to our conduct the more and faster our assets will be sapped. As the resources of the country decline so will the need for retrenchment increase. Paying staff salaries while they have no work to do is not the fault of employees, but it exasperates the problem and drives the economy more rapidly towards total collapse.

Despite the pain, government departments ought to do what is best for the country. The dilly-dallying around with real problems like this is typical of our politicians. They have placed Jamaica between a rock and a hard place. They created the problems out of greed for power at the expense of country and they are still looking for ways to keep power while staff is employed to sit around with no work for them to do. Laying them off means less votes and loss of power. So they have never really cared for country, it is all about power. Here again is the opportunity to do the right thing: remove the corruption to increase investment, increase production, increase employment and rid us of the entitlement culture.

Let us see the IMF as a hand from some divine source, sent to deliver us from corruption and incompetence. Not a handout.

The Security Forces

We have increased our reliance on ex military personnel for top jobs in Jamaica. The discipline that accompanies them helped to slow the rate at which the nation is slipping but they have not been allowed access to solving the root problem. So they have acted mainly as disciplined 'band aids.' The former Commissioner of Police Col. Trevor MacMillan was one such person. He slowed but couldn't fix corruption in the police force despite the integrity he carried into the force. The real problems emanated from above that level, and Commissioner Macmillan found that out the hard way.

"Politicians get in the way of justice and they wield the power to keep themselves in the way" he once told me. His hands were tied; so were those of Commissioner Lewin and so are those of Commissioner Ellington and I don't expect change anytime soon. A commissioner can have criminals arrested and charged, but we all know what happens past his level?

It remains common knowledge that any Police Commissioner who is honest is guaranteed to fail at his job. No matter how earnest and resolute on the job.

The recent experiences in Sierra Leone are little different from what happens in Jamaica. Political corruption at all levels was directly responsible for the lack of indictments of public officials in Sierra Leone over a 7 year period despite the existence there of an anti-corruption agency. It took something different to correct that. It took the thing that Jamaican politicians fight to prevent: the placing of prosecutorial powers in the hands of an independent body.

I know of no better way to start the corruption removal process than an independent anti-corruption body with prosecutorial powers and an expansion of the Office of the Contractor General to hold similar powers. I expect continued strong opposition to this. This deathblow to corrupt leaders in society is a path to paradise for all Jamaicans. I am hoping that it will come to pass and that with these changes all efforts to limit the effectiveness of such agencies will be strongly opposed by those who should care for the future of Jamaica such as the church and civic bodies, some of which did little to prevent our slide. I believe that results beneficial to stamping out present corruption in high places will also bring about freedom to investigate past occurrences, make corrections, and allow for the history books to send the message so that it never happens again.

Likewise, the horrendous acts of genocide as happened in Bosnia are still being treated with action, which sends the message that the international community will hunt down and turn offenders over for trial. This kind of message can't hurt, not only by deterring offenders today but by deterring those who might be inclined to try genocide anywhere and anytime in the future.

Thankfully Jamaica has avoided similar atrocities, but from a legal perspective a similar approach is required. Meaningful efforts—by way of investigations, exposures, and indictments where necessary, of leaders who have presided over and have been part of the destruction of Jamaica—seem the only pinch of hope for this country today.

Broken Promises

Jamaican governments, in their hunt for money, are in the habit of changing economic conditions very suddenly and with little warning, which ultimately severely affect entrepreneurs and manufacturers. Long-term investors don't like surprises. They like promises they can trust. They have seen what happened in the NHT raid; they see the Courts in disarray; they wonder what would happen to the millions they've invested if something bad were to happen. What if they don't (or can't) pay? What government department can they rely on for honest guidance?

The FINSAC story might never be logged truthfully or in its entirety in our history books, but the people who were there know the truth. The generation following FINSAC is already being denied a proper accounting, as the inquiry into the debacle has been plagued with obfuscation and delays. This therefore continues to add distrust to the mix. We must complete the inquiry report fairly and without further delay and debate it for years if necessary. We must expose to future generations the reasons why Jamaica collapsed in the 90s while every country in the civilized world was growing. We must ask, where did all the money go? We must expose all.

We need integrity from our lenders in the First World, not complicity. First world countries have consistently given shelter to those who have helped to fleece the people in developing countries of their assets and of their rights, forcing them into lives of poverty. The USA, Canada, Britain, Holland, France and other first world countries are complicit in the corruption process when they harbor and protect them. Jamaica cannot be expected to cooperate with First World countries by helping them to reduce the scourges of terrorism, crime, and drug addiction while they are protecting the very offenders who are fleecing us and funding the very scourges that they themselves seek to avoid. We need to demand their full cooperation, or refuse our own.

Additionally, the part played in corruption by developed countries has always been clear. They have traditionally made funds available as "loans" and "grants". They cannot deny knowing that these funds are consistently misappropriated. Yet they continue to give and lend knowing that it places countries like Jamaica into more debt while at the same time helps to mold a culture that destroys future Jamaican generations. They are also facilitating the very problems we now own by lending on easy conditions that are not policed for accountability. They are strong and they are able to state loan conditions just like the IMF does. In fact it is their money, they are the lenders and they can lend on whatever conditions they wish. They, more than anyone else, can insist on conditions of independent anti-corruption bodies. They can either contribute to destroying this country or they can act responsibly and help us reestablish 'paradise'.

Debt forgiveness can be a force for good only if applied properly. Too often it is too easy to create debt that is so overwhelming that it can never be repaid. This usually happens in the absence of due diligence or from corruption on the part of one or both parties. The chances of debt forgiveness increase astronomically when the climate is a just one. Qualification for forgiveness comes easier as the spinoffs from independent anti-corruption bodies bear fruit; the same bodies that should be in place at the insistence of lenders. A debt write-off should never come about without conditions that will guarantee the removal of corruption.

Huge contributors to the dilemma in developing countries are private contractors. Competition for major works in developing countries often drives large contractors, local and overseas, to bend the standards in ethics and to do whatever is necessary to win bids or negotiations for major jobs. Kickbacks become a way to curry favor with leaders who seek to enrich themselves as they handout some of the proceeds to their voters and hang on to power. This strengthens the perception internationally that kickbacks are a prerequisite for all projects undertaken, particularly in the developing countries.

Common sense reasoning would suggest that there are hardly any sizeable projects done in Jamaica by international contractors that have been completed without kickbacks. Competition among international contractors would surely support the belief that the kickbacks of the 90s are nowhere near those of today, as bidders increase kickbacks when competing for work. Funds from kickbacks continue to find safe haven in first world countries and seem to be spared harassment from authorities in those countries who have no difficulty looking the other way. It is as if they accept it as a norm.

Much of the proceeds end up in personal foreign accounts of politicians, their cohorts and friends. This happens only because foreign authorities allow shelter. Developed countries have access to the accounts of these politicians and their assets that are overseas. Their embassies must be aware. They know more than we do in that regard. We must therefore insist on their cooperation that will help us, and help us to help them. These developed countries like to appear as if they do not interfere in the affairs of other nations, especially those which had been more recently colonized. However, developed countries would be well advised to take lessons from the path travelled by many nations that escaped the control of their colonial masters only to be victims of the same fate as Jamaica. Corruption ran unhindered in African countries as western democracies looked the other way. The result was that these countries gave in to the present state of extremism and terrorism.

I have no doubt that many of these former colonies— like Nigeria, Kenya, Somalia, and Sudan— became exposed to extremism and terrorism only after experiencing the level of corruption and injustice as seen in Jamaica.

The creation of a breeding ground for extremism and terrorism is not a farfetched thought. It appears more real every day as countries like Jamaica fall victim to the type of poverty and suffering that allows for little choice between death by starvation and life by route of extremism. Surely the message here must that Jamaica's turn at terrorism is not very far away. Jamaica, from as far back as I can remember, was the role model for many of the Caribbean Islands. Other nations have adopted Jamaican culture to some extent, and this cannot be comfort to the western world and the USA in particular. If terrorism in Africa is worrisome to them, terrorism in their backyard must surely get their attention.

America and Europe should not see the West Indies as business as usual. They have good reason to fight corruption from inside their territories. If we are to assume that the First World countries want us to thrive, they will discourage any complicity from within their boundaries and will see us through fiscal responsibility by not recklessly lending or granting funds without absolute transparency and accountability on both sides. Likewise, I expect exposure of bank accounts held by Jamaican citizens in political office or in positions that would connect them in any way to kickback funds taken from the Jamaican taxpayers' kitty. Those Jamaicans who amass large accounts overseas may have earned it legitimately but ought to offer explanations that would clear them of complicity in corruption.

Attorneys, who abuse their privileges to protect and even create schemes like "Estate Planning", a tool so convenient for laundering and funding crime, even to the extent of terrorism, should find no shelter in first world countries. "Estate Planning" schemes have found their way into various tax haven countries, usually through Law firms and financial institutions that seem to enjoy protection almost everywhere. They should find no protection from the microscopes of law enforcement in the first world.

Ponzi schemes don't operate and continue to exist outside of banks and lawyers. Jamaican officials who are complicit in supporting Ponzi schemes through their cohorts, relatives and bank connections, and who enjoy protection under professional guises must not be allowed to hide from international law enforcement. They should be exposed and held to account. David Smith was not a lone wolf in the Olint Ponzi scheme. Many of those who are sheltered overseas somehow seem to find room among the untouchables, free to influence even the very staff in their Jamaican organizations. Yes, they lead by their example and seem to do so using protection from many developed countries.

Here I am not asking for handouts. I ask for cooperation in seeing to justice for the all the people of Jamaica and in first world countries.

We have heard talk by the Portia Simpson Government of some kind of 'agreement' that will allow prosecutorial powers, but this was put forward casually with a caveat "subject to some kind of oversight" intervention powers by the DPP" . . . or something of the sort.

What hogwash! We must not continue to accept this kind of political trickery.

Jamaica has suffered through most of what Sierra Leone has already tried in their quest to solve their problems. That didn't work for us either. We continue to be a step behind the politicians. A similar promise with a caveat didn't work for Sierra Leone even with an independent agency in place for an extended period. Somehow Sierra Leone's independent body was constantly bypassed by political influence in the absence of prosecutorial powers. The moment that independent prosecutorial powers came into action, funds started flowing to the benefit of all their people like magic. We must bear this in mind.

Why should we keep repeating these blunders? Why do we allow the politicians to constantly linger one step behind justice?

Most of my allegations may appear to many outside of Jamaica as too outrageous, and I quite understand why it can be misinterpreted as embellishment. Indeed Jamaica's problems can be best described at best as outrageous. Out of fear that I may be seen as overstating, it is important that I quote from qualified well meaning contributors.

The local 'Observer' paper of Sunday, January 16, 2011, featured an article by Trevor Munroe titled "Catching 'Big Fish': The need for a single anti-corruption agency" [3] which is in line with my experiences and reads in support of my convictions:

> "The 'continued success or failure' of the struggle against corruption... depends on the vigour with which the country's system of justice can investigate, arraign, prosecute and convict key 'big fish' accused of corruption.

Helping to identify and eliminate impediments to the successful pursuit of this goal has been one of our central goals.

> ......"
>
> "These successes against previous 'untouchables' in Sierra Leone were a direct result of the fulfillment of a political commitment made by the newly elected president Ernest Koroma (in 2007) to strengthen Sierra Leone's Anti-Corruption Commission to give it powers of investigation, arrest and prosecution.
>
> ....."
>
> "The commission before 2007 was nicknamed 'the toothless bulldog'. It would make a lot of publicity. It would make a lot of noise about people who had been arrested but then... nothing seemed to be happening because these cases would then tend to be stuck once sent to the Attorney General's Office for whatever reason, whether it was political or administrative." (Interview with Glenna Thompson, October 14, 2010).
>
> This situation changed dramatically when after being elected in 2007 President Koroma fulfilled his pledge, the Constitution was amended and the relevant statute changed to give the ACC prosecutorial powers.
>
> ....."
>
> "...the Anti-Corruption Commission is a success story in Sierra Leone... the one department or the one government (agency) that comes out on top of others... is the Anti-Corruption Commission because the success rate is high." (Interview with Glenna Thompson, October 14, 2010).
>
> ....."
>
> "If we are to curb corruption in Jamaica, tough and enforceable laws are needed as a first step. Ordinary people must begin to see more corrupt officials being held

> accountable to be fully punished by the judiciary process. The rich and politically powerful must not be allowed to buy their way out of accountability! Secondly, we need to treat the drive against corruption as a major campaign on the same scale as if we were fighting a deadly infectious disease. Thirdly, we need an intense campaign to educate the general population to recognise corruption as a destructive force aimed at the moral foundations of our nation."

In further support, an article in the *Observer* by a 'journalist and public affairs commentator' Claude Robinson on Sunday, February 03, 2013 titled "Seize the opportunity to create a strong, single anti-corruption agency" [4] is also worth reading. However, Jamaica is too far past redemption for me to agree with his opinion that:

> "Under new arrangements, the DPP would still have ultimate prosecutorial authority and could enter what the lawyers call a nolle prosequi, thus discontinuing a prosecution if s/he felt the matter should not proceed."

What then would be point for giving powers of prosecution when our history shows what is likely to happen? What if the 40 or so matters given to the DPP by the Contractor General had come from such an agency? And why should we refuse to learn from the experiences of Sierra Leone?

Claude Robinson writes:

> I have often written in support of an agency with investigative and prosecutorial powers to give some bite to the bark; to reduce the risks of allegations that make headlines but don't get to the level of prosecution; and to bring earlier resolution to matters which now seem to drag on and on to the distress of the individuals concerned and the cynicism of the public.

Of course, any granting of prosecutorial powers to the new body should not diminish the constitutional protections given to the office of the DPP in these matters. Under new arrangements, the DPP would still have ultimate prosecutorial authority and could enter what the lawyers call a nolle prosequi, thus discontinuing a prosecution if s/he felt the matter should not proceed…."Claude Robinson added:

"Lessons from Sierra Leone…

We can also draw on other experiences, including the West African nation of Sierra Leone whose head of the Anti-Corruption Commission, Joseph Kamara, was on a one-week visit to the island last week at the invitation of National Integrity Action (NIA) for just that purpose".

Speaking to reporters Monday he said, to knowing smiles and nods in the audience: "We created an anti-corruption agency in 2000 [because] we realised that corruption was endemic in the society—you pay for a driver's license, you pay for medical treatment, you bribe your way through traffic, you pay for classes, you bribe lecturers to pass exams."

In 2008, the country made legislative changes which gave the commission the power to prosecute and freeze assets. Since then, according to Kamara, there has been a "tremendous increase in the number of cases before the courts…".

"From 2008 until now we've witnessed the topmost officials being taken to court... Fifteen government ministers were tried and convicted by the court," he added, listing the ministers of finance, foreign resources, and health among them. High-level civil servants have also been brought to book. Overall, their prosecution success rate was 70 per cent."

Ironically, paying for driver's license and bribing one's way through is standard conduct in Jamaica.

CHAPTER 17
CLOSURE

Jamaica is an independent nation disfigured by endemic corruption. All the promises of cleaning up corruption have proven to be a farce. However, I believe that many Jamaican people want to do what is right, but they worry that playing by the rules will get them “shafted”.

Every nation is destined to repeat the things hidden from history. Whatever is omitted from the history books of any country is tantamount to a sentence to purgatory for future generations. The mistakes and the successes of one generation, documented and made available to future generations, are shortcuts to maturity, growth, and success of following generations.

My experiences in a single case, visiting the steps of the Jamaican high courts on more than 70 occasions, communicating with more than four government-controlled bodies on the matter, pursuing my cause for more than 12 years, and fighting for fairness in the corrupt Jamaican justice system ought to be available as a cautionary tale. My hope is that these pages help reduce the pain of generations that follow.

Indeed it is from my experience as a private businessman and as a victim of the “connected” culture that I can confirm the reason why dons are essential to the survival of the uneducated. From this, I draw the conclusion that short of immediate and resolute action, there is absolutely no hope for the poor or oppressed in this generation —or even the next—in Jamaica.

So often we as citizens discover how oblivious we are to the things happening around us because we are not exposed to them. If we are not located near certain communities, have no interaction with them, and fail to understand the type of life they endure, then we cannot change the future of our nation. Sometimes it takes one's own demise to create real awareness. Sometimes this new awareness is received with disbelief and shock. For one to overlook this and do nothing about it would be an unpatriotic act, contributing to the very injustice that destroys one's own country.

The damage that my family and I have suffered is irreversible, and therefore I have nothing to gain by any selfish pursuit of personal justice. It is for exactly this reason that my experiences and observations ought to be placed in the public forum with the hope that others will step forward and make their contribution to taking back this nation from the tentacles of the corruption cruelly organized and controlled from in high places.

An appeal to Jamaicans living overseas

To all Jamaicans living and working overseas, to the Jamaican Diaspora I say: You have worked hard, made huge sacrifices, unwittingly funded shortfalls, and indeed you need to continue. You were there to cheer on Bob Marley, Usain Bolt, and Tessanne Chin as she swept *The Voice* in the USA. You in the Jamaican Diaspora have powerful voices. You must use it to again make Jamaica the paradise it once was. More than anyone else, I believe that each person in the Jamaican Diaspora has the wish to see this; all that is needed is the conviction to see it through. Your work has helped to build other countries while providing funds to help sustain your families in Jamaica. Those countries are appreciative of your input, and it is only reasonable that you seek fair treatment for the country that grew, nurtured, and educated you and your parents from birth. You remain overseas where you experience a difference in governance and justice that no doubt has allowed you to also improve on your worth. We need your support to again make that same justice readily available in Jamaica.

Your voices should be heard in support. Your calls must be heard for cooperation in investigating and indicting corrupt overseas contractors who dishonestly pay bribes by any means and operate in the countries where you labour. Your calls must be heard for investigating and indicting launderers, scammers, gunrunners, drug traders, and all the cohorts or connections who have led Jamaica down this path while stashing away millions of dollars overseas. Your voices must be heard for vigilance and exposure of financial institutions that fund Jamaican projects while exposing Jamaican taxpayers to enormous wasted charges in interest and principal. You must demand due diligence on loans, and for pressure to be applied for the formation of independent bodies with the power to bypass political departments all of which have been already corrupted.

By not suppressing the pen, I am prepared to share these experiences without care or fear of the consequences that I know are inevitable, with the hope that it can contribute, even in a small way, to the cause of equal rights and justice for all Jamaicans. These inalienable rights are taken for granted in progressive countries, but they are sorely missed here in Jamaica. Short of applying severe physical abuse, I don't believe that there is any additional injustice that can be meted out to me today that is much worse than what I have already received. I believe there are hundreds of thousands in Jamaica whose rights are trampled on and whose suffering, without doubt, dwarfs mine. Yes, I know what it is like to be dealt tremendous injustice for more than twelve years. Many bear it for a lifetime.

My contribution here is not just giving an opinion or just simply reasoning things through. I have experienced the nightmare and the injustices that so many in Jamaica continue to suffer in silence out of fear for their lives and for those of their families. The poor often go to the streets and call for justice. I don't see their relief, but I see that they keep trying. I too, must.

I consider myself to be in a more fortunate position than many in Jamaica who have succumbed to these frustrations with anger and have taken the law into their own hands. Few of them know how much and how often I empathized with their frustrations.

To those who have supported and encouraged me in many ways; to those who have called me anonymously with tip-offs of rackets in the system; I thank you and I am grateful. I hope Jamaica will be grateful to you as well. To those who have confided in me that they have been through similar experiences but have kept silent or have chosen to protect their family from persecution, I appreciate your honesty.

Having lost many years in the prime of my life—my ordeal began at 54, and today I am 68—I know that full exposure of injustice and corruption in Jamaica will in future provide many with emotional and material gain. I am convinced that it will not be corrected by the politicians who governed Jamaica over the past 40 years. Those years that I lost cannot be recovered, but there will be some consolation for me if there is any success in opening some eyes. The satisfaction I will gain would be if others can be spared the same fate; that to me will be enough reward. Greater reward would be to witness the day when this will never again be accepted by Jamaicans as the norm.

At this stage of my life, taking a stand is really with the next generation in mind, hoping that it will help to change things for them, and soon. I have always taken a stand against injustice by doing what is right, but that is not enough in today's world. I am now convinced that there is no effective way but to expose the ills I see all around. I am convinced that failure to speak out has been a contributor to our decline. Pain is the great teacher, and the hardship of even a single person must help to pave the way to a better future for others. I see exposure therefore as a critical ingredient of change, development, and progress in every country and every generation, especially in countries riddled with corruption.

Silence over the years is a friend of the scourge that we now endure. One of my regrets in this regard is that it is impossible to cover all that I need to say in a single volume.

I reflect on my learning and observation course in thoroughbred horse husbandry back in the late 60's when Mr. Elmer Heubeck Jnr., the then manager of a farm in Ocala Florida who allowed me a stint on a thoroughbred farm where I was allowed to occupy a room adjoining a barn of race horses; a room specifically in place for employees on the farm, at that time reserved for whites only. I was the only colored sleeping on any such farm in Ocala. This caused objections by some employees but Mr. Heubeck took a stand. When I got wind of it I recall telling him that if he wished I would leave in order to avoid problems that might affect the smooth running of the farm. His reply was a firm "Hell, no." Looking back, the risk that he took in those days, could have cost him his life. Mr. Heubeck has since passed on, probably without realizing that he made a contribution to justice in America—a small step that added to others. I know that he had absolutely nothing to gain and I believe he did it without caring about the consequences. However small his contribution might now appear, I truly believe that he expected nothing in return. Possibly unknown to him, his was one of the millions of contributions that appear miniscule but without which a colored person could never become President of the United States. We owe it to fellow Jamaicans to make similar contributions, however small they appear and the only payback we should wish for is a better future for all other Jamaicans.

ABOUT THE AUTHOR

Dwight Clacken was born in Kingston Jamaica in 1947. He enjoyed a colorful childhood that was dotted by typical boyhood mischief and bravado but who was also kept in line by strong familial community bond where the entire village took responsibility for each other's welfare. The son of upright middle class parents, Dwight was influenced by their religious values which shaped his perception of ethics, justice and fairness. Even as a student he was quick to identify the mistreatment of others and was fearless in rejecting it.

A businessman by profession, he has vast experience working in different fields as his career began in his youth. As an adult he worked long hours as he was passionate about building his dream business, EML. Dwight is enthusiastic about nation building, justice and fighting the cause of the poor and the oppressed. He is motivated to write this novel having witnessed the rise and fall of successive governments, the brunt of their failures on the ambitions of a fledgling country and also the depreciation of our values over time. His own struggles in the treacherous justice system vividly juxtapose the Jamaica of his boyhood idyllic perception and the stark and brutish reality that now jeers him.

He has great concern that Jamaica his island home is being decimated by the greed and selfishness of politicians and professionals. Where did the love, decency and integrity go? Where have these cold, greedy and cynical people come from? Dwight fears that the values and attitudes that were once the pride and selling point of Jamaica have been eroded by corruption and may be irreversible if there is no urgent collective will and courage to take the stand necessary to bring about change.

Dwight is married to his beautiful and supportive wife Lynne. They share five children.

Facebook: /dwightclacken

Linkedin: Dwight Clacken

dclacken4@gmail.com

NOTES

Preface

1. ***"Hustling" or "Hustlin" (in a negative context)***...... Many kinds of activities from which there is monetary gain derived from beating the system...usually illegal or against the law.
2. **'dawg a go nyam dawg** '.... . Jamaican saying that things will be at rock bottom ... couldn't be worse.

Chapter 1

1. ***'Runnins'*** .... The trend, culture or norm usually bypassing the rules ... inner workings, usually opposite to laws, values and attitudes ... street language.

Chapter 2

1. **"*Post Mistress*"**.... The lady in charge of each post office branch throughout Jamaica and who was a well respected member of the community.
2. **"*Gig*"**.... Same as a 'spinning top'
3. ***"O level" grade"*** ... The British exam level in Jamaican high schools which was at that time roughly equivalent to grade 12 in USA High school.

Chapter 3

1. ***"Higher School Certificate (A level GCE equivalent)"*** .... The British exam level in high school which at that time was roughly equivalent to first year in US College.
2. ***'DaCosta Commission of inquiry'*** .... An inquiry into the corruption that occurred during the 60s and early 70s.

Chapter 4

1. ***"Crash Program".*** … Same as the Jamaican JEEP program. A program designed by political interest groups to provide speedy and short term menial employment....usually for the working class. This program is generally theorised as a political strategy to secure votes because it is usually unsustainable in its capacity to provide long term employment solution for the poor which would ultimately lead to poverty alleviation.

Chapter 5

1. "***bandooluism***," … Conduct less than honest. Trickery used to gain financially or for favours.

Chapter 6

1. **"*higgler*" .....**Informal commercial trader. Vendor who buys everything that she sells. Trade usually takes place in a market or roadside
2. '***FINSAC***' …. Financial Sector Adjustment Company. …
3. ***Prominent FINSAC'd failures were***:- .....Life of Jamaica Limited, Island Life Insurance Co Ltd., National Commercial Bank Ltd., Paul Chen Young & Co Ltd., Jamaica Citizens Bank Ltd., Island Victoria Bank Ltd., Crown Eagle Life Insurance Co Ltd., Workers Bank Ltd., Century National Bank Ltd., Caldon Finance Ltd. . . . and many more big companies.

Chapter 7

1. **"*Boss mek mi get a man fi done dem fi yu*" ….** Means: "let me find somebody to do a hit on them for you".
2. **"*wa wrong wid yu boss . . . .yu na go deal wid dem?...* .** Means: what is the matter with you? Aren't you going to kill them?
3. ***"Boss, yu must be tun eediat"…*** *M*eans: have you become stupid?

Chapter 8

1. ***'Runnins'*** …. The trend, culture or norm usually bypassing the rules ... inner workings, usually opposite to laws, values and attitudes … street language.

2. ***Trafigura Scandal****....* Involving Trafigura Beheer, a Dutch company - Trading globally in businesses, including the supply and off take of crude oil, petroleum products, liquefied petroleum gas (LPG), metals, ores and concentrates. Trafigura had paid over some J$30 million which ended up in a private account connected to the governing PNP
3. ***Cuban Light Bulb Scandal*** .... Light bulbs donated by the Cuban government to the Jamaican people were allegedly sold and the funds pocketed by individuals.

Chapter 9

1. **"Serving Notice on Jamaica" ...** article by *Lowrie – Chin, Jamaican journalist.*
2. ***Queens Council*** .... A UK term for a Lawyer/Barrister who, having practiced law with distinction for at least ten years, is given the honour to earn the right to take precedence over other Barristers in the court. A similar honour makes an attorney 'Senior Counsel' in British commonwealth countries. After being appointed Q.C., the lawyer may use the initials "Q.C."
3. ***'Runnins'*** ... The trend, culture or norm usually bypassing the rules ... inner workings, usually opposite to laws, values and attitudes ... street language.

Chapter 10

1. ***'Runnins'*** ... The trend, culture or norm usually bypassing the rules ... inner workings, usually opposite to laws, values and attitudes ... street language.
2. ***'Eat a food'*** .... A term used to express handing out funds without expecting commensurate work of production. It is an opportunity to collect funds freely to feed oneself without working for it productively. A similar phrase would be to "let off" ..... let off money (typically for little or no work done in exchange) ... . in some contexts it means survival. The big man is expected to "let off" so I can eat a food.

   OR

A term which generally means 'to gain money or favours through cracks created in the system by unscrupulous individuals who have devised a way to cheat the system, Usually by a link/connections within the system that dole out the opportunities to people who are unqualified and or who will receive payment for little or no work done

Chapter 11

1. ***'bruk dung"*** … . Broken down (like a vehicle down for repairs) often used punning regarding the "JEEP" program
2. ***'eat a food' ….*** as at [2] chapter 10
3. ***'curried goat, oxtail' …*** popular Jamaican food normally too high priced for the poor, but a welcome dish.
4. ***"Greg Christie writes to Portia"***... **Wants corruption issues addressed** ... On January 09, 2012 | 1:33 PM) CONTRACTOR General Greg Christie from the Office of the Contractor General (OCG) wasted no time in writing to newly appointed Prime Minister Portia Simpson Miller, to convey more than 25 Office of the Contractor General (OCG) anti-corruption recommendations for urgent consideration and implementation by the People's National Party (PNP) administration. http://www.jamaicaobserver.com/news/Greg-Christie-writes-to-Portia http://www.ocg.gov.jm/website_files/media_releases_issued/media236.pdf
5. ***"Reputable persons on the run because of Ponzi schemes"*** **Article in** Observer, April -25 - 2012 http://www.jamaicaobserver.com/news/Reputable-persons-on-the-run-because-of-Ponzi- schemes---Franklyn_11333220

   and

   "Jamaica has made advances in corporate and public governance, but" **...** Article in Observer Mar-18-2012. http://www.jamaicaobserver.com/columns/Jamaica-has-made-advances-in-corporate-and-public-governance--but---_11045595
6. ***'bling' …..*** Flashy lifestyle where one displays or seeks after the latest most trendy styles in clothing, jewelry, motor cars, houses etc.

7. "***Eradicate the culture of impunity around the lottery scam***" … Article published by Claude Robinson in Observer of March 17 2013. http://m.jamaicaobserver.com/mobile/columns/Eradicate-the-culture-of-impunity-around-the-lottery-scam_13872254
8. "***Lotto scamming, bling and morality***" ….. Journalist Ian Boyne says it clearly http://jamaica-gleaner.com/gleaner/20130310/focus/focus1.html
9. ***'Moral Dis-ease Making Jamaica Ill?: Re-engaging the Conversation'***… reference to 66-page booklet by Boston College and Cambridge University trained Dr. Ana Perkins. http://www.gracekennedy.com/images/lecture/grace_lecture_moral-dis-ease-2013_final.pdf
10. ***"Only in this country!"*** ….. Commentary in the *Jamaica Gleaner* of March 27, 2013 by "George Davis is a journalist. http://mobile.jamaica-gleaner.com/gleaner/20130327/cleisure/cleisure2.php
11. "***The appearance of injustice***" …. Article published by Peter Espeut, a sociologist and Roman Catholic deacon, in the Jamaica Gleaner of Friday March 22, 2013,. ***http://jamaica-gleaner.com/gleaner/20130322/cleisure/cleisure2.html***
12. "***Between a rock (the police) and a hard place (the gunman)***"…. Article in the Observer newspaper on March 21, 2013 by a seasoned veteran journalist Mark Wignall. http://www.jamaicaobserver.com/columns/Between-a-rock--the-police--and-a-hard-place--the-gunman-_13900067
13. "***Rogue cops killing faith in police force***"… Reverend Roy Notice, known for his integrity and fearless sermons of truth, in a letter to the Editor of a local newspaper, The Gleaner, on June 5, 2013. http://mobile.jamaica-gleaner.com/gleaner/20130605/letters/letters1.php

Chapter 12

1. ***'Is The IMF To Blame For J$ Depreciation?'*** … . Article by Aubyn Hill is the CEO of Corporate Strategies Limited and was an international banker for more than 25 years. Published in Gleaner: Friday May 31, 2013. http://jamaica-gleaner.com/gleaner/20130531/business/business9.html

2. ***'TRAPPED! IMF rep says without key policy changes, Jamaica will remain in economic rut'*** .... supported by Dr Damien King Head of the Department of Economics at the University of the West Indies. http://mobile.jamaica-gleaner.com/gleaner/20130613/lead/lead1.php
3. "***Azan, Defiance And Impeachment"*** … . Gary Spaulding, Political Affairs Reporter in a Gleaner commentary of April 21, 2013. … http://jamaica-gleaner.com/gleaner/20130421/cleisure/cleisure2.html

Chapter 13

1. ***"Dem tief, dem get buy out"*** ….. Means "they are thieves" … . "they have been bribed" … . "they have been bought."
2. ***'Runnins'*** … The trend, culture or norm usually bypassing the rules ... inner workings, usually opposite to laws, values and attitudes … street language.
3. ***"di whole a unu understand mung unu self but di whole a we tink unu is tief."***… .. Attorneys and judges among themselves can understand each other but the average man believes they are all thieves.
4. ***"Him nah go no weh"*** … . ***"Police seh him wi tek $2 million"*** … He won't be going to any jail … . police willing to take $2million to bypass jail.
5. ***"Fear fuels not-guilty verdicts"***… Headline in the Gleaner newspaper January 2013, http://jamaica-gleaner.com/gleaner/20130120/lead/lead2.html
6. "***Mirror image of justice system***" and sub-headed "***Accountability***"…. A letter to editor March 21, 2013, regarding Ponzi schemes. http://jamaica-gleaner.com/gleaner/20130321/letters/letters1.html
7. ***Dirk Harrison And The Burden Of Precedent*** … A Gleaner Editorial February 27, 2013. **http://jamaica-gleaner.com/gleaner/20130227/cleisure/cleisure1.html**
8. ***Jamaica's losing battle with corruption*** … Article by Ian Boyne in Gleaner March 8, 2009 http://mobile.jamaicagleaner.com/20090308/focus/focus1.php

9. ***"Greg Christie hits bull's eye"*** **– ... A must read -** published July 1 2012 in the Daily Gleaner *by* Ian Boyne, a veteran journalist, is the 2010-11 winner of the Morris Cargill Award for Opinion Journalism. http://jamaica-gleaner.com/gleaner/20120701/focus/focus4.html
10. "***The will to fight corruption'*** ....An article by Delroy Chuck - an attorney-at-law and Opposition Member of Parliament. http://old.jamaica-gleaner.com/gleaner/20001115/cleisure/cleisure2.html
11. ***"Corruption Choking the Courts"*** ... October 10, 2011 article by *Gleaner* writers Arthur Hall and Nedburn Thaffe. http://jamaica-gleaner.com/gleaner/20111010/lead/lead5.html
12. ***Integrity Of Justice System Intact – Golding ...*** Gleaner article by Tyrone Reid - February 12, 2012 http://jamaica-gleaner.com/gleaner/20120212/lead/lead4.html
13. ***"Why the Buckfield case fell flat"*** .... DPP explanation verbatim in Daily Gleaner, March 20, 2013 part 1. http://mobile.jamaica-gleaner.com/gleaner/20130320/cleisure/cleisure3.php March 21, 2013 Part 2. http://jamaica-gleaner.com/gleaner/20130321/cleisure/cleisure4.html
14. ***"Ethically challenged"*** .... Peter Espeut, in his article of September 27, 2013 in the Gleaner. **http://mobile.jamaica-gleaner.com/gleaner/20130927/cleisure/cleisure3.php**
15. "***Garrisonisation***" ... A deliberate act by politicians or dons to create and seclude an area that is 'acculturised' and socially conditioned to think, behave and vote in accordance with the ideologies and motives of the architect . This community usually shows blind allegiance to the political party that influenced its creation; and control is generally exercised by the ruthless dons who carry through the orders of their superiors; and who also ensures that the borders (and also the culture) are not infiltrated.

Chapter 14

1. '***bandooluism***' .... Conduct less than honest.. Trickery used to gain financially or for favours.
2. '***links***' .... Unfair connections

3. ‘*hustling*’… . .“***Hustling” or “Hustlin” (in a negative context)***…. Any kind of activity from which there is monetary gain derived from beating the system usually illegal or against the law.
4. ***‘Runnins’*** …. The trend, culture or norm usually bypassing the rules ... inner workings, usually opposite to laws, values and attitudes … street language.
5. ***‘Bly’*** …. Given a chance … a break after doing wrong or intending to.
6. ***‘ting’*** …. ’bribe’ or ‘unfair favour’
7. ***“nine day wonders”*** …. A very serious issue that attracts much sensationalism but is forgotten or swept under the carpet in a matter of days. The origin of the term 9 days comes from Jamaican folklore where the 9th day signals when something should happen … . like “nine night”, … . nine lives …. So in the case of “nine day wonder “ …. After 9 days we won’t hear the issue again.(hence the word wonder.)
8. ***‘bandoolu’*** … . Conduct less than honest.. Trickery used to gain financially or for favours.

   Not The Way To Go … Gleaner of September 1, 2010 refers to James Moss Solomon’s resignation. Also in the Observer and RJR media. http://m.jamaicaobserver.com/mobile/columns/Jamaica-farewell_13491976 **&** http://jamaica-gleaner.com/gleaner/20100901/lead/lead1.html & http://rjrnewsonline.com/local/james-moss-solomon-resigns-from-government-boards
9. ***“you can always stay deh chat, di whole a unoo lucky”***… . Stated in context of “we have better things to chat about and listen to ... you are OK ... you are lucky (facetiously) …. Regardless of how unscrupulous and underhanded something might appear we will not back down in the face of talk.

Chapter 15

1. ***“Didn’t we almost have it all?”*** … An article in Gleaner of October 7, 2012. **http://jamaica-gleaner.com/gleaner/20121007/letters/letters1.html**

Chapter 16

1. Greg Christie's "holistic surgical…approach" http://jamaica-gleaner.com/gleaner/20120701/focus/focus4.html & http://www.jamaicaobserver.com/columns/Greg-Christie-s-last-blow-against-corruption_12975920

1a. ***"nine day wonders"* …** A very serious issue that attracts much sensationalism but is forgotten or swept under the carpet in a matter of days. The origin of the term 9 days comes from Jamaican folklore where the 9th day signals when something should happen … . like nine night, … . nine lives …. So in the case of "nine day wonder " …. After 9 days we won't hear the issue again.(hence the word wonder.)

2. **"Tabled findings in the House"** ….Re Armadale http://rjrnews-online.com/local/pnp-wants-immediate-release-of-armadale-report http://jamaica-gleaner.com/gleaner/20100224/lead/lead91.html http://jamaica-gleaner.com/power/17087

3. "**Catching 'Big Fish': The need for a single anti-corruption agency"** … An article by Professor Trevor Munroe - the director of the National Integrity Action Forum, and Visiting Fellow at the Sir Arthur Lewis Institute of Social & Economic Studies, UWI in the Observer' paper of Sunday, January 16, 2011. "http://www.jamaicaobserver.com/catching--big-fish---the-need-for-a-single-anti- corruption-agency_8291637 http://www.jamaicaobserver.com/catching--big-fish---the-need-for-a-single-anti- corruption-agency_8291637#ixzz2K8jAYHvH

4. **"Seize the opportunity to create a strong, single anti-corruption agency"** … . Article in the *Observer* by Attorney Claude Robinson on Sunday, February 03, 2013 http://m.jamaicaobserver.com/MOBILE/COLUMNS/SEIZE-THE-OPPORTUNITY-TO-CREATE-A-STRONG--SINGLE-ANTI-CORRUPTION-AGENCY_13536888

Additional Notes of Interest

- Seaga renews call for impeachment ... In Gleaner of 13-Feb-2003 http://old.jamaica-gleaner.com/gleaner/20030213/lead/lead2.html

- From My Notebook(Blaming the media for our inaction is nuts) Star of 15-Mar-13 http://jamaica-star.com/thestar/20130315/features/features1.html
- LETTER OF THE DAY - Richard Azan A Law Unto Himself ... Gleaner of 22-Apr-13 http://jamaica-gleaner.com/gleaner/20130422/letters/letters1.html
- We want Justice! - Majority of Jamaicans say justice system is corrupt –UNDP in the Gleaner of 12-Feb-2012. http://jamaica-gleaner.com/gleaner/20120212/lead/lead2.html
- Media Release 19th March 2013 ...supporting Buckfield matter. http://dpp.gov.jm/sites/default/files/pressrelease/Media%20Release%20DPP-Lloyd%20Kelly%20Buckfield%20Matter(1).pdf
- Screams From Armadale ... Article 23-May- 2013 in Gleaner by Jaevion Nelson http://jamaica-gleaner.com/gleaner/20130523/cleisure/cleisure3.html
- 'Too much evil'...Article by Ingrid Brown - Observer staff 18-Jan-2008 http://www.jamaicaobserver.com/news/131503_-Too-much-evil-
- Prime Minister sends Armadale report to PSC for action .... In Observer of 13-Mar-10 http://www.jamaicaobserver.com/armadale-report

Made in the USA
Middletown, DE
04 January 2016